Jupyter Notebook 101

Michael Driscoll

Published by Michael Driscoll
Ankeny, IA

Cover art by Tyler Sowles

Contents

Introduction

Welcome to **Jupyter Notebook 101**! The Jupyter Notebook is an open source web application that you can use to create and share documents that contain live code, equations, visualizations and text. You can use a Jupyter Notebook for any of the following:

- teaching
- presentations
- learning a computer language
- numerical simulations
- statistical modeling
- data visualization
- machine learning
- and much more!

The Jupyter Notebook started out as the IPython Notebook but now supports over 40 programming languages! Jupyter Notebooks allow you to share your code in an easy to digest manner. They can be emailed, put on Github or run online via **nbviewer** (http://nbviewer.jupyter.org/), **binder** (https://mybinder.org/) or **Google Colaboratory** (https://colab.research.google.com).

You may also add HTML, images, Markdown, videos, LaTeX and custom MIME types to your Notebooks. Finally, Jupyter Notebooks support big data integration.

We will be using **Python 3** in this book. While there are versions of Jupyter Notebook that support Python 2, the Jupyter project is starting to drop support for it. For example, IPython 6.0 dropped Python 2 support entirely and Jupyter Notebook is built on top of IPython.

Note that while Jupyter Notebook can run code in many other programming languages, you are required to have **Python** installed.

About the Author

You may be wondering about who I am and why I might be knowledgeable enough about Python to write about it, so I thought I'd give you a little information about myself. I started programming in Python in the Spring of 2006 for a job. My first assignment was to port Windows login scripts from Kixtart to Python. My second project was to port VBA code (basically a GUI on top of Microsoft Office products) to Python, which is how I first got started in wxPython. I've been using Python ever since, doing a variation of backend programming and desktop front end user interfaces as well as automated tests.

I realized that one way for me to remember how to do certain things in Python was to write about them and that's how my Python blog came about: http://www.blog.pythonlibrary.org/. As

I wrote, I would receive feedback from my readers and I ended up expanding the blog to include tips, tutorials, Python news, and Python book reviews. I work regularly with Packt Publishing as a technical reviewer, which means that I get to try to check for errors in the books before they're published. I also have written for the Developer Zone (DZone) and i-programmer websites as well as the Python Software Foundation. In November 2013, DZone published **The Essential Core Python Cheat Sheet** that I co-authored. I have also written the following books:

- **Python 101** - June 2014
- **Python 201: Intermediate Python** - Sept. 2016
- **wxPython Cookbook** - Dec. 2016
- **wxPython Recipes** - Dec 2017
- **Python Interview: Discussions with Python Experts** - Feb. 2018
- **ReportLab: PDF Processing with Python** - June 2018

Conventions

As with most technical books, this one includes a few conventions that you need to be aware of. New topics and terminology will be in **bold**. You will also see some examples that look like the following:

```
myString = "Welcome to Jupyter!"
```

Most of the code in this book will be done either in Python files or in Jupyter Notebooks.

Prerequisites

I just want to emphasize this. Python is required to be able to install and use Jupyter Notebook.

Installing with Anaconda

Anaconda is a distribution of Python that focuses on data science. You can just download Anaconda's Python 3 version from https://www.anaconda.com for your specific operating system and install it. Anaconda comes with Jupyter Notebook along with many other scientific libraries for Python.

Installing with pip

Pip is Python's package manager. It now comes with the Python programming language starting in Python 2.7.9 and Python 3.4.

Setting up & Activating a Virtual Environment

If you don't want to add the Jupyter Notebook and all its dependencies into your system's Python installation, then you can use a virtual environment. In Python 2.x - 3.2, you would need to install a package called **virtualenv** to create a virtual environment for Python. The idea is that it will create a folder with a copy of Python and pip. You activate the virtual environment, run the virtual pip and install whatever you need to. Python 3.3 added a module to Python called **venv** that does the same thing as the virtualenv package, for the most part.

Here are some links on how all that works:

- https://docs.python.org/3/library/venv.html (Python 3 only)
- https://pypi.python.org/pypi/virtualenv (Python 2 and 3)

When you are using a Python Virtual Environment, you will need to first activate it. Activation of a virtual environment is like starting a virtual machine up in VirtualBox or VMWare, except that in this case, it's just a Python Virtual Environment instead of an entire operating system.

Creating a virtual sandbox with the **virtualenv** package is quite easy. On Mac and Linux, all you need to do is the following in your terminal or command prompt:

```
virtualenv FOLDER_NAME
```

To activate a virtual environment on Linux or Mac, you just need to run the following command

```
source FOLDER_NAME/bin/activate
```

On Windows, things are slightly different. To create a virtual environment, you will probably need to use the full path to virtualenv unless you have your Python's **Scripts** folder set up to be in your environment's path:

```
c:\Python37\Scripts\virtualenv.exe
```

Once that virtualenv is created, you can activate it by running the following on your machine:

```
FOLDER_NAME\Scripts\activate
```

Once activated, you can install any other 3rd party Python package.

Note: It is recommended that you install all 3rd party packages, such as Jupyter Notebook, in a Python Virtual Environment or a user folder. This prevents you from installing a lot of cruft in your system Python installation.

I would also like to mention that **pip** supports a –user flag that tells it to install the package just for the current user if the platform supports it. There is also an –update flag (or just -U) that you can use to update a package. You can use this flag as follows:

```
python pip install PACKAGE_NAME --upgrade
```

Now your package should be installed and up-to-date!

Note: Most Linux distributions still default to Python 2 when you run the python command. Keep thing in mind when you are working with Python as you might find that you are accidentally installing packages to the wrong Python version.

Installing

You can install the Jupyter Notebook package with Python 2.7 and Python 3.3 or greater. Here is how you would do it with pip:

```
python -m pip install --upgrade pip
python -m pip install jupyter
```

Note: If you have both Python 2 and Python 3 installed and you want to install for Python 3, then you need to call python3 instead of just python on the command line.

An alternative to using virtualenv directly would be to download and install **Pipenv** which will let you create a virtual Python environment and install packages to it in one command. You can learn more about Pipenv here: https://docs.pipenv.org/

Verify Jupyter Notebook Installation

To verify that your Jupyter Notebook installed correctly, open up a terminal and try running the following command:

```
jupyter notebook
```

You should see some output that looks like the following:

Fig. Intro-1: Console output from jupyter notebook command

Your default web browser should also launch and look something like this:

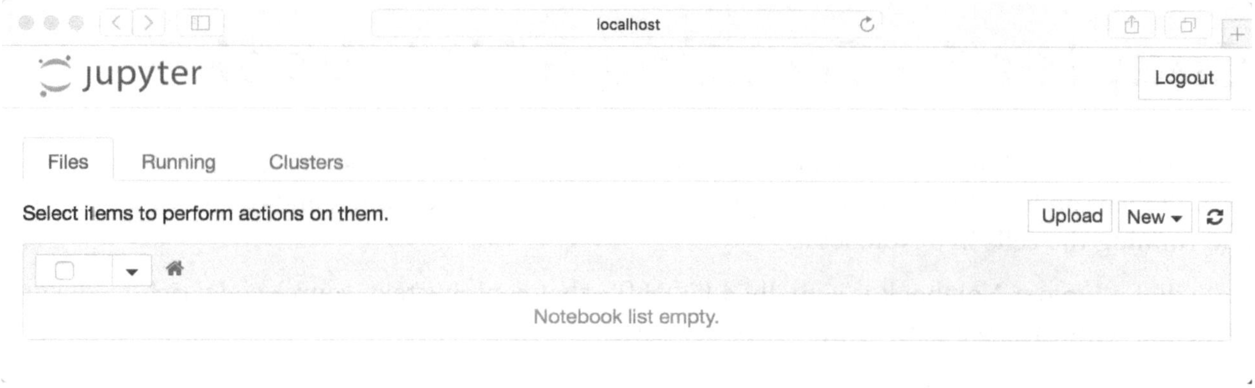

Fig. Intro-2: Jupyter Notebook initial page

Now you are ready to use the Jupyter Notebook!

Reader Feedback

I welcome your feedback. If you'd like to let me know what you thought of this book, you can send comments to the following email address:

comments@pythonlibrary.org

Errata

I try my best not to publish errors in my writings, but it happens from time to time. If you happen to see an error in this book, feel free to let me know by emailing me at the following:

errata@pythonlibrary.org

Code Examples

Code and Notebooks from the book can be downloaded from Github at the following address:

- https://github.com/driscollis/jupyternotebook101

Now, let's get started!

Chapter 1 - Creating a Notebook

Now that we have Jupyter Notebook installed, we can learn how you can use them. In this chapter, we will focus on learning how to run Jupyter Notebooks, create new ones, and the process of editing and running the cells in a Notebook.

Note that a Jupyter Notebook is actually a JSON file that contains text, source code, rich media and metadata with each segment of the JSON document stored in a cell.

To get started, open up a terminal or command prompt and navigate to the folder that you want to run your Notebook from. You can use the **cd** command for navigation in your terminal. Once you have changed directories to the folder you want to use for your Notebooks, you can start up Jupyter Notebook with the following command:

```
jupyter notebook
```

This will open your default web browser to the folder you specified and look something like this:

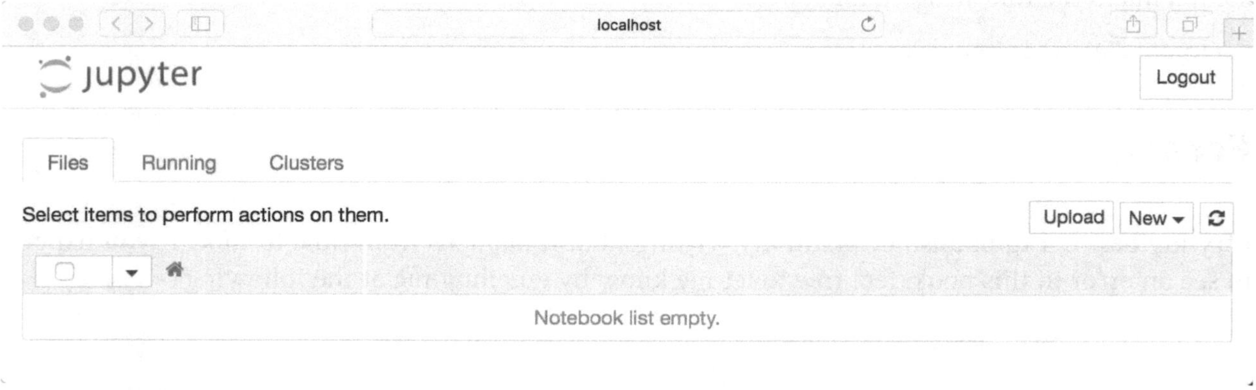

Fig. 1-1: Jupyter Notebook initial page

Now let's learn how to create a Notebook!

Creating a Notebook

Creating a Jupyter Notebook is actually really easy to do. If you want to create a Notebook, then you will need to click the button / combobox that is labeled **New** in the upper right hand side of the web browser. Here's a screenshot with the button circled in red:

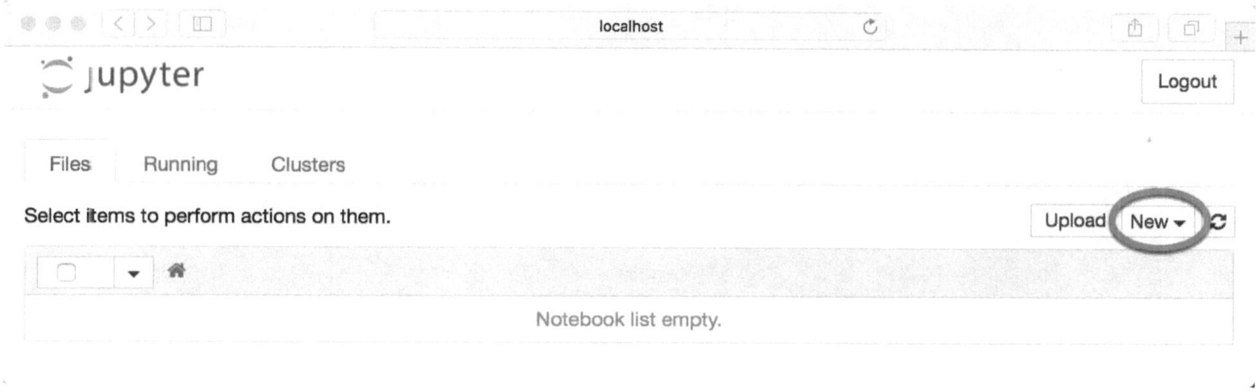

Fig. 1-2: Creating a new Notebook

If you have more than one Python version installed, then choose whichever Python version you would like the Notebook to use from within the combobox. When you have chosen your Python version, a new tab or window in your browser will open and you will have an empty Notebook that looks like this:

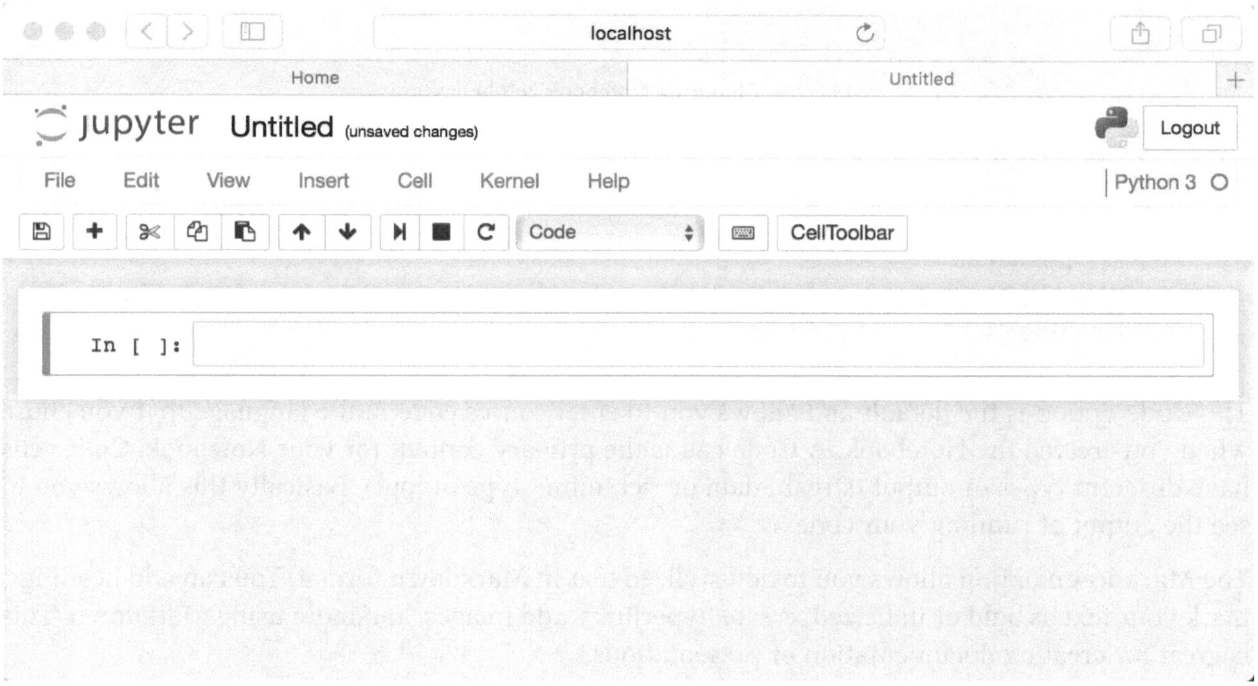

Fig. 1-3: An empty Notebook

By default, the Notebook's cells expect you to add code to them. A **cell** appears visually as a multi-line text box, kind of like a comment form on a website. These cells allow you to write code, Markdown and other types of text. To change cell's default behavior you can click on the combobox that is in the middle of the toolbar at the top of the page:

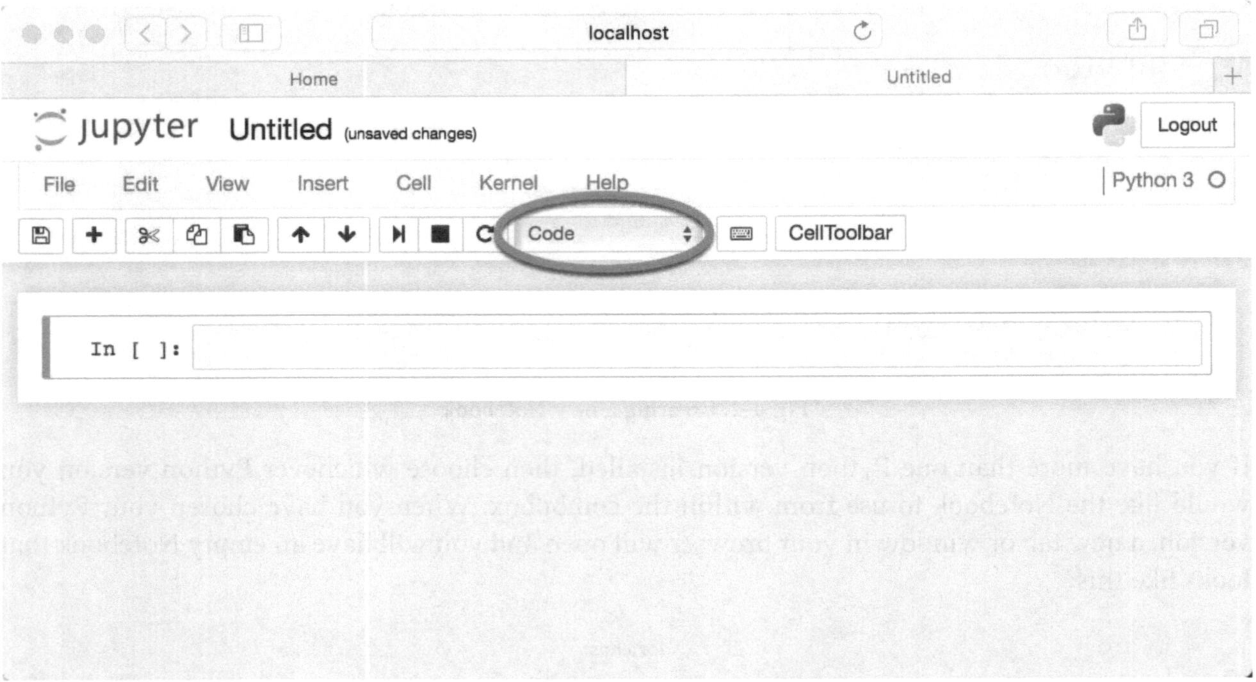

Fig. 1-4: Changing Notebook cell behavior

Here you can choose from the following four options:

- Code
- Markdown
- Raw NBConvert
- Heading

The **Code** option is the default and allows you to enter source code in the language that you chose when you created the Notebook. A Code cell is the primary content for your Notebook. Code cells have different types of output (stream data or rich mime-type output). Basically this allows you to see the output of running your code.

The **Markdown** option allows you to add stylized text in Markdown format. You can add headings, mark your text as bold or italicized, create hyperlinks, add images, and more using Markdown. This is great for creating documentation or presentations.

The **Raw NBConvert** is used for *unmodified* output for **nbconvert**, which is a tool that comes with Jupyter Notebook for converting the Notebook to other formats, such as PDF. The raw cell could be used for entering LaTeX to make converting the Notebook to PDF easier or you might enter some other markup, such as restructuredText if you want to convert your Notebook to Sphinx, which is Python's documentation library.

If you choose the **Heading** option you will see the following message:

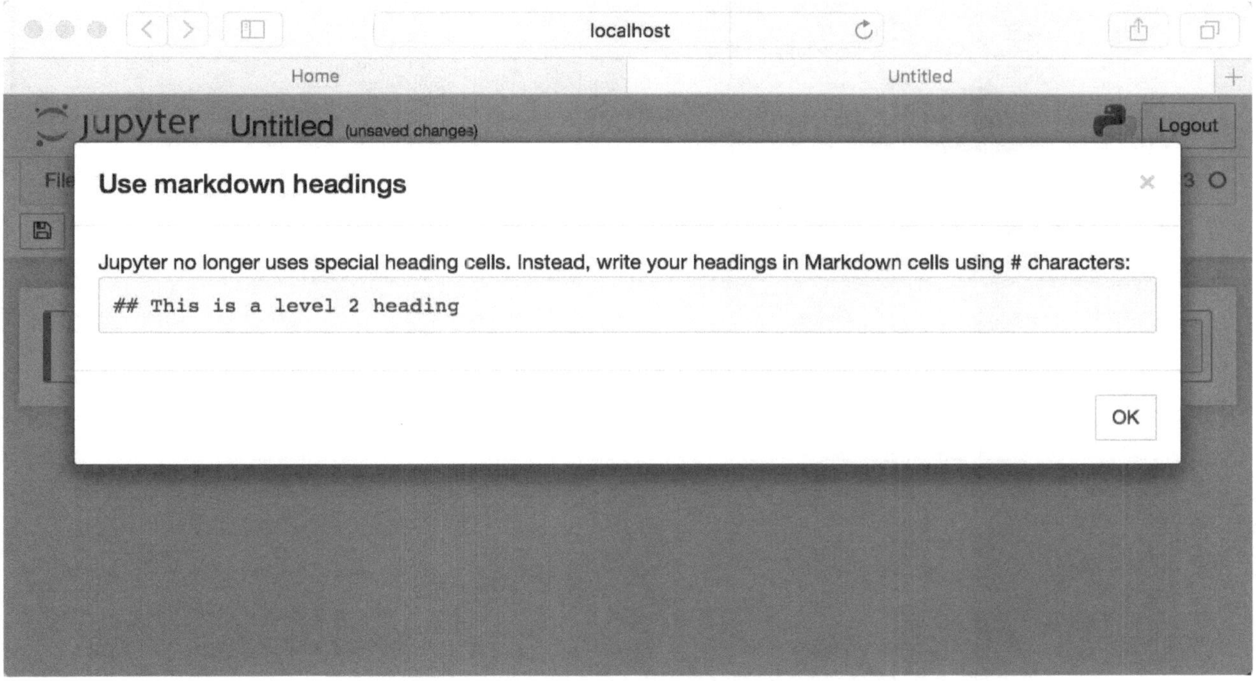

Fig. 1-5: Heading warning message

As you can see, the Heading option is no longer supported since you can add headings by just using Markdown.

Naming a Notebook

You might have noticed that the Notebook is currently labeled "Untitled". I circled it in the screenshot below to make it more obvious:

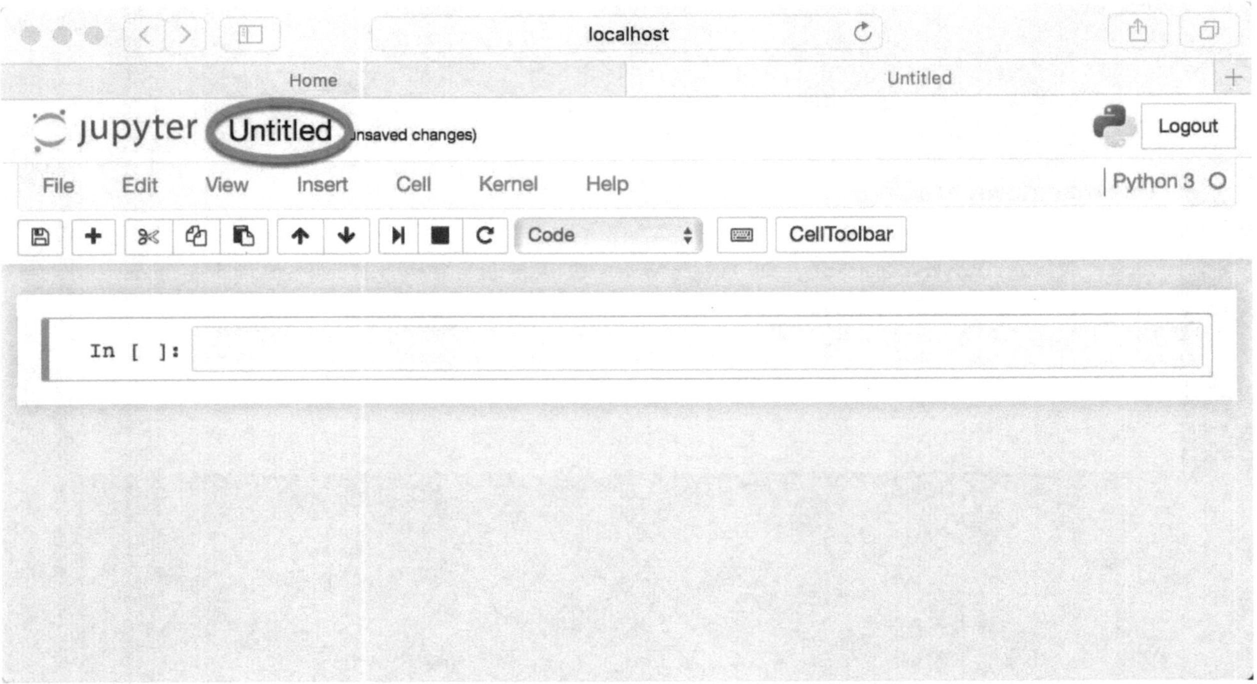

Fig. 1-6: Opening the rename Notebook dialog

You usually want to name your Notebook, so to do that, just click on the current title and you should see the following dialog appear:

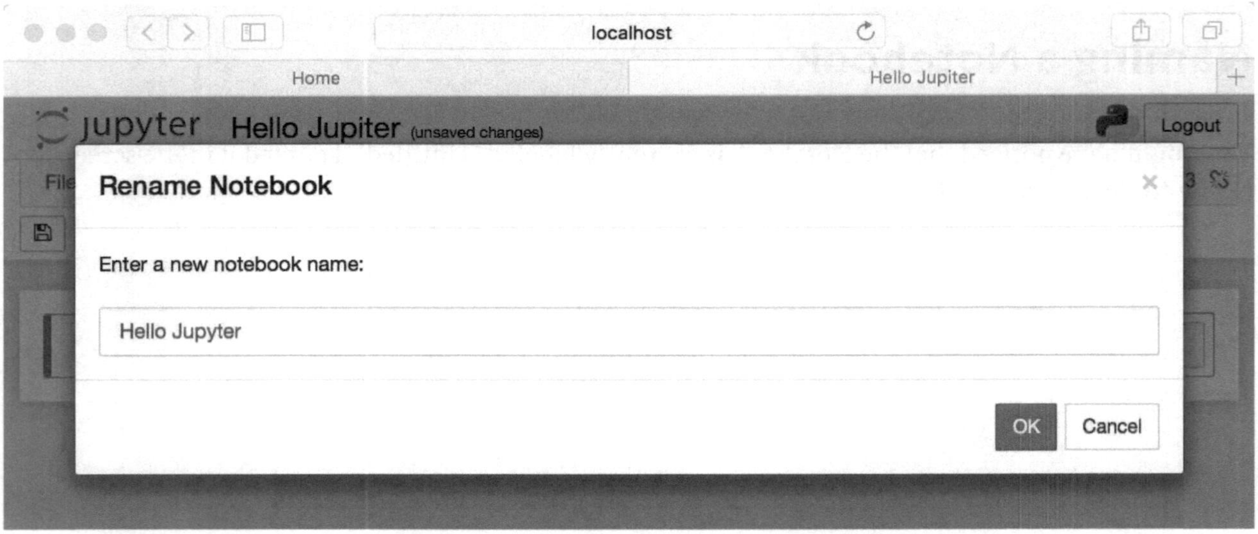

Fig. 1-7: Changing the title of the Notebook

Now you can enter any name that you desire. For this example, I put in "Hello Jupyter". Just be sure to press the **Rename** button when you are done to save your changes.

Running a Cell

The primary purpose of the Notebook cells is running code. The default programming language is Python, so let's take a moment and learn how we add code to a cell and run it. To make sure we are all on the same page, I am going to circle the cell in a screenshot of my current Notebook:

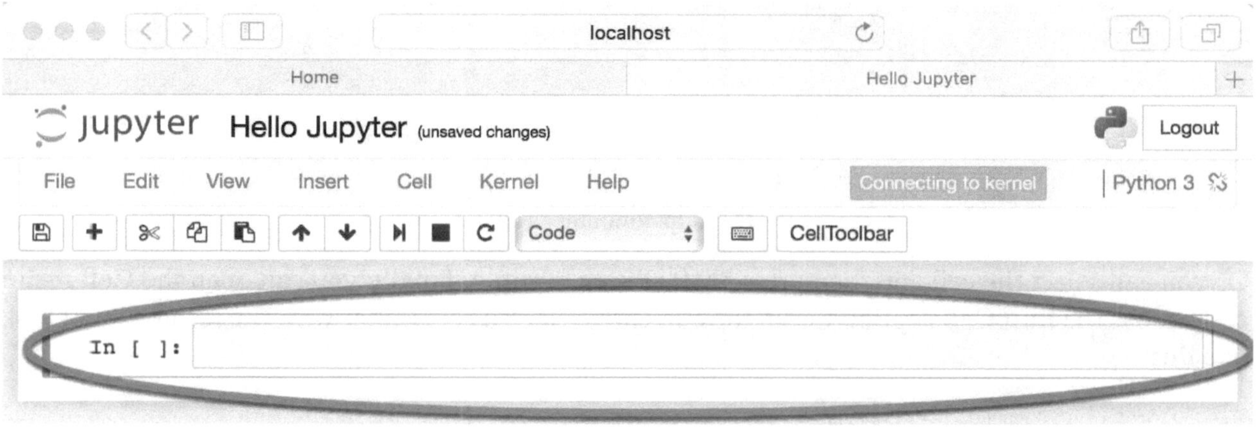

Fig. 1-8: The Notebook's cell

Now type the following code into your cell:

```
print('Welcome to Jupyter!')
```

Your cell should now look like this:

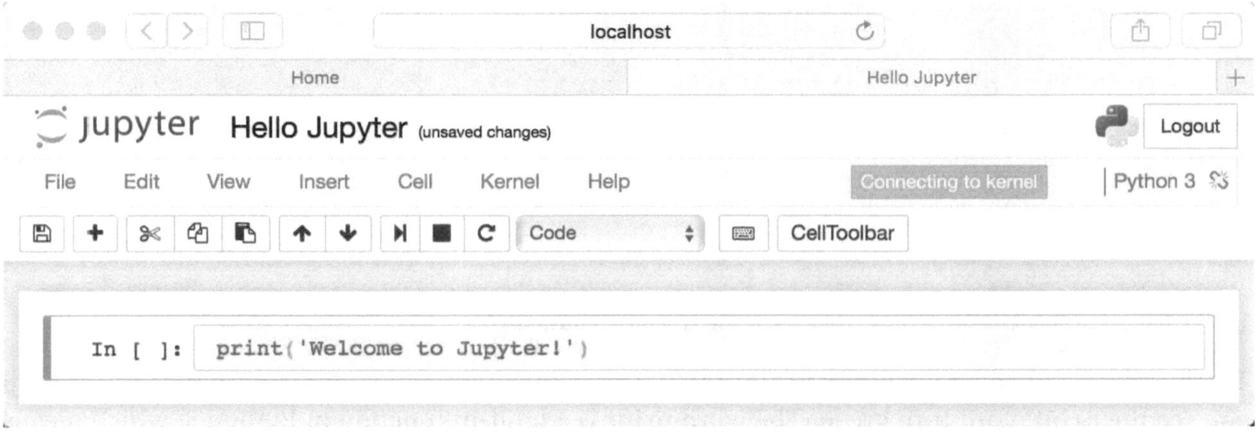

Fig. 1-9: Editing the cell

To run this code in your Notebook, you just need to press the **Run** button (circled below):

Fig. 1-10: Running a cell

Or you can select the cell and then press **Shift+Enter** to run it. Finally you can open the **Cell** menu and choose the **Run Cells** option to run the currently selected cell. Either way, the result should look like this:

Fig. 1-11: Cell output

The Jupyter Notebook will automatically apply syntax highlighting to your code, which is why you you see the **print** word turn green. The word **print** is a built-in function in Python 3, which means that you shouldn't use "print" as the name of one of your own variables.

If you have a typo in your code, Jupyter Notebook will print out the traceback when you run the code. Let's modify our code example so it has a typo in it by removing the closing parenthesis from the print statement:

```
print('Welcome to Jupyter!'
```

Now when you run the code, you should see the following:

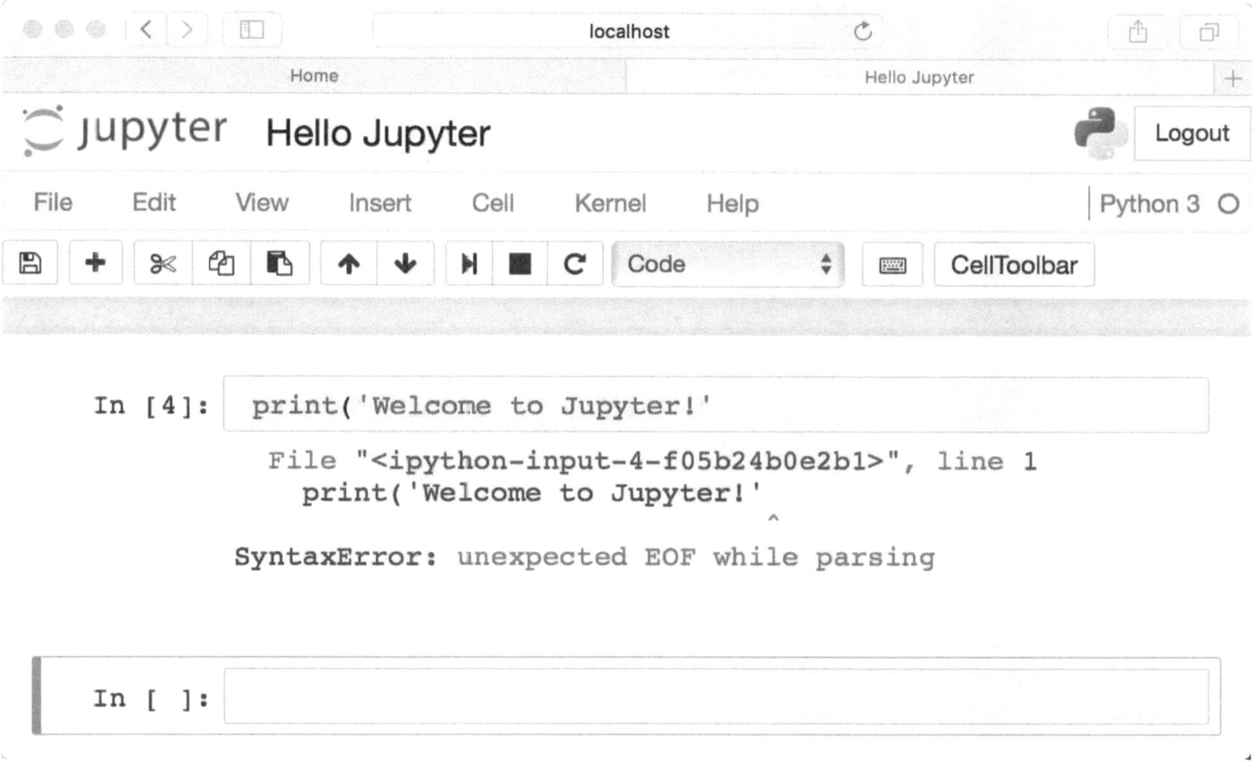

Fig. 1-12: Cell output of a typo

This is really helpful in debugging your code examples in the Notebook environment.

Coding Across Cells

One thing that isn't obvious at first is that when you create a variable in one cell, it can become available in subsequent cells. This only happens if you run the cells in order though. Let's create a quick example. In your Notebook, create two cells. It should look like this:

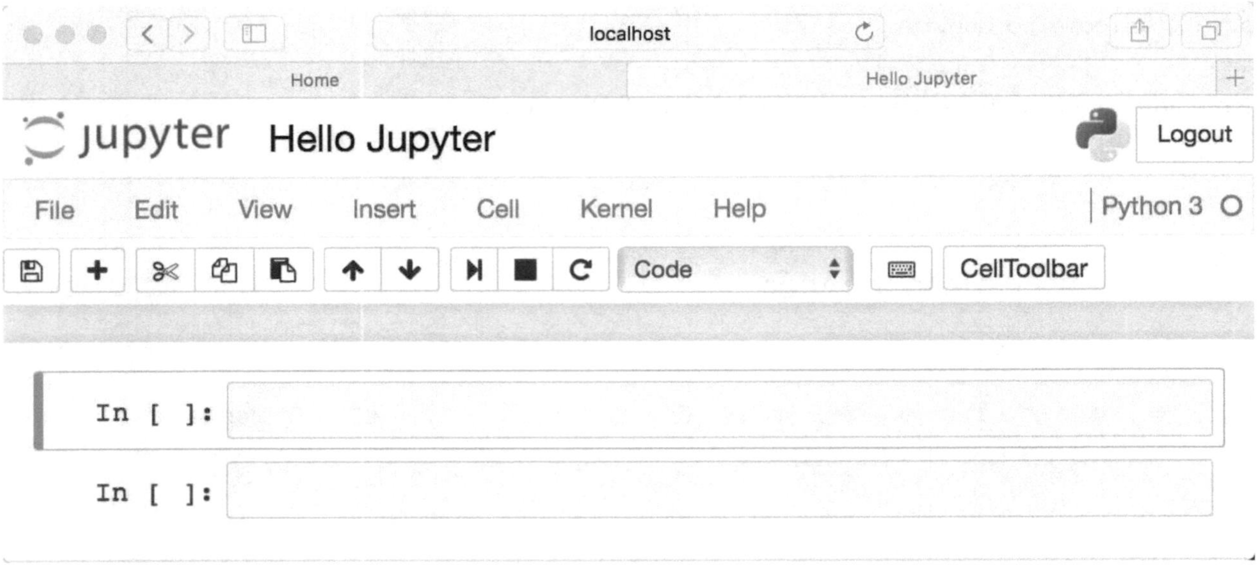

Fig. 1-13: Two cells

Now enter the following code in the first cell:

```
name = 'Jupyter'
```

Then in the second cell, enter the following:

```
print(name)
```

Your cells should now look like this:

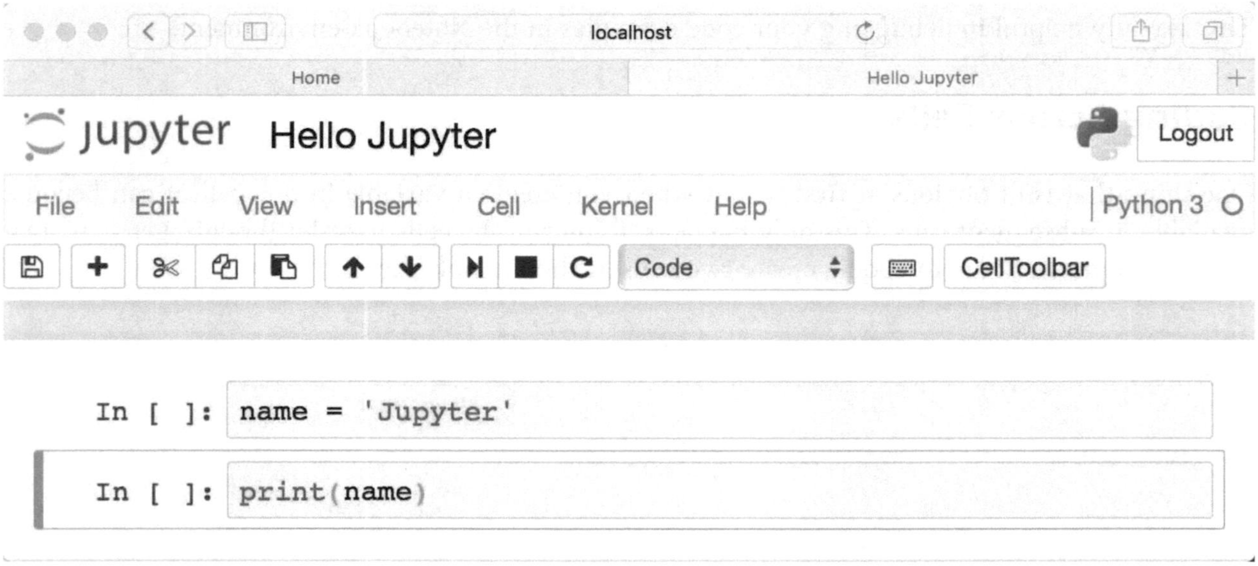

Fig. 1-14: Code in two cells

Try running the second cell and you should get a **NameError**:

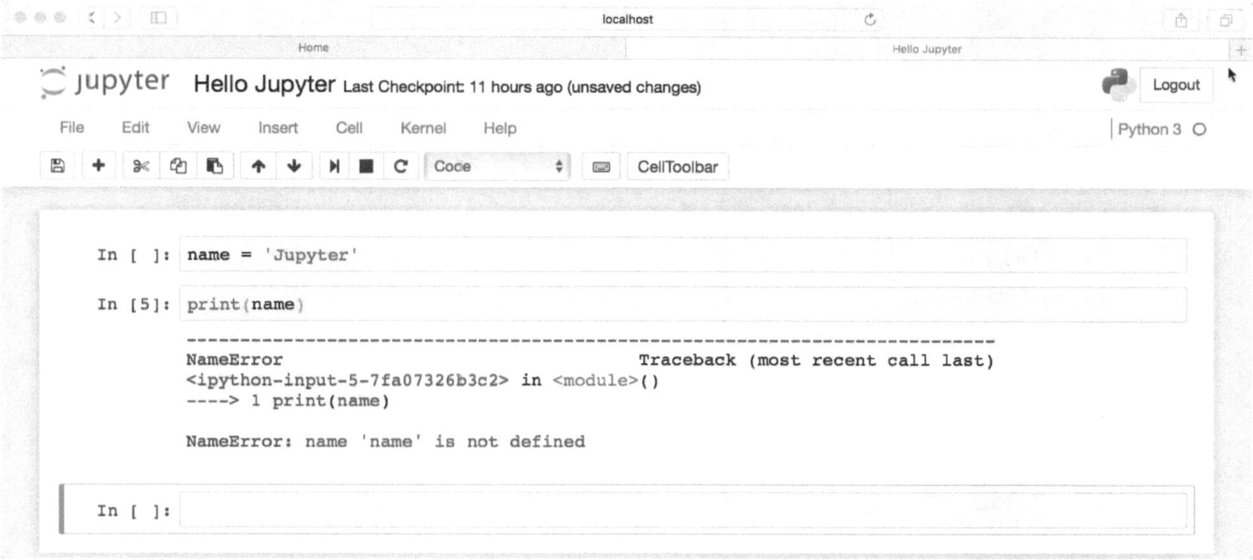

Fig. 1-15: Cells run out of order

However if you run the first cell and then the second cell in order, your code will work and the output will look like this:

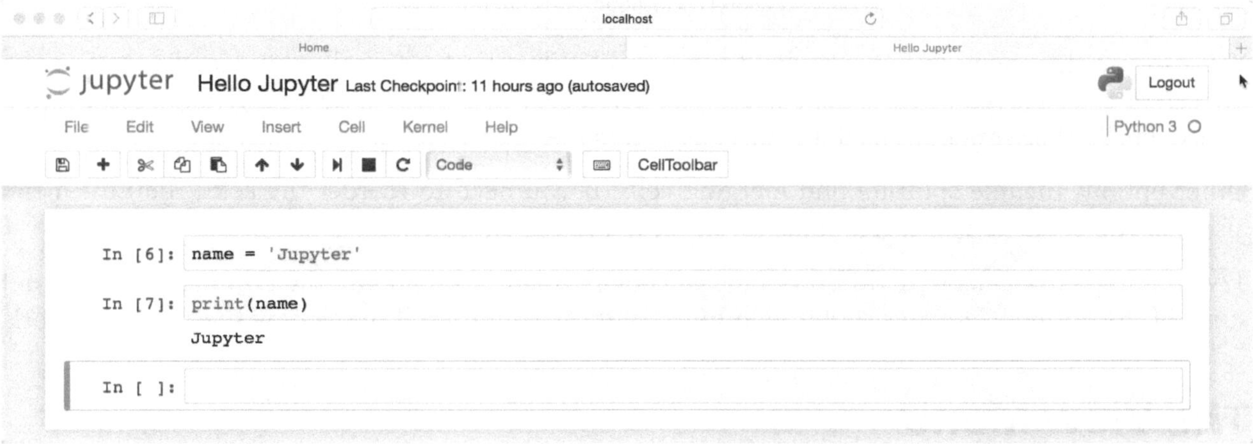

Fig. 1-16: Cells run in order

This kind of coding is very useful when you are presenting topics, but it can be confusing when the code doesn't work because you forgot to run the examples in order.

Cell Management

Jupyter Notebook has a lot of fun options for cell management. Just open the **Edit** menu to get a listing of your options. Here is a screenshot that shows some of the options that are available:

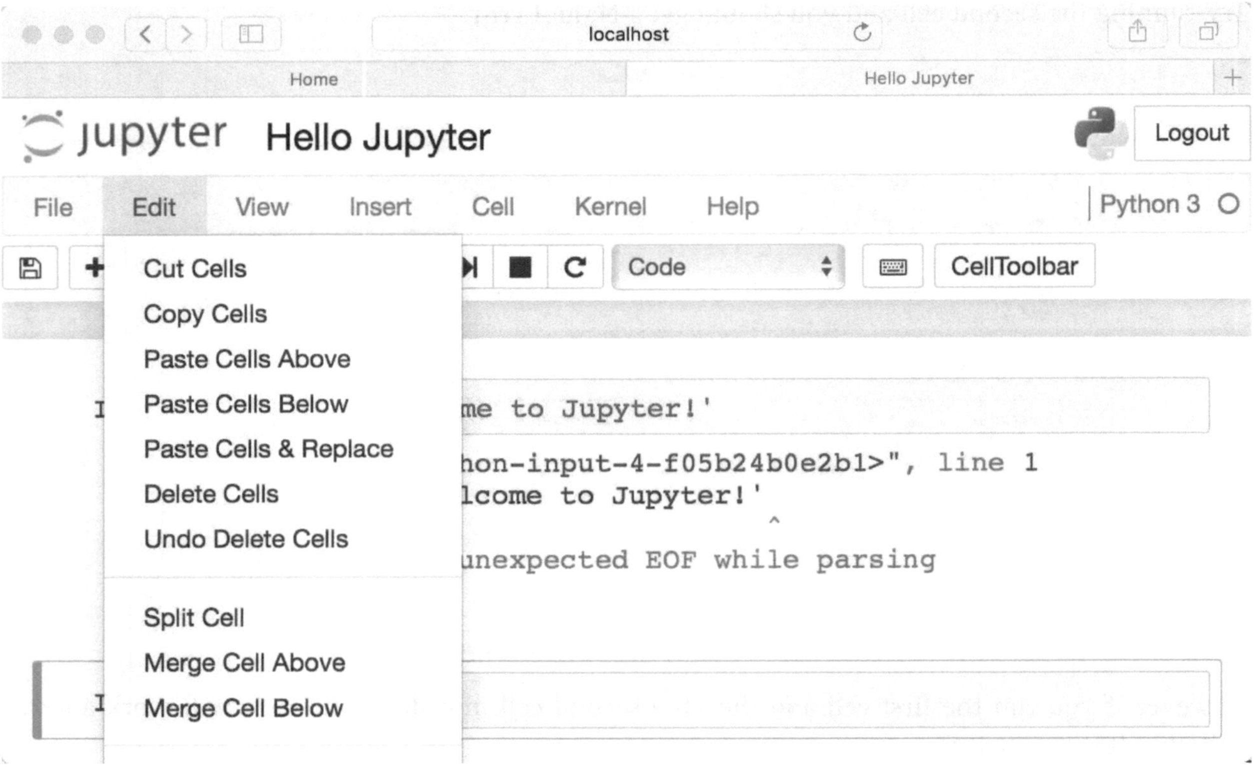

Fig. 1-17: Notebook Edit menu

You can use this menu to cut, copy and paste cells. When pasting a cell, you can choose to paste the cell or cells above or below the currently selected cell. You can also do a paste that replaces that selected cell. There are options to delete cells in this menu as well.

Other options include splitting and merging cells. If you need to reorder the cells, the **Edit** menu also has you covered as it has options for **moving** cells up or down.

Try creating a few cells with different lines of code in them. Then go into the Edit menu and try out some of the options. I always find it helpful to try things out myself to see how they actually work.

The View Menu

You can use the **View** menu (screenshot below) for toggling the visibility of your Notebook's header / title. You can also toggle the visibility of the toolbar here and the line numbers in your cells.

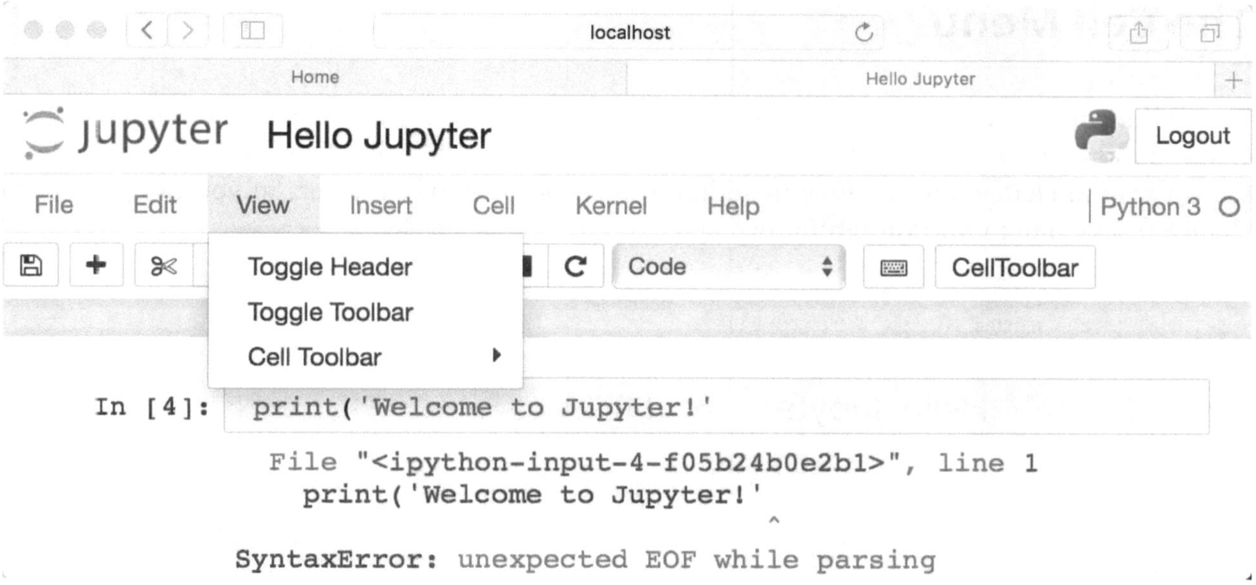

Fig. 1-18: Notebook View menu

There is also a sub-menu in the **View** menu called the **Cell Toolbar**. Here you will find different ways to edit or add metadata to the cells, among other things.

The Insert Menu

The **Insert** menu is used for inserting cells either above or below the currently selected cell. That's all it is currently used for.

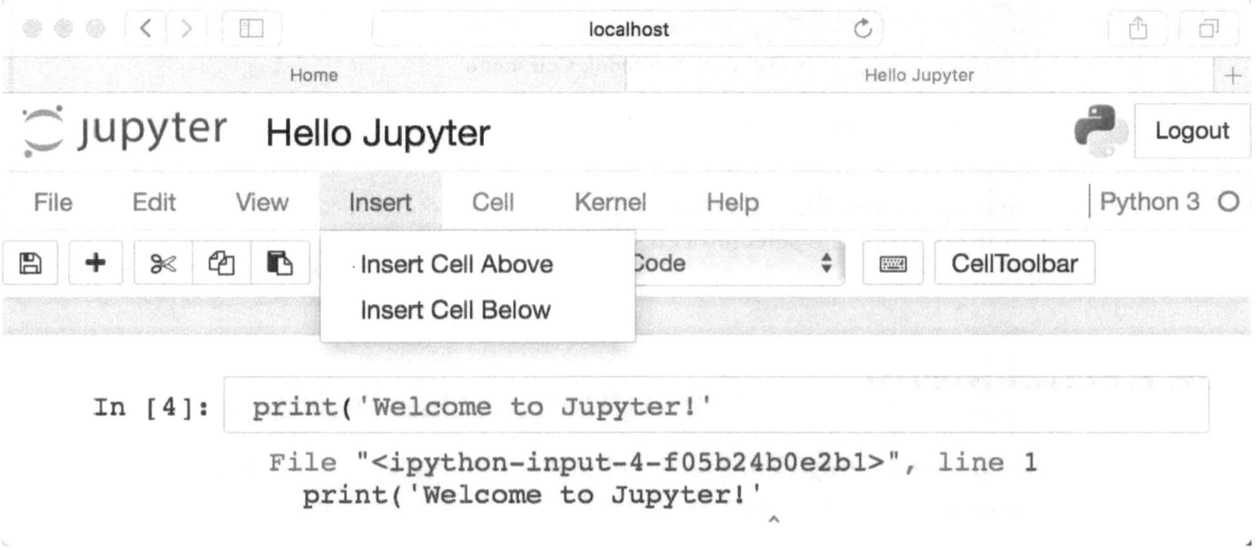

Fig. 1-19: Notebook Insert menu

The Cell Menu

The **Cell** menu is where you go to run the cells. You can run the selected cell by choosing the "**Run Cells**" option. You can also run all the cells or a selection of the cells. This menu also provides a second way to change the cell type in addition to using the handy toolbar. So you can go here to change from **Code** to **Markdown** for example.

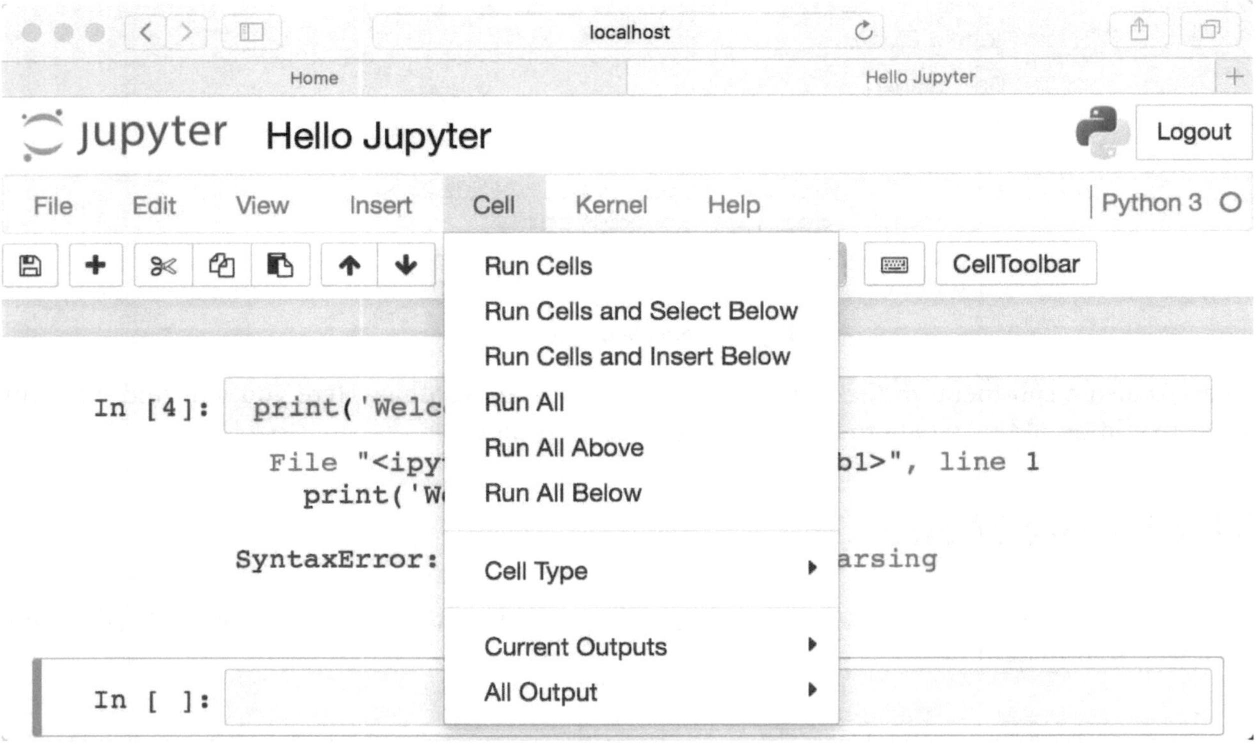

Fig. 1-20: Notebook Cell menu

You may also do the following tasks from the cell menu:

- toggle the output from the cells on or off
- clear the output from the selected cell
- clear all the cells

The Kernel Menu

The **Kernel** menu is for interacting with the kernel that is running your code behind the scenes. In this instance, the Kernel refers to Python (i.e. IPython). Here is a screenshot that shows some of the options available:

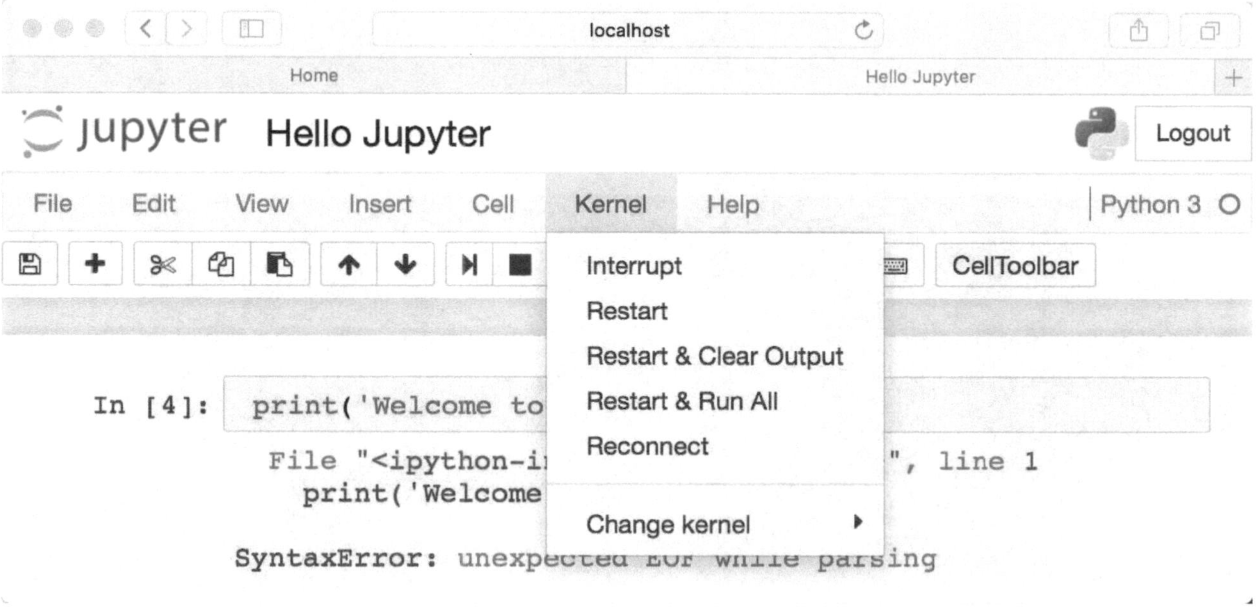

Fig. 1-21: Notebook Kernel menu

You can restart it here in a number of different ways. For example, you can just restart the kernel or you can restart and clear output. You can also interrupt, reconnect and shutdown the kernel.

If you have multiple kernels on your machine, such as Python 2 and Python 3, you can switch between them from this menu as well under the **Change kernel** option

Starting a Terminal in the Browser

The Jupyter Notebook **Home** page has some other options beside just creating new Notebooks. For example, you can also create a **Text File**, a **Folder** or a **Terminal** form the **New** combobox. The first two are pretty self-explanatory, however the **Terminal** option is interesting. If you choose that option, a new tab or window will appear with a terminal-like session running in your browser. Here is what it looked like on my machine:

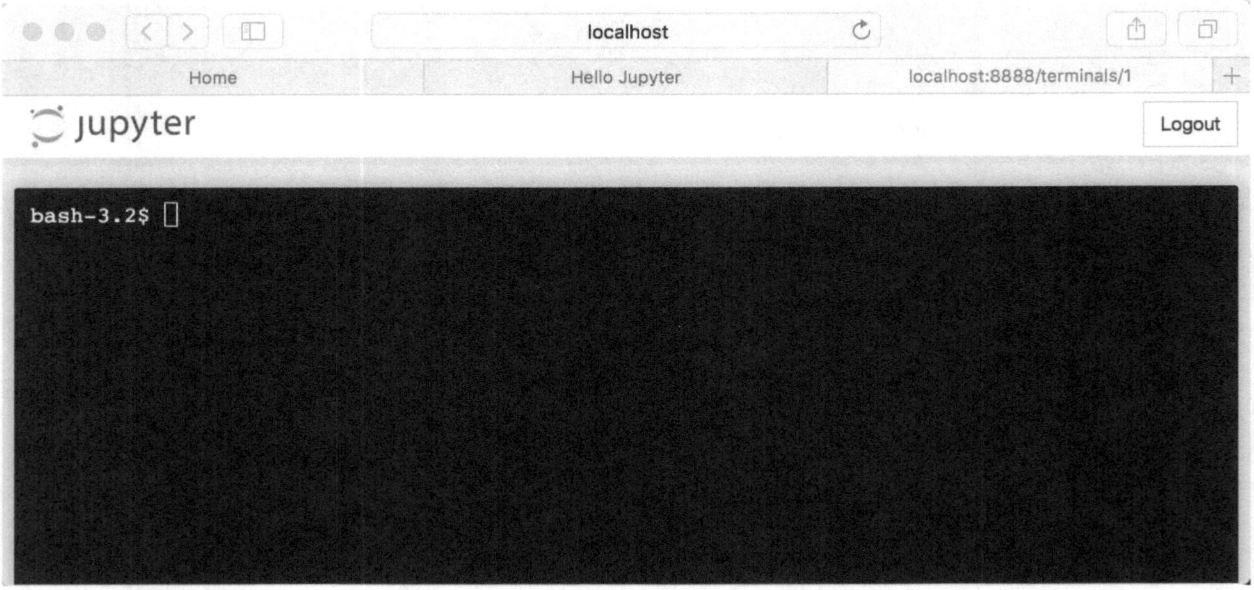

Fig. 1-22: Terminal in a browser

You can use this terminal to run terminal commands like **ls** in the folder that you are currently in. This is useful for debugging your environment.

Note: When I ran this on my Windows 7 machine, I got a Powershell terminal. I would assume you would get cmd.exe if Powershell was not installed.

Managing Notebooks

Another handy feature of the Home page is that you can click on the **Running** tab to see what Notebooks or Terminals are running. Here is a screenshot of the Running tab circled:

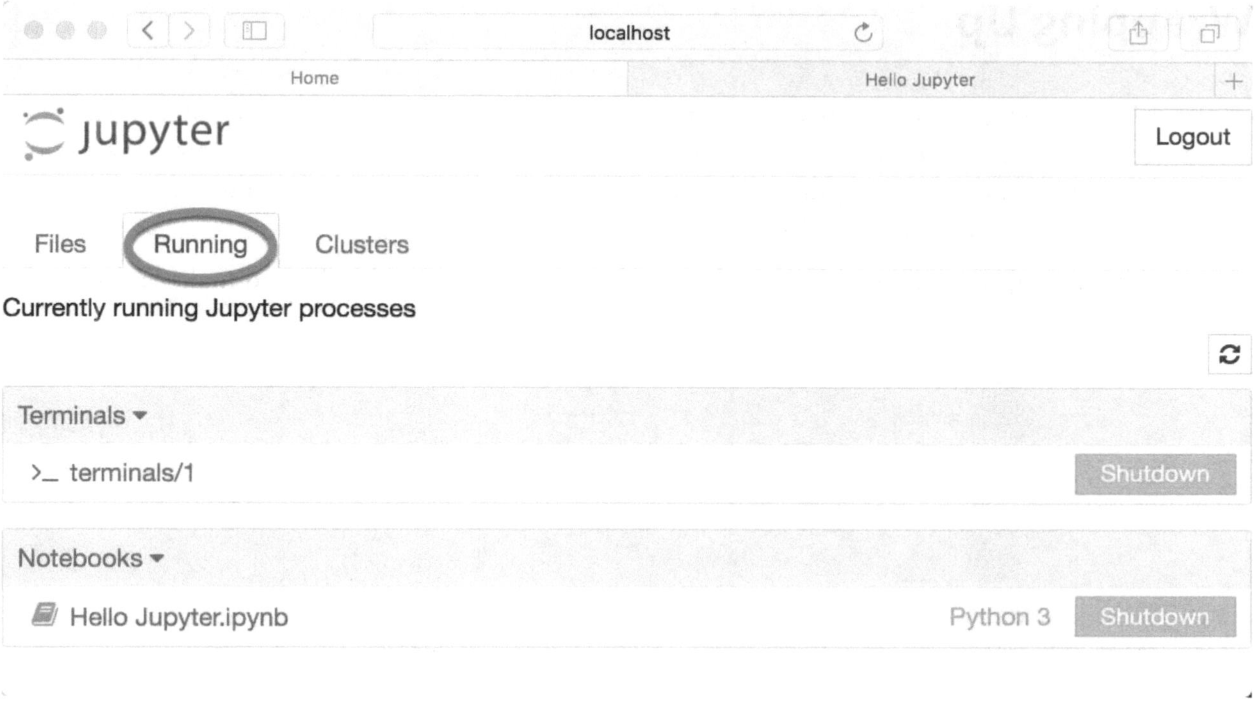

Fig. 1-23: The running tab

When you have the Running tab selected, you can use it to shutdown running Notebooks and Terminals.

Jupyter Clusters

If you have a Jupyter cluster set up, you can get access to those features via the **Clusters** tab:

Fig. 1-24: The clusters tab

Note that you will need **IPython parallel** installed to use Clusters.

Wrapping Up

We have learned a lot about how to create Jupyter Notebooks. In this chapter we created a Notebook and a Terminal. We learned how to create cells and run them. We also learned about the various menus that you can use to manipulate the cells. The toolbar holds the most commonly used menu functions, so be sure to play around with those as well.

In the next chapter, we will learn how to format the Jupyter Notebook cells and make rich content.

Chapter 2 - Creating Rich Text in Notebooks

There is a lot more to Jupyter's Notebook cells than just running code. You can also use a markup language called **Markdown** for creating rich text in your cells. Rich text is basically text that you can style like you would in Microsoft Word or LibreOffice. You can use Markdown to bold text, add headings and much more. This is useful for comments and descriptions about your code. You can create hyperlinks to documentation that relates to what you are working on. You can add images that correlate with your code. You can also create charts and graphs in Python and have them display in your output.

In this chapter you will learn about all of these features. Let's get started!

Styling a Cell

This book isn't a Markdown guide, but I will cover the basics here so you can use it in your Jupyter Notebooks effectively. There are many resources of the web that you can use to supplement what you learn here. Here are a couple that I have found helpful:

- https://www.markdownguide.org/
- https://guides.github.com/features/mastering-markdown/

To get started using Markdown in your Jupyter Notebook, you need to change the cell type to **Markdown** from the combobox:

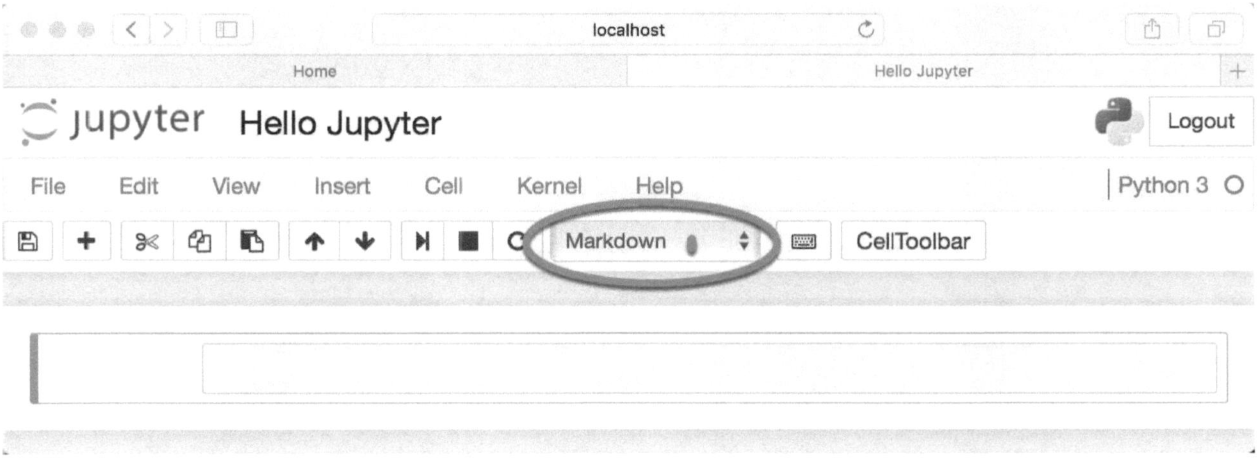

Fig. 2-1: Changing the cell type to Markdown

Headers

Jupyter Notebooks support 5 levels of headings. These are controlled via the octothorpe or pound sign (#). A single pound sign equals **Heading 1**. Add additional pound signs up to five to create the other headings. Here is an example of what it looks like in a Markdown cell before the cell is run:

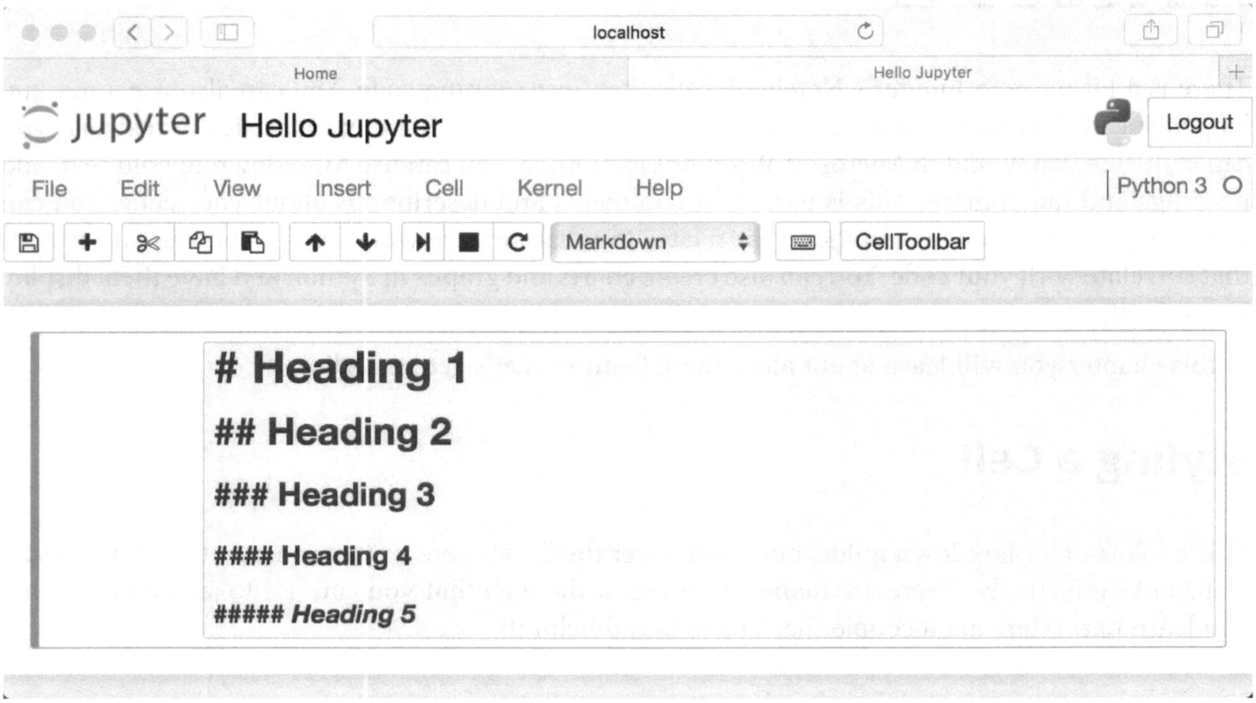

Fig. 2-2: Five different heading styles in Markdown

When you run the cell, it will look like this:

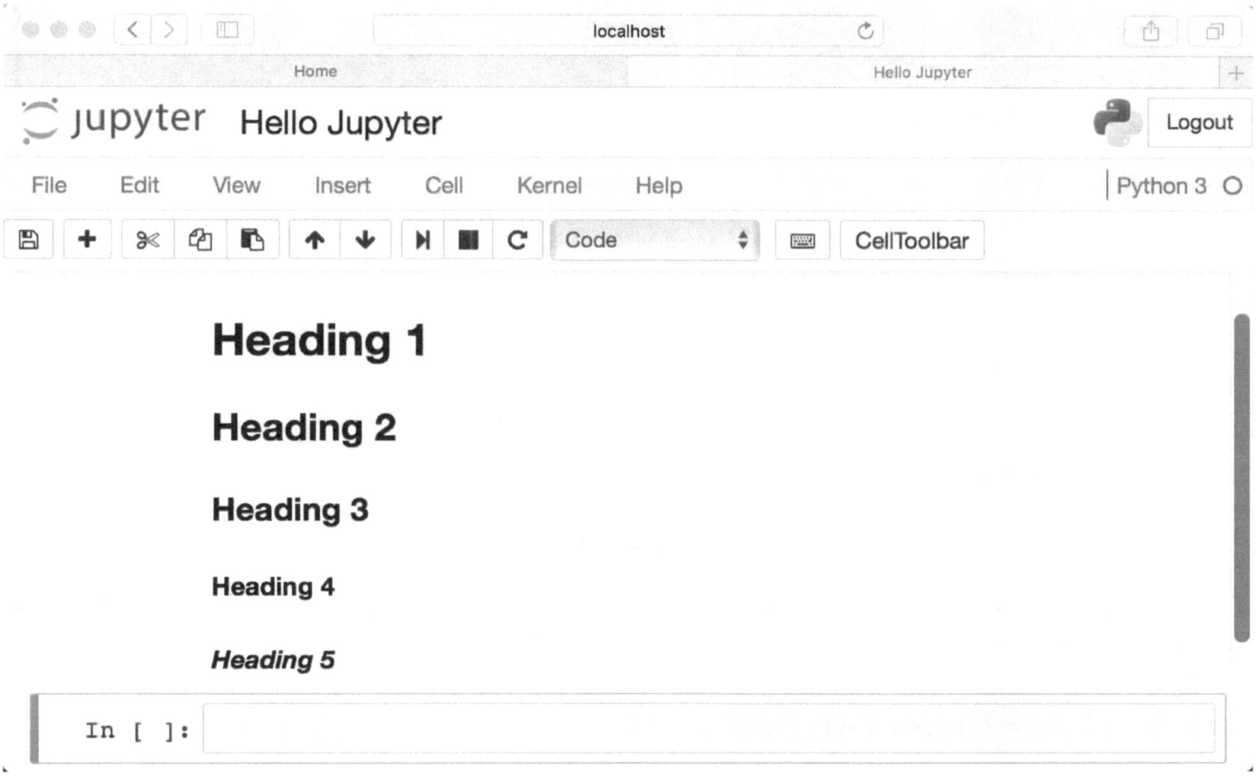

Fig. 2-3: Heading formatting when the cell is ran

That looks pretty nice.

If you want to edit it again, just double-click on the text and the cell will return to editing mode.

Styling Text

Jupyter Markdown supports bold, italics and strike-through. To make your text bold, you can use two asterisks before and after the text that you want to make bold. If you would prefer to add emphasis (or italicize) your text, just use one asterisk before and after. Finally, for strike-through, you need to use two tildes. Here is what it looks like in a Notebook cell:

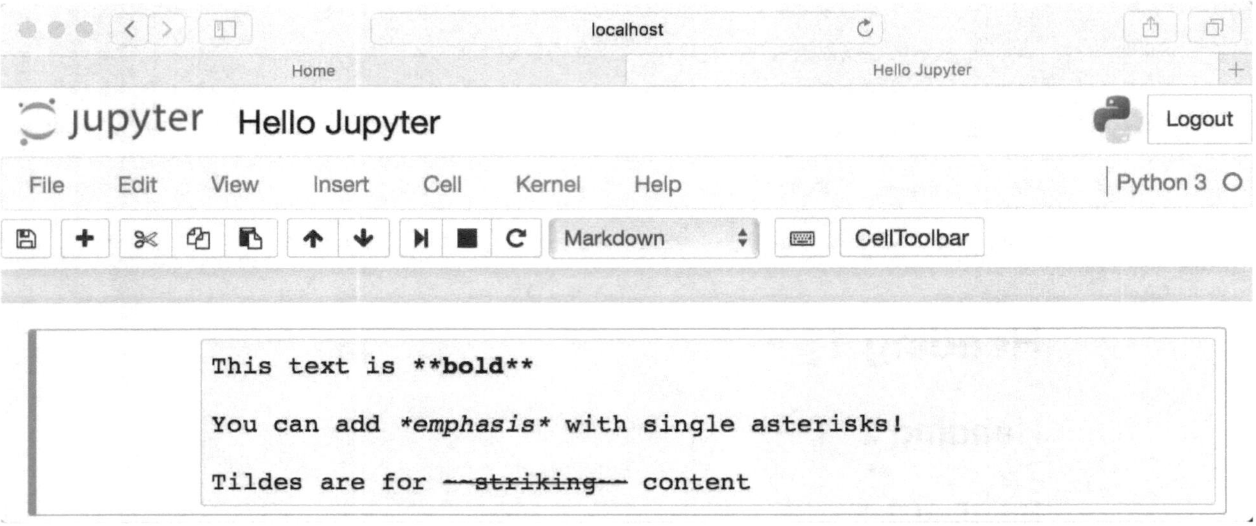

Fig. 2-4: Adding styling to your text

If you would like to change the text's color, then you can use HTML tags for that. Just enter the following text into your cell:

```
<font color='green'>Green text</font>
```

Note that this is deprecated in HTML5, but it works just fine in Jupyter Notebook. However you can also use the new HTML5 standard way of changing text color:

```
<span style="color:red">Red text</span>
```

Here is what the code looks like in the cell before we run it:

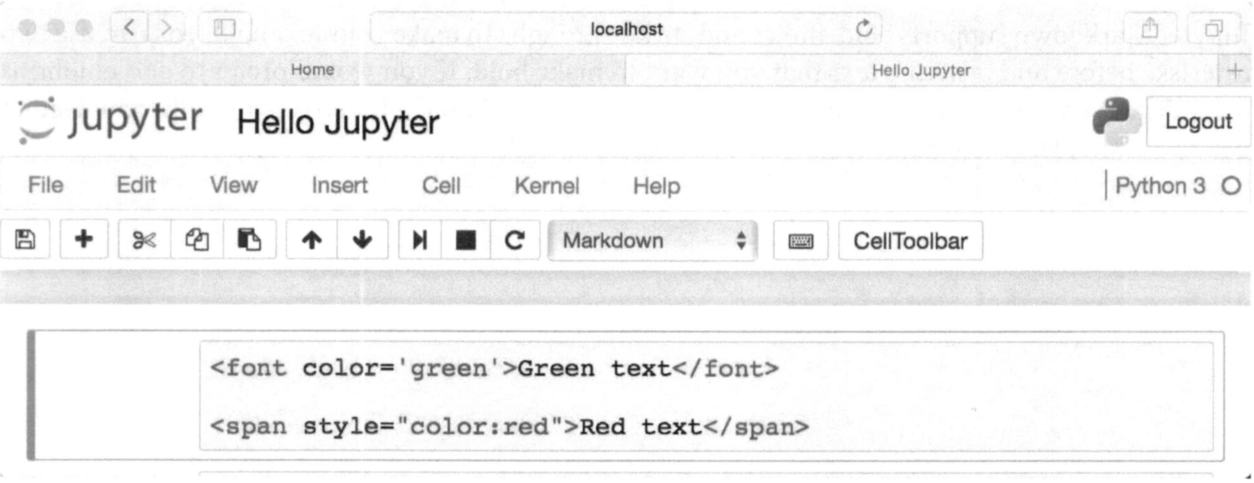

Fig. 2-5: Using HTML tags to change text color

Now let's run the cell and see what it looks like:

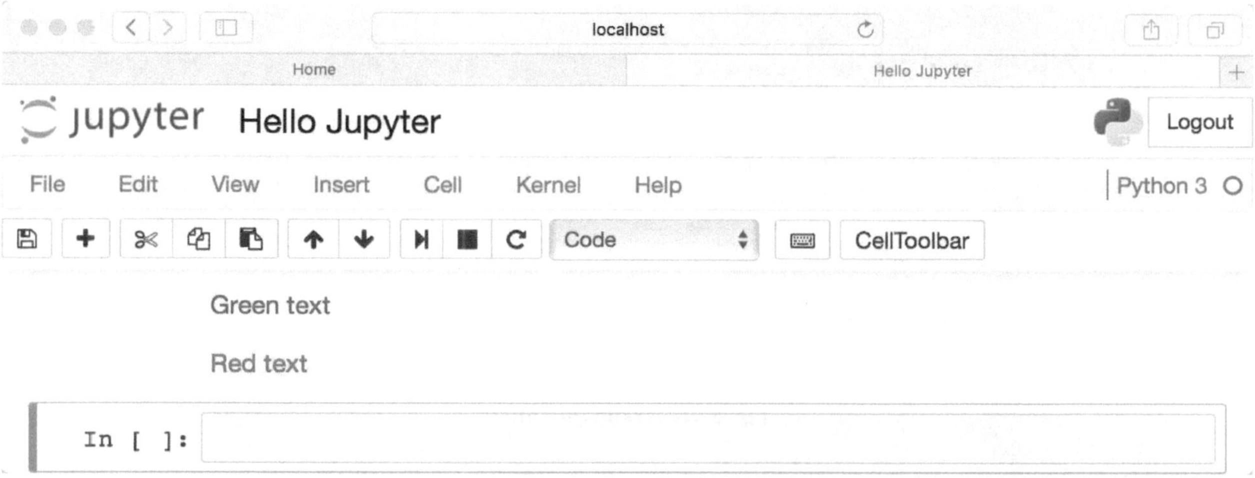

Fig. 2-6: Text in full color

Pretty neat! If you know how to use CSS, you can also apply style to your Jupyter Notebook that way. If you want to set up a custom theme, you will need to save it here:

```
~/.jupyter/custom/custom.css
~/.jupyter/custom/custom.js
```

There are actually pre-made themes out on the web for the Jupyter Notebook. You should look them up and try a few out to see if you prefer using one of those over the default theme.

Lists (Bullets)

Markdown has a pretty simple method for creating bulleted lists. All you need to do is use a dash, an asterisk or a plus. Here is an example:

```
- List item 1
+ List item 2
* List item 3
```

If you add the above to a Notebook cell and then run the cell, you should see the following:

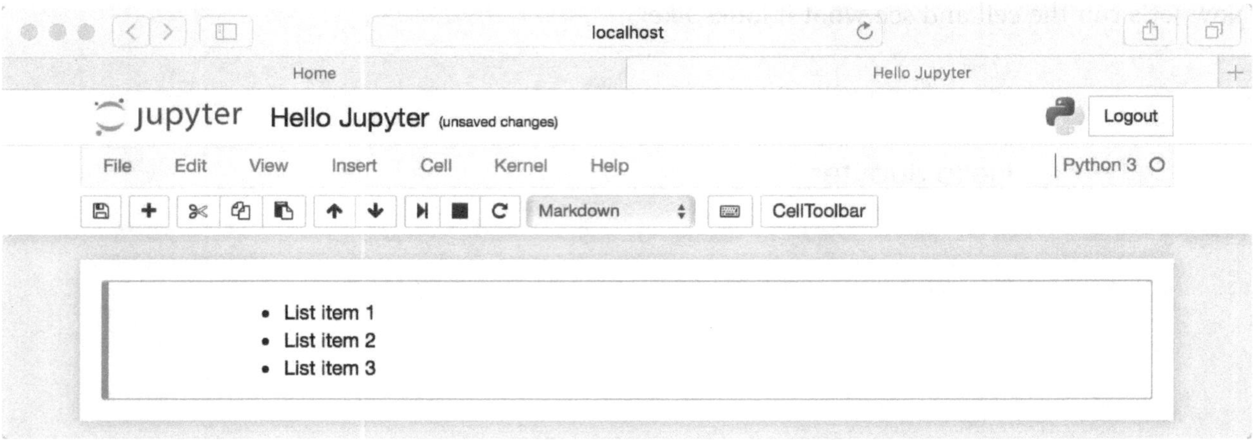

Fig. 2-7: Markdown bullets

These lists also support properly indented paragraphs. Here is an example of a paragraph using the ipsum lorem text:

- Lorem ipsum dolor sit amet, consectetur adipiscing elit, sed do eiusmod tempor incididunt ut labore et dolore magna aliqua. Ut enim ad minim veniam, quis nostrud exercitation ullamco laboris nisi ut aliquip ex ea commodo consequat. Duis aute irure dolor in reprehenderit in voluptate velit esse cillum dolore eu fugiat nulla pariatur. Excepteur sint occaecat cupidatat non proident, sunt in culpa qui officia deserunt mollit anim id est laborum

If you run this in your Notebook, you will see that the paragraph wraps and indents as you would expect:

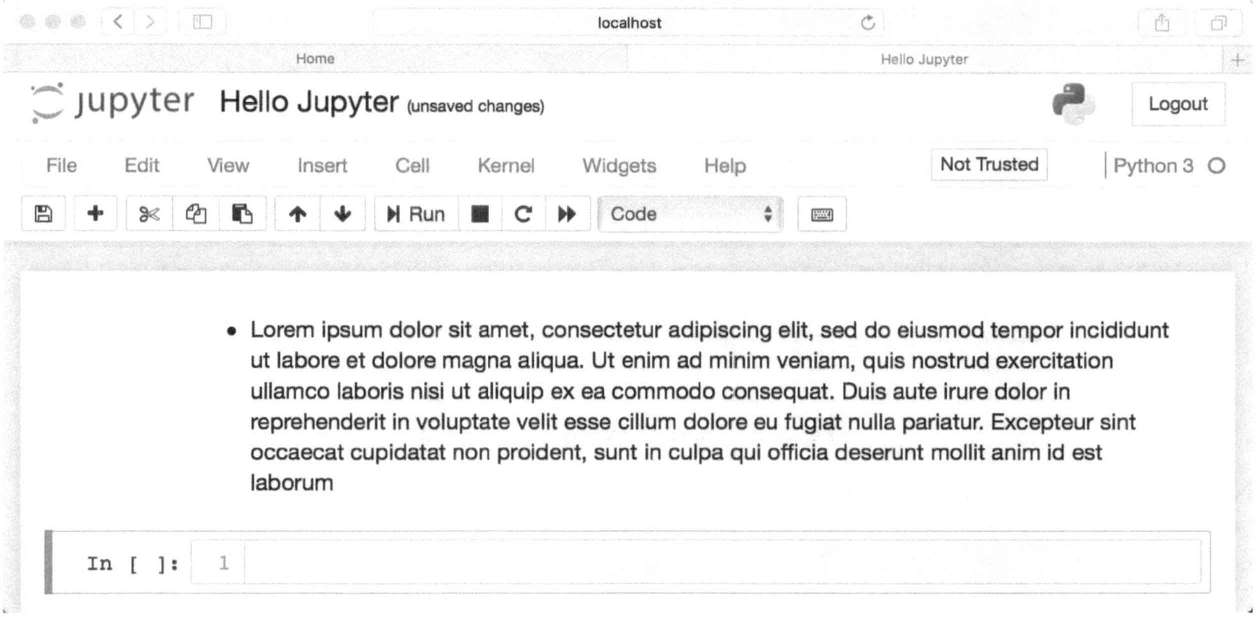

Fig. 2-8: Markdown bullet paragraph

Hyperlinks

You can also add hyperlinks to your Jupyter Notebooks in Markdown. Here is the syntax that you need to use to insert a hyperlink:

```
[Text](http://www.my_website.com)
```

You will note that the text that you want to turn into a hyperlink must start and end with a square bracket. Then to add a link, you must immediately follow the closing square brace with an open parentheses followed by the URL that you want the hyperlink to map to, which is then finished with a closing parentheses. Here's a more realistic example:

```
Python [website](http://www.python.org)
```

Let's enter the code above into a Notebook cell:

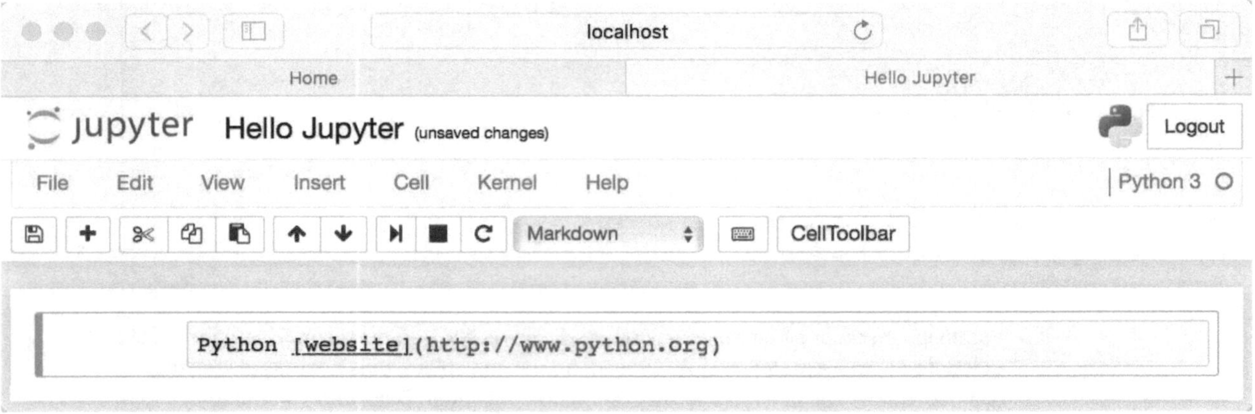

Fig. 2-9: Hyperlink example before run

Now when you run this cell, you will see that it looks like this:

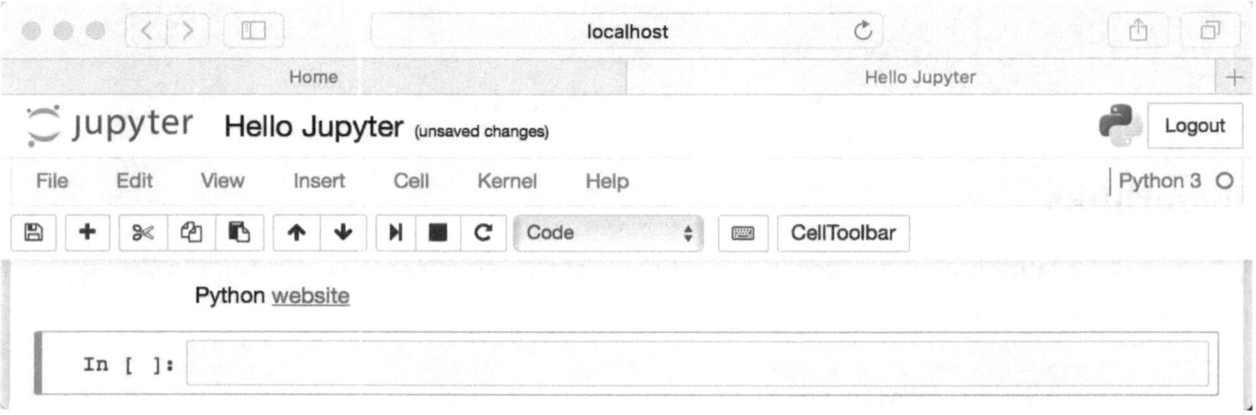

Fig. 2-10: Hyperlink example after run

Now let's learn how to add images to our Notebooks.

Adding Images

Markdown also supports adding images to your Jupyter Notebooks. You can easily add an image by using the following syntax if you want to display an image that is on your local machine:

```
![title](snakehead.jpg)
```

Note that this syntax is very similar to the hyperlink syntax except that it has an exclamation point at the beginning. also note that this will **not** embed the image in your Jupyter Notebook. what this means is that if you were to convert the Notebook to another format, the image may not survive the conversion.

You can also use this syntax to load an image from the Internet:

```
![title](http://www.somewebsite.com/picture.jpg)
```

You can also use the **IPython** module to insert Images and easily control the size of the image that you want to insert into a cell. Here is some sample code you can use in your Notebook cell to add an image that is 100x100 pixels in size. Note that you need to change the cell type back to code to use this though since this is no longer Markdown.

```
from IPython.display import Image
from IPython.core.display import HTML
Image(url="snakehead.jpg", width=100, height=100)
```

When you run this code in your browser, you will note that the image shows up as output instead of just replacing the cell like it does when you run Markdown.

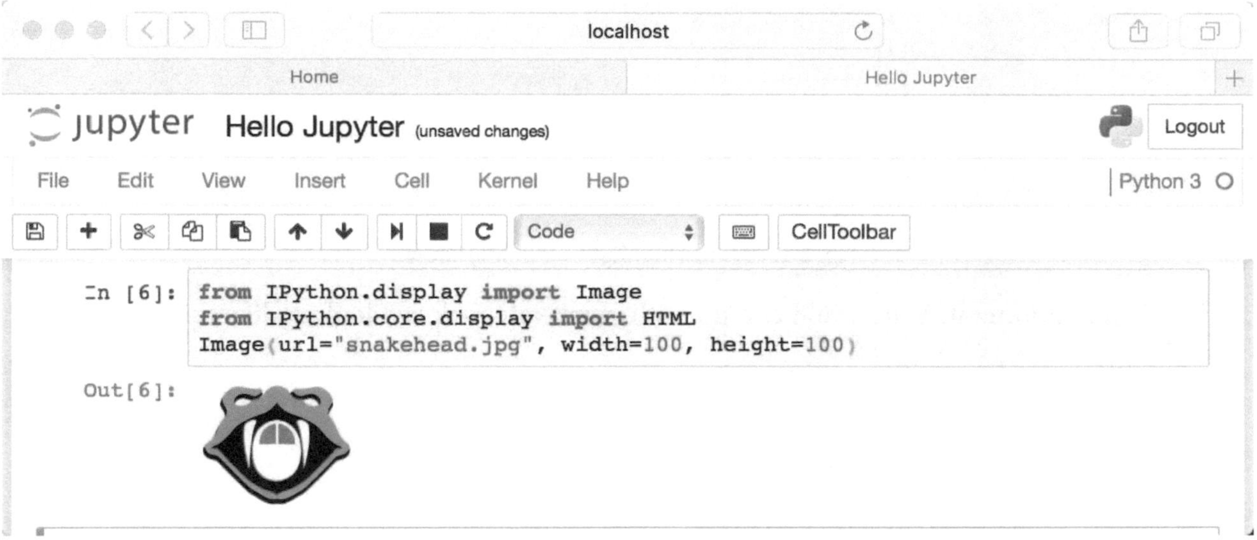

Fig. 2-11: Inserting an image with the IPython module

You can also insert images using an IPython "magic" keyword, but we will look at that in another chapter.

Code and Syntax Highlighting

You can also use Markdown in your Jupyter Notebook to highlight code both inline and in blocks of code. Let's look at an inline code example first. To mark code inline, just put a single back-tick at the beginning and end of the word:

```
This `code` is called Inline code and has to have back-ticks around it
```

If you want to add syntax highlighting to a block of code, then you need wrap it with 3 back-ticks at the beginning and end of the block of code. You can also just indent the block of code four spaces, but that won't apply any syntax highlighting. Also note that to apply a specific language's syntax highlighting, you can specify the programming language by entering it immediately following the beginning 3 back-ticks.

Let's try it out. Enter the following code in a Notebook cell:

Fig. 2-12: Syntax highlighting in Markdown

Now let's try running it. You should end up with your Notebook cell looking like this:

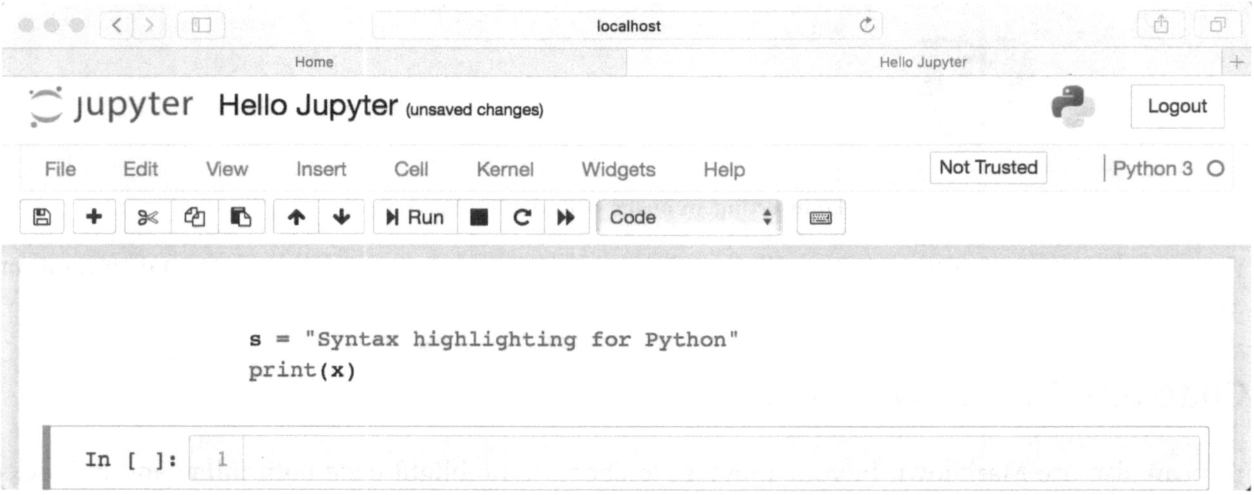

Fig. 2-13: Running the Syntax highlighting code

Try modifying this example by changing it to show Javascript or some other programming language.

Wrapping Up

In this chapter we learned how to add rich text to your Jupyter Notebook's cells. We can do this because Jupyter Notebook supports using the Markdown markup language. We can use this markup to make text bold and italicized. You can also use it to add lists (bullets), hyperlinks and code. You can even add syntax highlighting to your code. Finally we learned how to display images with Jupyter Notebook.

Chapter 3 - Jupyter Notebook Configuration

The Jupyter Notebook provides a fairly rich set of configuration options. The most popular areas of the Notebook that are configured on a regular basis are the following:

- The common configuration system
- The Notebook server
- The front-end client
- Extensions for the Notebook

We will look at all of these. But first, let's find out how we can learn about the defaults!

Notebook Defaults

You can get a listing of the options you can use when running a Notebook by running the following command in a terminal or cmd.exe on Windows:

```
jupyter notebook --help
```

When you run this command, the output will look something like this:

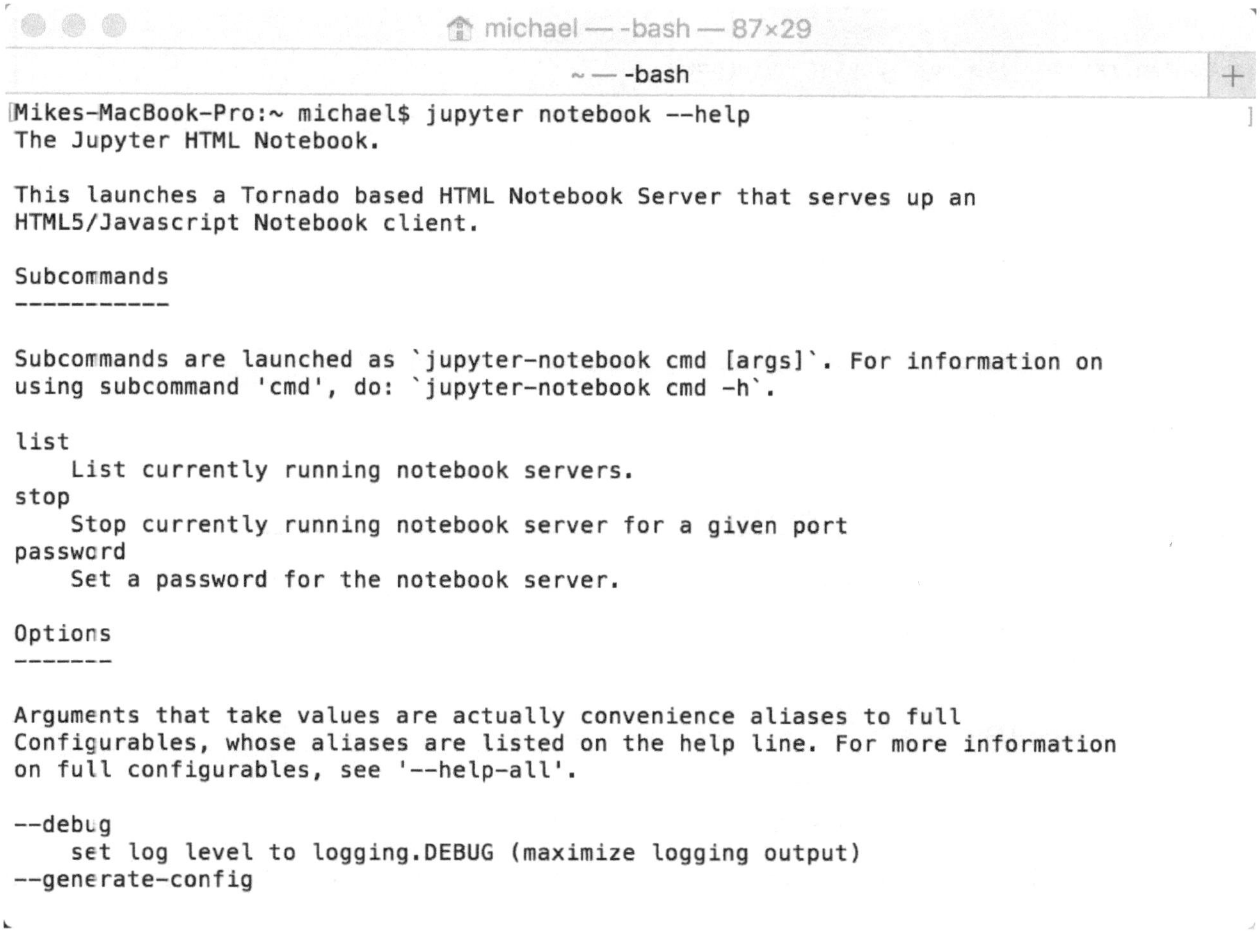

Fig. 3-1: Output from the –help command

You can also set up the defaults for your Notebooks by creating a file called **jupyter_notebook_-config.py** which you will want to place in your Jupyter folder. This is in your home directory, **\~/.jupyter**.

To actually create this file, all you need to do is run the following command in your terminal:

```
jupyter notebook --generate-config
```

This will generate the file with all the defaults commented out. Here is a screenshot of the top of the file:

jupyter_notebook_config.py

```
# Configuration file for jupyter-notebook.

#------------------------------------------------------------------------------
# Application(SingletonConfigurable) configuration
#------------------------------------------------------------------------------

## This is an application.

## The date format used by logging formatters for %(asctime)s
#c.Application.log_datefmt = '%Y-%m-%d %H:%M:%S'

## The Logging format template
#c.Application.log_format = '[%(name)s]%(highlevel)s %(message)s'

## Set the log level by value or name.
#c.Application.log_level = 30

#------------------------------------------------------------------------------
# JupyterApp(Application) configuration
#------------------------------------------------------------------------------

## Base class for Jupyter applications

## Answer yes to any prompts.
#c.JupyterApp.answer_yes = False

## Full path of a config file.
#c.JupyterApp.config_file = ''

## Specify a config file to load.
```

Fig. 3-2: Output from the –generate-config command

Now we are ready to learn more about the common items that people usually configure for their Notebooks.

The Common Configuration System

The Jupyter project uses a common configuration system and a common config directory. The default config director is \~/**.jupyter**. If you are using multiple kernels (i.e. languages), and the kernel uses config files, they will be organized in separate directories per kernel. For example, if you are Python, then you will have the IPython kernel which will be stored in the IPython directory, which is most likely \~/**.ipython/**.

When you edit the configuration file, be careful to use the correct spelling as incorrect names will be silently ignored. You can also change the configuration via the command line. Let's look at an example of changing the Notebook's port number via the command line. Open up your terminal and enter the following:

```
jupyter notebook --NotebookApp.port=8888
```

The most used options will have shorter aliases. So you could swap out **–NotebookApp.port** for **–port** instead, for example. When running a command on the command line, it will just override what is in the config file, not replace it. Thus if you ran your Notebook without passing the flag above, the port would default to whatever is in the config.

Common Directories and Files

There are some so-called "common directories and files" within Project Jupyter that I think are worth mentioning. The config files, as was already mentioned, are stored in **\~/.jupyter** by default. However you can override that location by setting the **JUPYTER_CONFIG_DIR** environment variable. Jupyter also has a search path of alternate locations for the config file. On Unix, the following two locations are checked in order:

- {sys.prefix}/etc/jupyter/
- /usr/local/etc/jupyter/ /etc/jupyter/

Windows has only one alternate location currently:

- %PROGRAMDATA%jupyter

If you would like to list out the config directories, you can run the following command:

```
jupyter --paths
```

Jupyter will also use a search path to find installable **data files**. Examples include kernelspecs and notebook extensions. Jupyter will only search up until it finds something, so if you happen to have a file that is in a path that is lower in precedence, it is possible that it may not be found if something in a higher precedence location has the same name. An example search path that Jupyter will use are the kernels subdirectories.

You can set custom search paths by setting the **JUPYTER_PATH** environment variable. You can set a series of paths by separating the paths with a semicolon on Windows or a regular colon on Unix. Paths that are in this environment variable are searched before all others.

On Linux, the following paths are the defaults (in order):

- \~/.local/share/jupyter/
- {sys.prefix}/share/jupyter/
- /usr/local/share/jupyter /usr/share/jupyter

Mac has only one search path:

- \~/Library/Jupyter

Windows has two search paths:

- %APPDATA%jupyter
- %PROGRAMDATAjupyter

Finally Jupyter has the concept of **runtime files**, which are files that are only useful during the lifetime of a process, such as a connection file. On Linux, the location used for finding this type of file is:

- $XDG_RUNTIME_DIR/jupyter

All other platforms use the **runtime/** subdirectory of the userâ€™s data directory.

If you would like to use a custom location, you can set this via the **JUPYTER_RUNTIME_DIR** environment variable.

Notebook Server

The Notebook server is what actually runs the language kernel behind the scenes when you are running your Notebook. It communicates with the front-end Notebook client, which is what you see in your browser.

There are specific configuration settings in the **jupyter_notebook_config.py** that we generated at the beginning of this chapter that apply to the server. An example of this is the **NotebookApp.password**, which is something you can use to secure your notebook server. Look through the config file for anything that is prepended with **NotebookApp** to see other settings that you can modify.

The Front-End Client

The front-end UI can also be configured, but is not currently completely configurable. The documentation states that the current method of changing the front-end is as follows:

- Acquire a handle of a JavaScript object which is configurable
- Access its configuration attribute
- Change that attribute using a JSON patch

There are only a couple of examples in the official documentation which you can find here:

- http://jupyter-notebook.readthedocs.io/en/stable/frontend_config.html

I would recommend reading through that if you really want to change the Notebook's user interface.

Notebook Extensions

Notebook extensions can be used to extend the behavior and / or feature set of your Notebook. We won't be covering how to do this in this book, but we will look at how we can install and use extensions in a later chapter. Feel free to read the documentation on this subject if you want to extend your Notebook though:

- https://jupyter-notebook.readthedocs.io/en/latest/extending/index.html

Wrapping Up

In this chapter we learned about how to generate a configuration file for the Jupyter Notebook. We also learned about some of the Notebook's defaults and its common configuration system that the Notebook shares with the rest of Project Jupyter. I highly recommend opening up the configuration file and reading through it as it has pretty extensive comments that explain what each and every setting does.

Chapter 4 - Distributing Notebooks

Let's pretend that you have just finished putting together an amazing Jupyter Notebook file that demonstrates your work. Now you want to share it with your colleagues. How do you do that? We will look at some of the most popular methods employed for sharing Notebooks in this chapter.

- Github
- binder - https://mybinder.org/
- Google's Colaboratory - https://colab.research.google.com
- Microsoft Azure Notebooks - https://notebooks.azure.com/
- Running a notebook server - http://jupyter-notebook.readthedocs.io/en/stable/public_server.html

Using Github

Github is one of the most popular methods of sharing code and that include Jupyter Notebooks. Of course, you can use pretty much any free source control host, such as Bitbucket or GitLab if you wanted to. Github just happens to be the most popular currently.

There are also different kinds of source control you can use. The most popular right now are Git, Subversion (SVN), Mercurial and Perforce. We will focus on Git. You will need to go to https://git-scm.com/ to download a copy of the software and follow their instructions for installing it on your operating system.

Once you have it installed, you will want to create a repository on your machine. A repository is just a fancy word for a folder on your machine that contains all your source code. The reason we call it a repository instead of a folder is that when you create it with Git, the Git program will create some metadata in the folder to allow it to track changes in the files that are in your folder.

Open up a terminal and navigate to a location where you would like to create a repository. Next create the folder that you want to store your code or Notebooks in. Now let's turn that folder into a repository! In your terminal, use the **cd** command to change directories into your newly created folder and run the following command:

```
git init
```

This will turn your folder into a Git repository. Now you can copy your work into this folder or just start from scratch and create all new files in this folder. It is usually recommended that you save your changes frequently. This is known as "committing" your work to the "repository". Here is the command I usually use:

```
git commit -a
```

The **-a** on the end just tell git to add all your changes to the committed changelist or changeset. A "changeset" is a term used to describe the changes that you are saving. It is usually represented by a number once your changes are saved. This allows you to roll back your changes to a previous changeset if you realize you made a mistake or you just want to review a previous version of your work.

Another way to add your changes before committing is to call this command:

```
git add .
```

Then you could just call **git commit** without the **-a** flag as the file(s) are already added.

Anyway, when you call **commit**, it will open a text editor in your terminal or possible just open your default text editor, such as Notepad. This allows you to write a note about the changes you are saving. Most developers keep it brief. If you are fixing a bug, it is usually a good idea to put the bug's ID number in your commit message so you can track down your fix later, if need be.

Now that you have your first commit, I would recommend creating an account with Github, Bitbucket, or some other source code website that offers free accounts. This allows you to save your changes to the cloud which is a nice way to backup your work. It also allows you to share your work with others as you will now have a unique URL that you can give out.

Let's pretend that you have created a Github account. Now you just need to click on their little plus (+) sign that is on the top right of all their web pages. Choose **New repository** and give it a name. It will walk you through a couple of things and then it's ready to go.

Now let's add your code to Github. All you need to do is run the following in your terminal:

```
git remote add origin URL
```

Note that you must use the URL to your Github repository that you just created instead of the word "URL". This command just sets the Github repository as the remote master, which means it is the "master" copy. To actually send your code to Github, you need to run one more command:

```
git push origin master
```

What this does is push your local changes to the cloud, which is the master.

There is a lot more that you can do with Git. I recommend reading the documentation as covering everything you can do with Git would take up a book in and of itself.

binder

There is a neat website called **binder** that was designed to be used with Github or a similar repository that is full of Jupyter Notebooks. You can find it at the following URL:

- https://mybinder.org/

This website can be used to share your Jupyter Notebooks as well. The main difference is that it will actually run them in the browser so you can share your Notebooks live. The end user doesn't need to download or install anything. They just need to go to your Binder URL.

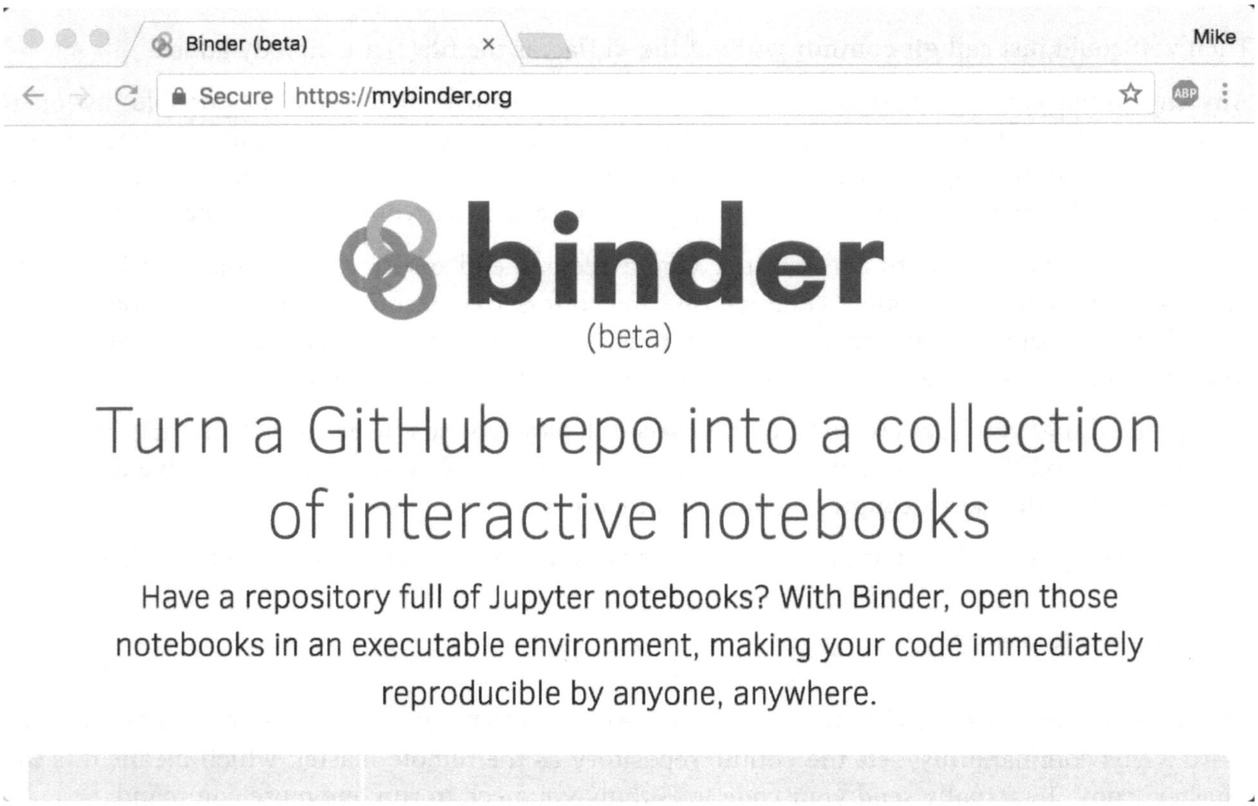

Fig. 4-1: The binder website

The cool thing about Binder is that it will create a Docker image of your Github repository. Docker is basically a virtualization utility for applications. You don't really need to know anything else about it, but if you are curious feel free to check their website out here: https://www.docker.com/

Anyway, as I was saying. Binder created a Docker image and uses your Github Repository's **requirements.txt** or **environment.yml** files to generate dependencies. These files are used to tell your users that you need some external packages outside of what is included in Python. Since Jupyter Notebooks are used a lot by data scientists, they tend to use 3rd party packages for Python, such as **matplotlib**, **numba**, **pandas** and others. You can use **requirements.txt** to specify which of these packages and which versions you require for your Notebook to run properly. Binder will read these files and install those extra libraries in the Docker image.

Once your image has been built, it will load your Notebook when you go to the Binder URL that you created. This Docker image only gets rebuilt when you commit new changes to your Github repository. It's actually pretty slick.

Underneath the covers, Binder uses a **JupyterHub** server to host your repository's contents. You can read more about JupyterHub here: https://jupyterhub.readthedocs.io/en/latest/ . It is free and open source and you can run one yourself in your own organization if you prefer to have full control over your content.

Google's Colaboratory

Google has its own Jupyter Notebook hosting site that it is calling the **Colaboratory** (https://colab.research.google.com). It allows you to upload your Notebooks directly to their site. Alternately, you can also use a Github URL in much the same way as you can with Binder. They have a third option which is done by using your Google Drive account and accessing any Notebooks you may have stored there. You will need an account with Google to use the Colaboratory.

Their fourth and final option is to just create a new Notebook right in the browser. You can connect your Notebook to Google's servers or you can connect it to using a local port, although the cell code is stored in Google Drive by default.

Here is what a brand new Notebook looks like in Colaboratory:

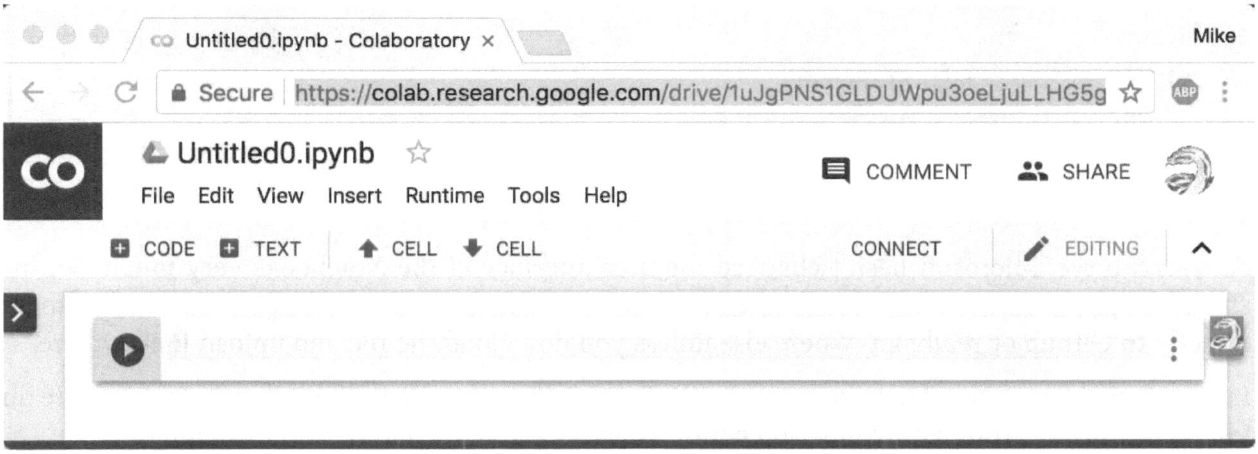

Fig. 4-2: The Google Colaboratory Notebook

You will notice that the user interface is a bit different than using Jupyter Notebook on your machine.

A nice bonus feature of using Colaboratory is that it allows you to use TensorFlow in the browser so you don't have to mess with setting it up. They also have a collection of interactive machine learning examples that they call the **Seedbank** that you can use to learn from.

When you go to save a Notebook, you can save it to Google Drive, Github Gist or Github itself. Once saved in one of those locations, you can share it quite easily. The Colaboratory is more about editing the Notebooks than really sharing them directly.

Microsoft Azure Notebooks

Microsoft also has a Notebook solution that they call **Microsoft Azure Notebooks** (https://notebooks.azure.com/). They support R and F# in addition to Python. You are required to have a Microsoft account to use Azure Notebooks. Here is an example notebook that I cloned from their sample Notebooks:

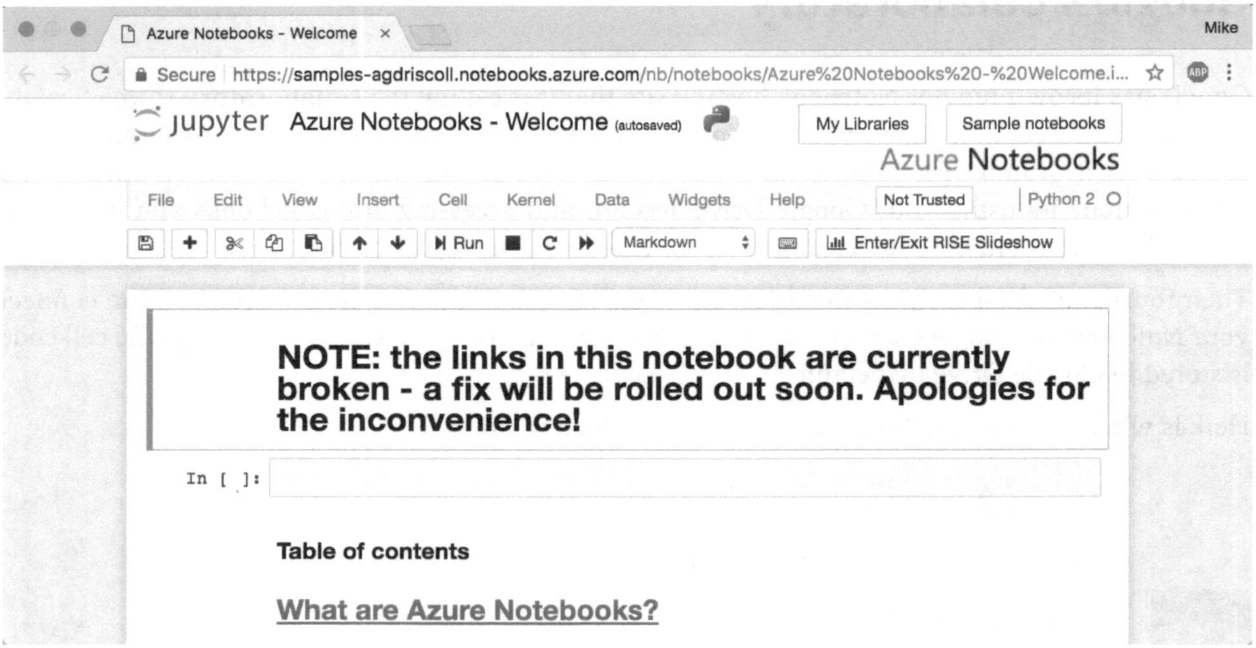

Fig. 4-3: The Azure Notebook

As you can see, Microsoft hasn't changed the user interface of the Notebooks very much. So this should be pretty familiar looking. Azure Notebooks save directly to Azure. You cannot save them directly to Github or really anywhere else unless you download the file and upload it elsewhere.

Interestingly, Azure Notebooks include the RISE plugin pre-installed. RISE allows you to create an interactive presentation with your Notebook. We will learn more about RISE in chapter 8.

You can add pre-made Notebooks to Azure by uploading them from your computer or by importing them from the Internet, such as Github.

Their website appears to work well, but it is not intuitive. It is not obvious how you get to your own Notebooks. They also use the generic term "Library" to refer to a group of Notebooks. You can create a new Library by creating a Notebook or importing from Github. This is what that looks like:

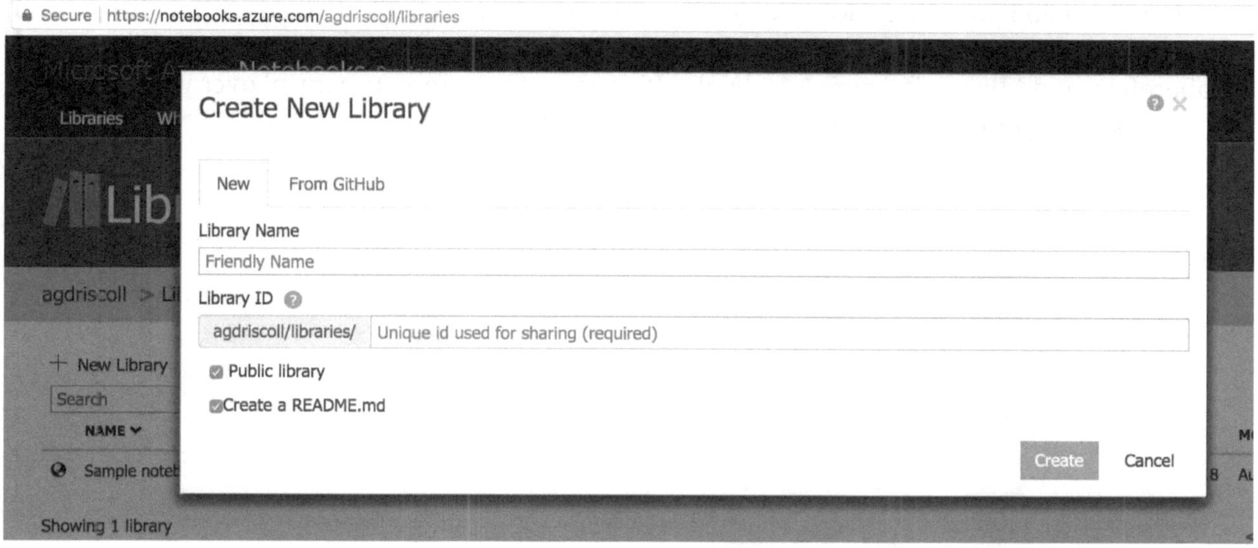

Fig. 4-4: A New Azure Library Dialog

Note that it defaults to making your library public. I think this one is worth a whirl as its URLs are nicely formatted and easy to share. They also have a "Share" button that makes sharing your Notebooks via social media, link or email, extremely easy to do.

Running a Notebook Server

There is another popular method that is used by some people for distributing / sharing their work and that is running their own home grown Notebook server or JupyterHub. I won't go over all the details here, but suffice it to say that you are basically going to configure a public server that needs to be secured. This method of sharing your work should probably be done by your IT team to prevent you from causing security issues for your company.

However, if you do go this route then you have the ultimate control over how people can access and use your Notebooks. For additional information on Jupyter Notebook servers, see the following:

- https://jupyter-notebook.readthedocs.io/en/stable/public_server.html

JupyterHub is a separate product from the Jupyter Project that allows you to create a multi-user Hub that will span, manage and proxy multiple instances of a Jupyter Notebook server. You can learn more about that here:

- https://github.com/jupyterhub/jupyterhub

Wrapping Up

In this chapter we learned about several different ways that you can use to distribute your Notebooks. Most people tend to just email them or use Github. Github is nice in that you can rollback changes since it will version your files. However you can't view your Notebooks live on Github. If you want to share them live, there are lots of good choices. In this chapter we looked at 3: Binder, Google Colaboratory and Microsoft Azure Notebooks. If you want the ultimate control over your data, then you can also roll your own Jupyter server or JupyterHub.

Chapter 5 - Exporting Notebooks

When working with Jupyter Notebook, you will find yourself needing to distribute your Notebook as something other than a Notebook file. The most likely reason is that you want to share the content of your Notebook to non-technical users that don't want to install Python or the other dependencies necessary to use your Notebook. The most popular solution for exporting your Notebook into other formats is the built-in **nbconvert** tool. You can use **nbconvert** to export to the following formats:

- HTML (–to html)
- LaTeX (–to latex)
- PDF (–to pdf)
- Reveal JS (–to slides)
- Markdown (md) (–to markdown)
- ReStructured Text (rst) (–to rst)
- executable script (–to script)

The nbconvert tool uses Jinja templates to convert your Notebook files (.ipynb) to these other static formats. Jinja is a template engine for Python. The nbconvert tool depends on Pandoc and TeX for some of the conversions that it does. You may need to install these separately on your machine. This is documented on ReadTheDocs:

- https://nbconvert.readthedocs.io/en/latest/

Using nbconvert

The first thing we need is a Notebook that we want to convert. I did a presentation on Python decorators where I used a Jupyter Notebook. We will use that one. You can get it from this book's source code on Github. If you would like to use something else, feel free to go download your favorite Notebook. I also found this gallery of interesting Notebooks that you could use for too:

- https://github.com/jupyter/jupyter/wiki/A-gallery-of-interesting-Jupyter-Notebooks

The Notebook that we will be using is called **Decorators.ipynb**. The typical command you use to export using nbconvert is as follows:

```
jupyter nbconvert <input notebook> --to <output format>
```

The default output format is HTML. But let's start out by trying to convert the Decorators Notebook into a PDF:

```
jupyter nbconvert Decorators.ipynb --to pdf
```

I won't mention this for every nbconvert run, but when I ran this command, I got the following output in my terminal:

```
[NbConvertApp] Converting notebook Decorators.ipynb to pdf
[NbConvertApp] Writing 45119 bytes to notebook.tex
[NbConvertApp] Building PDF
[NbConvertApp] Running xelatex 3 times: [u'xelatex', u'notebook.tex']
[NbConvertApp] Running bibtex 1 time: [u'bibtex', u'notebook']
[NbConvertApp] WARNING | bibtex had problems, most likely because there were no cita\
tions
[NbConvertApp] PDF successfully created
[NbConvertApp] Writing 62334 bytes to Decorators.pdf
```

You will see something similar when you convert your Notebook to other formats, although the output will differ obviously. This is what the output looked like:

Fig. 5-1: Decorators Notebook Converted to PDF

If you convert a Notebook to reStructuredText or latex, than nbconvert will use **pandoc** underneath the covers to do the conversion. That means that pandoc is a dependency that you may need to install before you can do a conversion to one of those formats.

Let's try converting our Notebook to Markdown just to see what we get:

```
jupyter nbconvert Decorators.ipynb --to markdown
```

When you run this command, you will get output that looks like this:

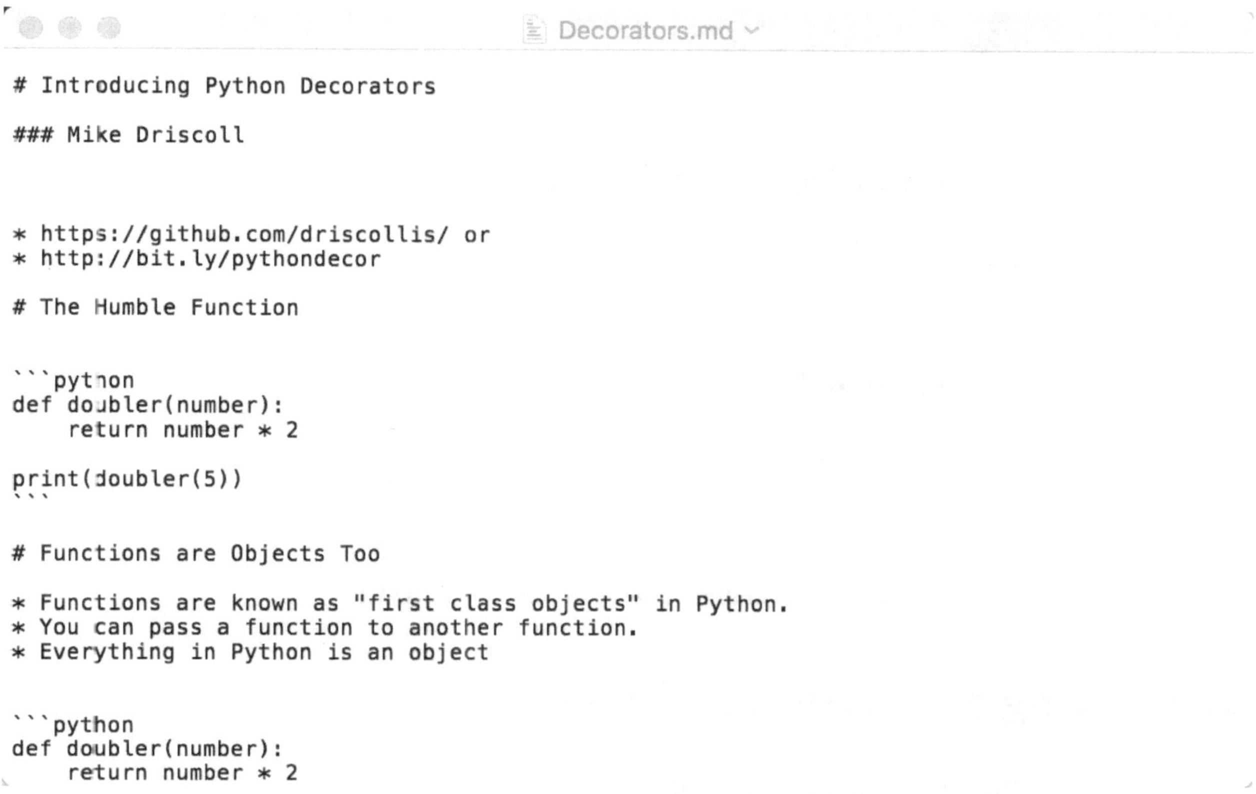

Fig. 5-2: Decorators Notebook Converted to Markdown

Let's do one conversion of our Notebook. For this conversion, we will turn our Notebook into HTML. The HTML conversion actually has two modes:

- –template full (default)
- –template basic

The full version will make the HTML render of the Notebook look very much like a regular Notebook looks when it is in its "interactive view" whereas the basic version uses HTML headers and is mostly aimed at people who want to embed the Notebook in a web page or blog. Let's give it a try:

```
jupyter nbconvert Decorators.ipynb --to html
```

When I ran this, I got a nice single HTML file. If you open the HTML in your web browser, you should see the following:

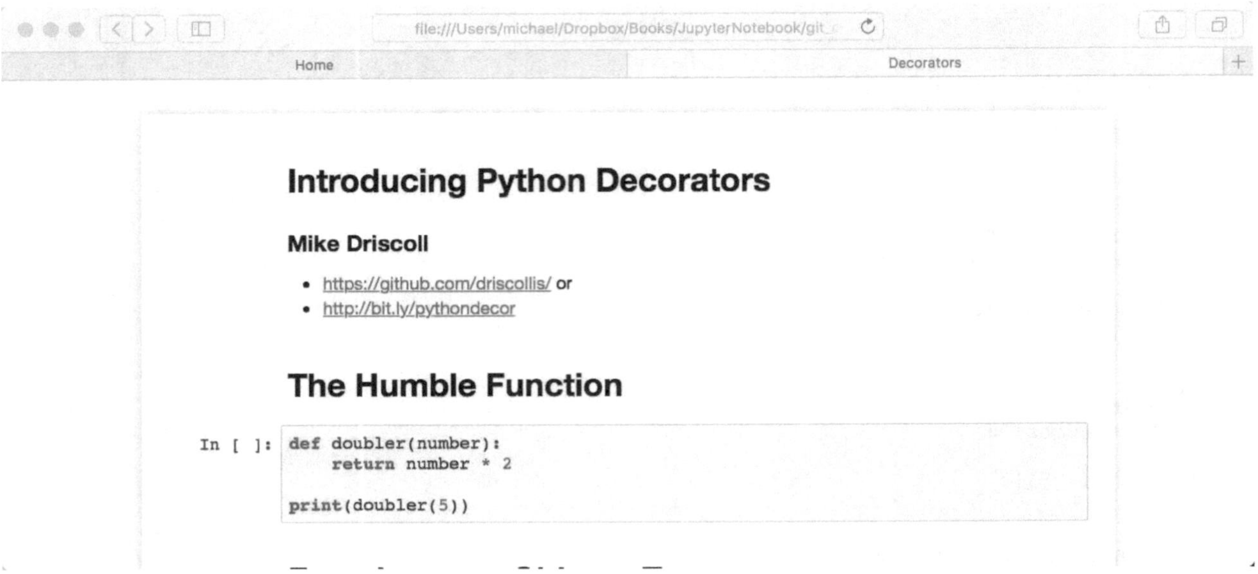

Fig. 5-3: Decorators Notebook Converted to HTML

Converting Multiple Notebooks

The nbconvert utility also supports converting multiple Notebooks at once. If you have a set of Notebooks with similar names, you could use the following command:

```
jupyter nbconvert notebook*.ipynb --to FORMAT
```

This would convert all the Notebooks in your folder to the format you specify as long as the Notebook began with "notebook". You can also just provide a space delimited list of Notebooks to nbconvert:

```
jupyter nbconvert Decorators.ipynb my_other_notebook.ipynb --to FORMAT
```

If you have many Notebooks, another method of converting them in bulk is to create a Python script that acts as configuration file. According to this documentation:

- https://nbconvert.readthedocs.io/en/latest/usage.html

you can create a Python script with the following contents:

```
c = get_config()
c.NbConvertApp.notebooks = ["notebook1.ipynb", "notebook2.ipynb"]
```

If you save this, you can then run it using the following command:

```
jupyter nbconvert --config mycfg.py
```

This will then convert the listed Notebooks to the format of your choice.

Executing Notebooks

As you might expect, most of the time, Jupyter Notebooks are saved with the output cells cleared. What this means is that when you run the conversion you won't get the output in your export automatically. To do this feat, you must use the –execute flag. Here is an example:

```
jupyter nbconvert --execute my_notebook.ipynb --to pdf
```

Note that the code in your Notebook cannot have any errors or the conversion will fail. This is why I am not using the Decorators Notebook in this example as I have some purposely created cells that fail for demonstration purposes.

Executing Notebooks with Python

You can also create a Python script that you can use to execute your Notebooks programmatically. Let's write some code that will run all the cells in my Decorators Notebook including the ones that will throw exceptions. Let's create an empty Python script and name it **notebook_runner.py**. Enter the following code into your editor:

```
# notebook_runner.py

import nbformat
import os

from nbconvert.preprocessors import ExecutePreprocessor


def run_notebook(notebook_path):
    nb_name, _ = os.path.splitext(os.path.basename(notebook_path))
    dirname = os.path.dirname(notebook_path)

    with open(notebook_path) as f:
        nb = nbformat.read(f, as_version=4)

    proc = ExecutePreprocessor(timeout=600, kernel_name='python3')
    proc.allow_errors = True
```

```
    proc.preprocess(nb, {'metadata': {'path': '/'}})
    output_path = os.path.join(dirname, '{}_all_output.ipynb'.format(nb_name))

    with open(output_path, mode='wt') as f:
        nbformat.write(nb, f)

if __name__ == '__main__':
    run_notebook('Decorators.ipynb')
```

The first items of interest are at the top of the code. Here we import **nbformat** and a preprocessor from **nbconvert.preprocessors** that is called **ExecutePreprocessor**. Next we create a function called **run_notebook** that accepts a path to the Notebook that we want to run. Inside of this function we extract the file name and the directory name from the path that we passed in.

Then we read the Notebook file using **nbformat.read**. You will note that you can tell nbformat what version to read the file as. Be sure to set this to match whichever version of Jupyter Notebook you are using. The next step is to instantiate the **ExecutePreprocessor** class. Here we give it a timeout and the kernel name. If you were using something other than Python this is where you would want to specify that information.

Since we want to ignore errors, we set the **allow_errors** attribute to **True**. The default is **False**. If we hadn't done this, we would need to wrap the next step in a **try/except** block. Anyway, we then tell Python to do the preprocessing via the **preprocess** method call. You will note that we need to pass in the Notebook data that we read as well as tell it where the Notebook is located via a dictionary of metadata. Be sure to update this if your path is different than the one used in this example.

Finally we create the output path and write out our the Notebook to a new location. If you open it up, you should see output for all of the code cells that actually produce output.

Configuration

The nbconvert utility has many configuration options that you can use to customize how it works. For full details, I recommend reading the documentation here:

- https://nbconvert.readthedocs.io/en/latest/config_options.html

Wrapping Up

In this chapter we learned how to export / convert our Jupyter Notebooks into other formats such as HTML, Markdown, and PDF. We also learned that we can convert multiple Notebooks at once in several different ways. Finally we learned different ways to execute a Notebook before exporting it. In the next chapter, we will learn how to extend our Jupyter Notebooks using extensions.

Chapter 6 - Notebook Extensions

There are several methods of extending the functionality of Jupyter Notebooks. Here are four of them:

- Kernels
- IPython kernel extensions
- Notebook extensions
- Notebook server extensions

For the purposes of this book, I will be focusing on the third item, **Notebook Extensions**. However, let's take a moment and talk about the other three so that you are aware of how they can affect your Notebook.

Kernels

We've mentioned this before, but the Kernel is basically the language run-time used. The default is Python via the IPython kernel. You can extend your Jupyter Notebook to use other languages besides Python. Check out the following URL for more information:

- https://jupyter.readthedocs.io/en/latest/projects/kernels.html

I won't be covering the installation of other kernels in this chapter as each kernel has different installation instructions. The URL above should be used as it has hyperlinks to the most up-to-date information on this topic.

You can also implement your own kernel if you want to. Here's a great primer on the topic:

- https://jupyter-client.readthedocs.io/en/latest/kernels.html

IPython Kernel Extensions

The IPython Kernel extension is just a Python module that can be used to modify the interactive shell environment. In Jupyter's case, these extensions would modify how code cells behave. You can use this type of extension to register new magics, define variables and modify the user's namespace. You can use the following three magics for managing IPython extensions:

- %load_ext
- %reload_ext
- %unload_ext

See **Appendix A** for more information on these magics.

Notebook Server Extensions

Jupyter Notebook also has the concept of "server extensions". A server extension is a Python module that loads when the Notebook's web server application starts. The current method of loading this type of extension is via Jupyter's configuration system, which we talked about in Chapter 3. You will need to specify which extensions to load in the configuration file or via the command line interface.

If you add a new extension while Jupyter Notebook is running, you will have to restart the Notebook process to activate the new extension.

Notebook Extensions

The type of extension that we care the most about in this chapter is the **Notebook Extension**. A Notebook extension (or nbextensions) are JavaScript modules that you can load on most of the views in your Notebook's frontend. They can access the page's DOM and the Jupyter JavaScript API which allows the extension to modify the user experience and interface. This type of extension is exclusive to the Notebook frontend.

Let's learn how you might install a Notebook Extension. The manual method of installing a Jupyter Notebook extension would look something like this, assuming you have already downloaded / pip installed the package that contains the extension:

```
jupyter nbextension install EXTENSION
jupyter nbextension enable EXTENSION
```

Note that you would replace **EXTENSION** with the name of the extension you are intending to install.

Another method that seems to have gained a lot of backing for managing Notebook extensions is by using the **Jupyter NbExtensions Configurator**. You can check out the project here:

- https://github.com/Jupyter-contrib/jupyter_nbextensions_configurator

This package is not part of the Jupyter Project, but it is quite helpful. You can use pip or conda to install the Configurator. Here's how to do it with pip:

```
pip install jupyter_nbextensions_configurator
```

If you use conda as your Python package manager, then you would install the Configurator like this:

```
conda install -c conda-forge jupyter_nbextensions_configurator
```

The Configurator is a Jupyter server extension and must be enabled. You will need to run the following command in your terminal before starting Jupyter Notebook (or you can restart the server):

```
jupyter nbextensions_configurator enable --user
```

When I ran this command, I got the following output:

```
Enabling: jupyter_nbextensions_configurator
- Writing config: /Users/michael/.jupyter
    - Validating...
      jupyter_nbextensions_configurator 0.4.0 OK
Enabling notebook nbextension nbextensions_configurator/config_menu/main...
Enabling tree nbextension nbextensions_configurator/tree_tab/main...
```

After starting up Jupyter Notebook, just click on the **Nbextensions** tab and you should see something like the following:

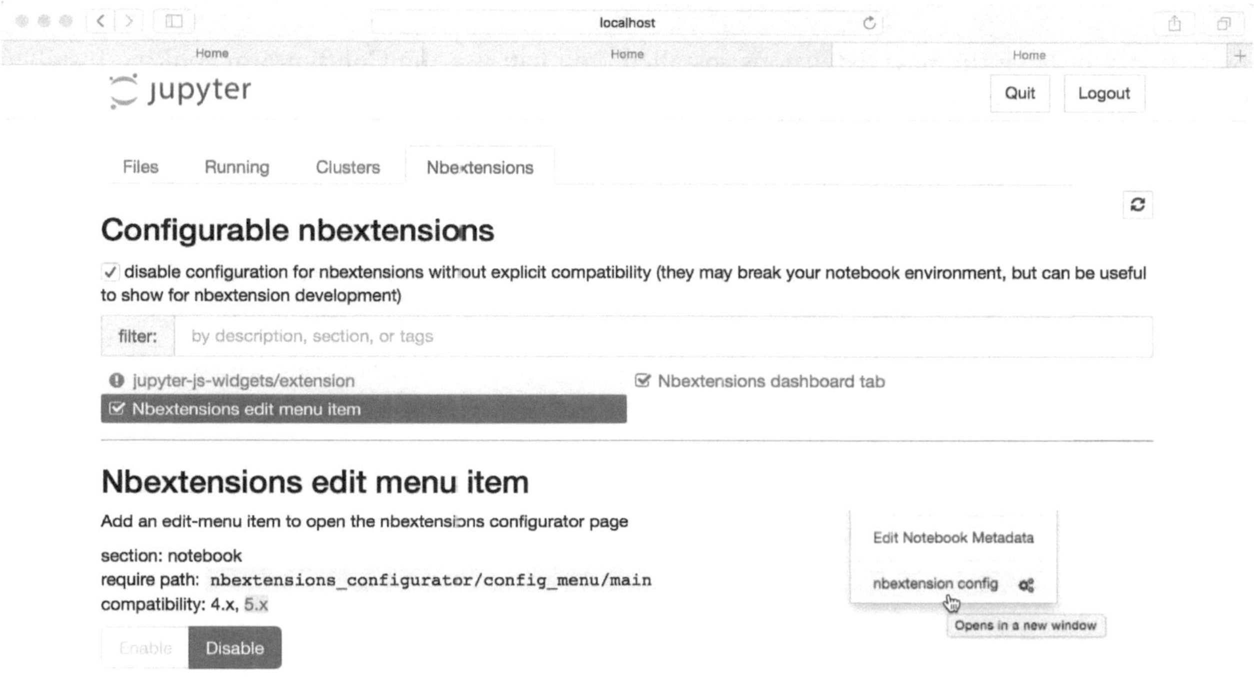

Fig. 6-1: The Jupyter NbExtensions Configurator

Since we don't have any extensions downloaded and installed, the Configurator looks kind of barren and can't really do all that much for us right now. Let's get some extensions to try!

If you were to search for Jupyter Notebook extensions, you would find the **jupyter_contrib_-nbextensions** pretty quickly. It is a collection of Notebook extensions provided by the Jupyter community. You can read more about the extensions that are included in this package at either of the following links:

- https://github.com/ipython-contrib/jupyter_contrib_nbextensions

- https://jupyter-contrib-nbextensions.readthedocs.io/en/latest/index.html

To install this set of extensions, you can once again use either pip or conda. Here is the pip command you will need:

```
pip install jupyter_contrib_nbextensions
```

And here is the conda command:

```
conda install -c conda-forge jupyter_contrib_nbextensions
```

Once you have this package downloaded and installed, you will need to use a Jupyter to install the javascript and css files to the right location so that the Notebook can access them. Here is the command you should run:

```
jupyter contrib nbextension install --user
```

Now that you have the new extensions installed, you can use the Configurator tool we installed earlier to easily enable or disable them:

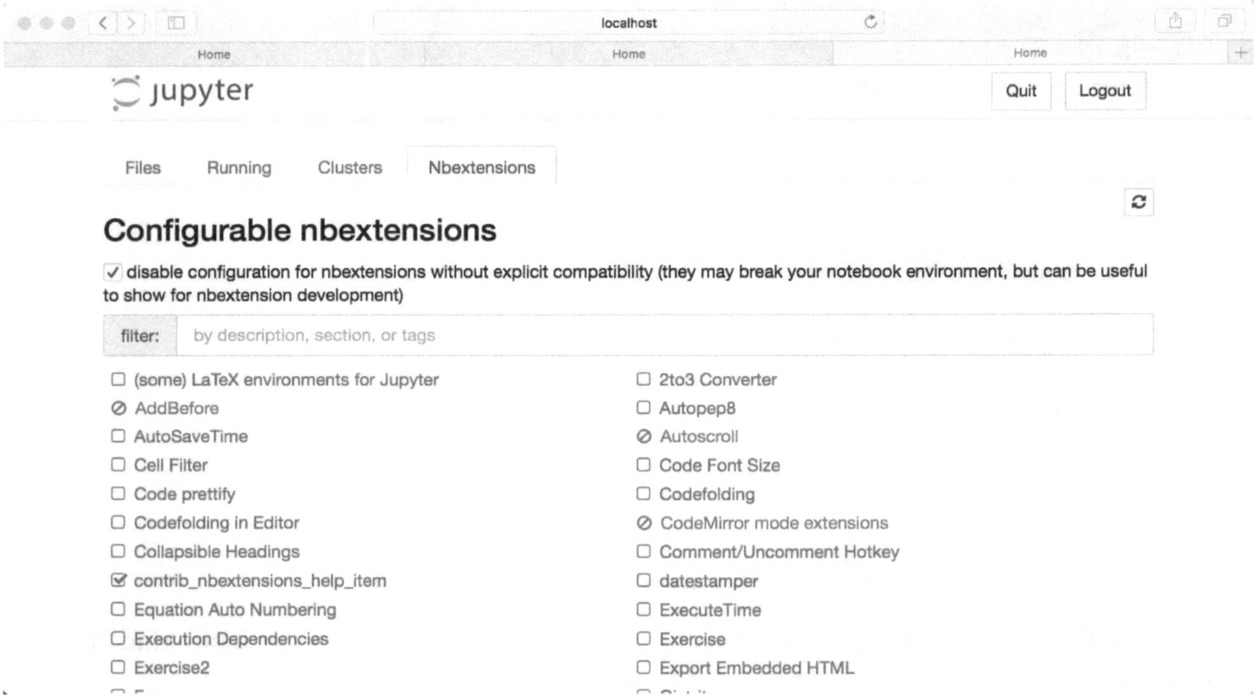

Fig. 6-2: The Jupyter NbExtensions Configurator with Extensions

As you can see in the screenshot above, there is now a LOT of extensions to play around with. The Configurator is really handy for figuring out which extensions you have installed and enabled. You can also enable and disable Notebook extensions by hand in the terminal using **jupyter nbextension enable EXTENSION** or **jupyter nbextension disable EXTENSION** respectively, but I personally find the Configurator easier to use.

Wrapping Up

In this chapter we learned about the different types of extensions you can use with Jupyter. The one we cared the most about were the Jupyter Notebook extensions. We then went on to learn the basics of installing extensions. We also learned how to enable and disable extensions using the terminal and also via the Jupyter NbExtensions Configurator package.

Chapter 7 - Notebook Widgets with interact

The Jupyter Notebook has a feature known as **widgets**. If you have ever created a desktop user interface, you may already know and understand the concept of widgets. They are basically the controls that make up the user interface. In your Jupyter Notebook you can create sliders, buttons, text boxes and much more.

We will learn the basics of creating widgets in this chapter. If you would like to see some pre-made widgets, you can go to the following URL:

- http://jupyter.org/widgets

These widgets are Notebook extensions that can be installed in the same way that we learned about in the previous chapter. They are really interesting and well worth your time if you'd like to study how more complex widgets work by looking at their source code.

Getting Started

To create your own widgets, you will need to install the **ipywidgets** extension.

Installing with pip

Here is how you would install the widget extension with pip:

```
pip install ipywidgets
jupyter nbextension enable --py widgetsnbextension
```

If you are using virtualenv, you may need to use the –sys-prefix option to keep your environment isolated.

Installing with conda

Here is how you would install the widgets extension with conda:

```
conda install -c conda-forge ipywidgets
```

Note that when installing with conda, the extension will be automatically enabled.

Learning How to Interact

There are a number of methods for creating widgets in Jupyter Notebook. The first and easiest method is by using the **interact** function from **ipywidgets.interact** which will automatically generate user interface controls (or widgets) that you can then use to explore your code and interact with data.

Let's start out by creating a simple slider. Start up a new Jupyter Notebook and enter the following code into the first cell:

```
from ipywidgets import interact

def my_function(x):
    return x

# create a slider
interact(my_function, x=20)
```

Here we import the **interact** class from **ipywidgets**. Then we create a simple function called **my_function** that accepts a single argument and then returns it. Finally we instantiate **interact** by passing it a function along with the value that we want interact to pass to it. Since we passed in an integer (i.e. 20), the interact class will automatically create a slider.

Try running the cell that contains the code above and you should end up with something that looks like this:

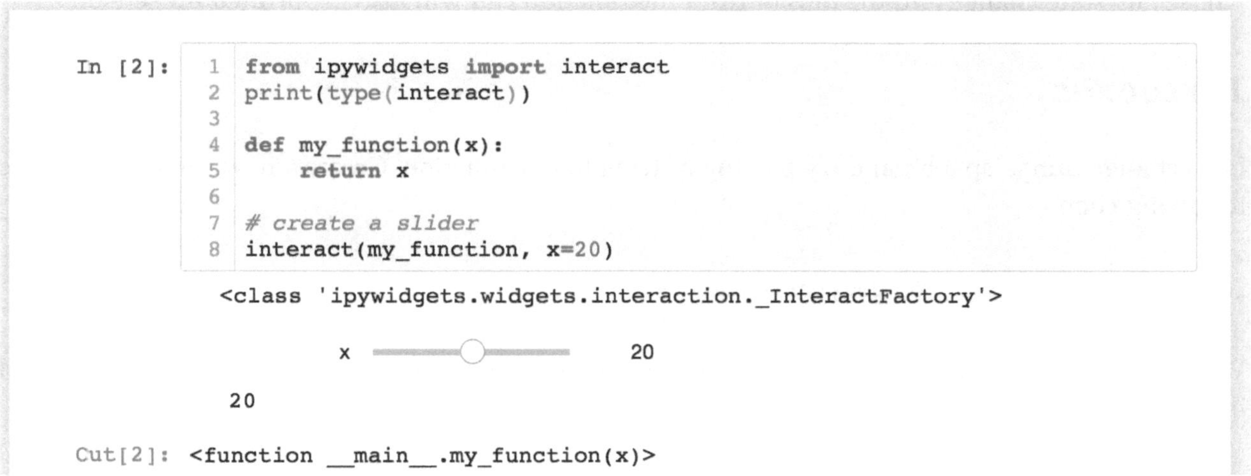

Fig. 7-1: Creating a slider with interact

That was pretty neat! Try moving the slider around with your mouse. If you do, you will see that the slider updates interactively and the output from the function is also automatically updated.

You can also create a **FloatSlider** by passing in floating point numbers instead of integers. Give that a try to see how it changes the slider.

Checkboxes

Once you are done playing with the slider, let's find out what else we can do with interact. Add a new cell in the same Jupyter Notebook with the following code:

```
interact(my_function, x=True)
```

When you run this code you will discover that interact has created a checkbox for you. Since you set "x" to **True**, the checkbox is checked. This is what it looked like on my machine:

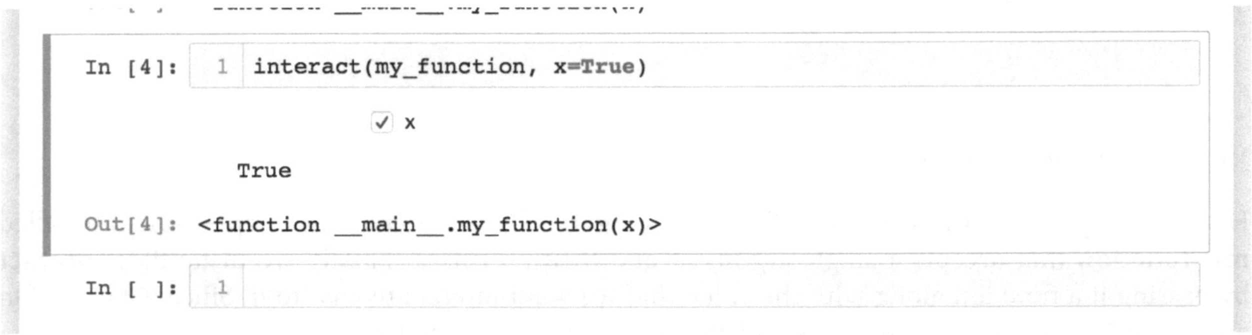

Fig. 7-2: Creating a checkbox with interact

You can play around with this widget as well by just checking and un-checking the checkbox. You will see its state change and the output from the function call will also get printed on-screen.

Textboxes

Let's change things up a bit and try passing a string to our function. Create a new cell and enter the following code:

```
interact(my_function, x='Jupyter Notebook!')
```

When you run this code, you will find that interact generates a textbox with the string we passed in as its value:

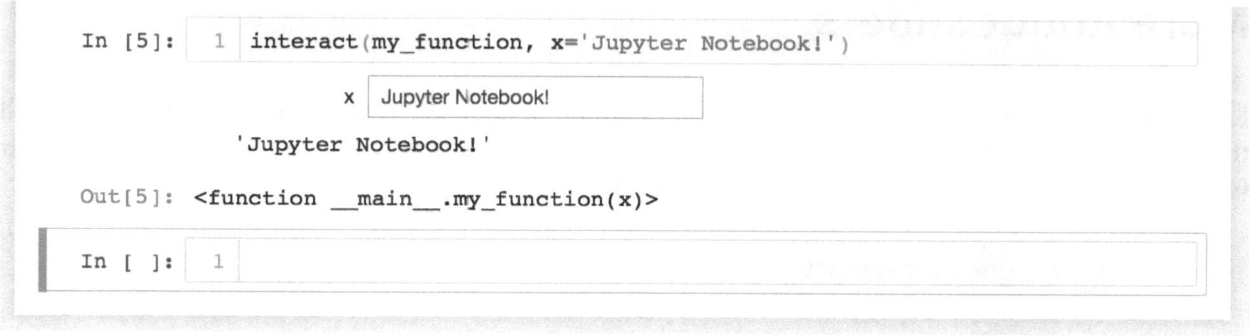

Fig. 7-3: Creating a textbox with interact

Try editing the textbox's value. When I tried doing that, I saw that the output text also changed.

Comboboxes / Drop-downs

You can also create a combobox or drop-down widget by passing a list or a dictionary to your function in interact. Let's try passing in a list of tuples and see how that behaves. Go back to your Notebook and enter the following code into a new cell:

```
languages = [('Python', 'Rocks!'), ('C++', 'is hard!')]
interact(my_function, x=languages)
```

When you run this code, you should see "Python" and "C++" as items in the combobox. If you select one, the Notebook will display the second element of the tuple to the screen. Here is how my mine rendered when I ran this example:

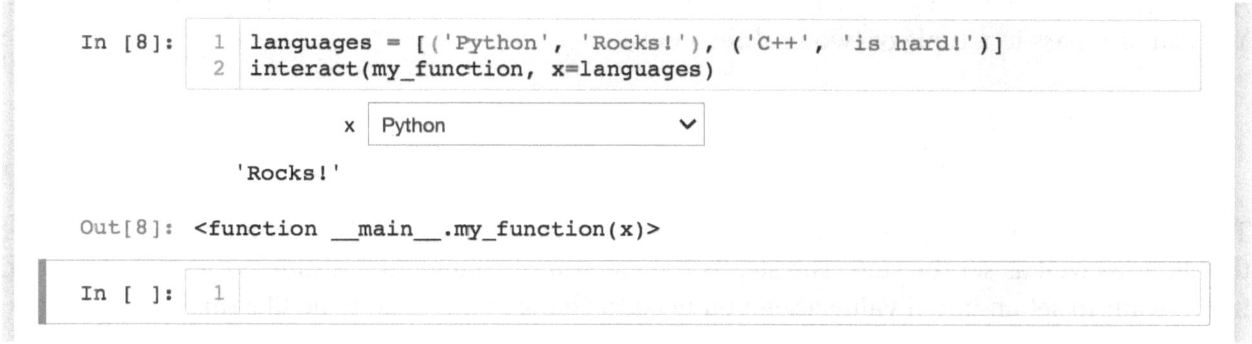

Fig. 7-4: Creating a combobox with interact

If you'd like to try out a dictionary instead of a list, here is an example:

```
languages = {'Python': 'Rocks!', 'C++': 'is hard!'}
interact(my_function, x=languages)
```

The output of running this cell is very similar to the previous example.

More About Sliders

Let's back up a minute so we can talk a bit more about sliders. We can actually do a bit more with them than I had originally let on. When you first created a slider, all you needed to do was pass our function an integer. Here's the code again for a refresher:

```
from ipywidgets import interact

def my_function(x):
    return x

# create a slider
interact(my_function, x=20)
```

The value, **20**, here is technically an abbreviation for creating an integer-valued slider. The code:

```
interact(my_function, x=20)
```

is actually the equivalent of the following:

```
interact(my_function, x=widgets.IntSlider(value=20))
```

Technically, Bools are an abbreviation for Checkboxes, lists / dicts are abbreviations for Comboboxes, etc.

Anyway, back to sliders again. There are actually two other ways to create integer-valued sliders. You can also pass in a tuple of two or three items:

- (min, max)
- (min, max, step)

This allows us to make the slider more useful as now we get to control the min and max values of the slider as well as set the step. The step is the amount of change to the slider when we change it. If you want to set an initial value, then you need to change your code to be like this:

```
def my_function(x=5):
    return x

interact(my_function, x=(0, 20, 5))
```

The **x=5** in the function is what sets the initial value. I personally found that a little counter-intuitive as the **IntSlider** itself appears to be defined to work like this:

```
IntSlider(min, max, step, value)
```

The interact class does not instantiate IntSlider the same way that you would if you were creating one yourself.

Note that if you want to create a FloatSlider, all you need to do is pass in a float to any of the three arguments: min, max or step. Setting the function's argument to a float will not change the slider to a FloatSlider.

Using interact as a decorator

The **interact** class can also be used as a Python decorator. For this example, we will also add a second argument to our function. Go back to your running Notebook and add a new cell with the following code:

```
from ipywidgets import interact

@interact(x=5, y='Python')
def my_function(x, y):
    return (x, y)
```

You will note that in this example, we do not need to pass in the function name explicitly. In fact, if you did so, you would see an error raised. Decorators call functions implicitly. The other item of note here is that we are passing in two arguments instead of one: an integer and a string. As you might have guessed, this will create a slider and a text box respectively:

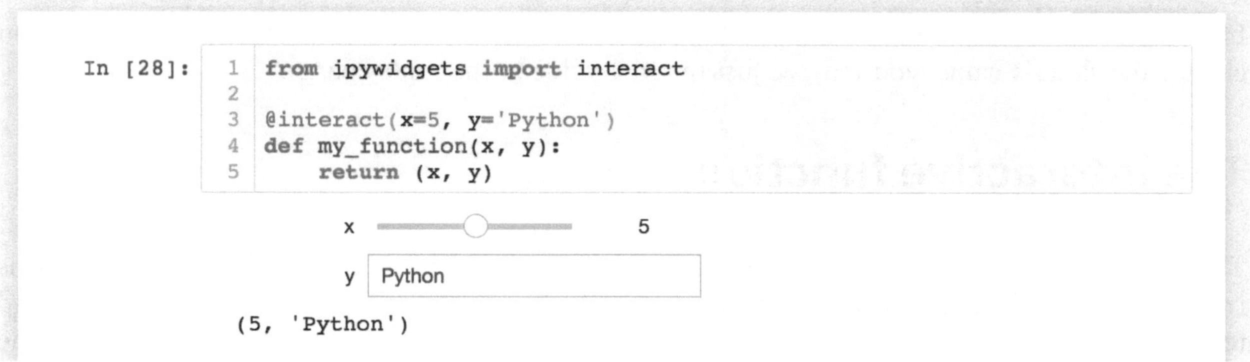

Fig. 7-5: Using interact as a decorator

As with all the previous examples, you can interact with these widgets in the browser and see their outputs.

Fixed Arguments

There are many times where you will want to set one of the arguments to a set or fixed value rather than allowing it to be manipulated through a widget. The Jupyter Notebook ipywidgets package supports this via the fixed function. Let's take a look at how you can use it:

```
from ipywidgets import interact, fixed

@interact(x=5, y=fixed('Python'))
def my_function(x, y):
    return (x, y)
```

Here we import the fixed function from ipywidgets. Then in our interact decorator, we set the second argument as "fixed". When you run this code, you will find that it only creates a single widget: a slider. That is because we don't want or need a widget to manipulate the second argument.

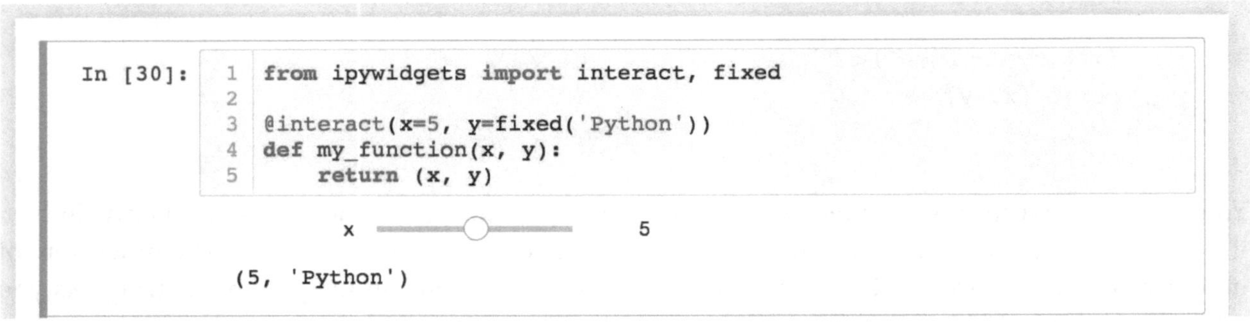

Fig. 7-6: Using interact with a fixed argument

In this screenshot, you can see that we have just the one slider and the output is a tuple. If you change the slider's value, you will see just the first value in the tuple change.

The interactive function

There is also a second function that is worth covering in this chapter that is called interactive. This function is useful during those times when you want to reuse widgets or access the data that is bound to said widgets. The biggest difference between interactive and interact is that with interactive, the widgets are not displayed on-screen automatically. If you want the widget to be shown, then you need to do so explicitly.

Let's take a look at a simple example. Open up a new cell in your Jupyter Notebook and enter the following code:

```
from ipywidgets import interactive

def my_function(x):
    return x

widget = interactive(my_function, x=5)
type(widget)
```

When you run this code, you should see the following output:

```
ipywidgets.widgets.interaction.interactive
```

But you won't see a slider widget like you did had you used the interact function. Just to demonstrate, here is a screenshot of what I got when I ran the cell:

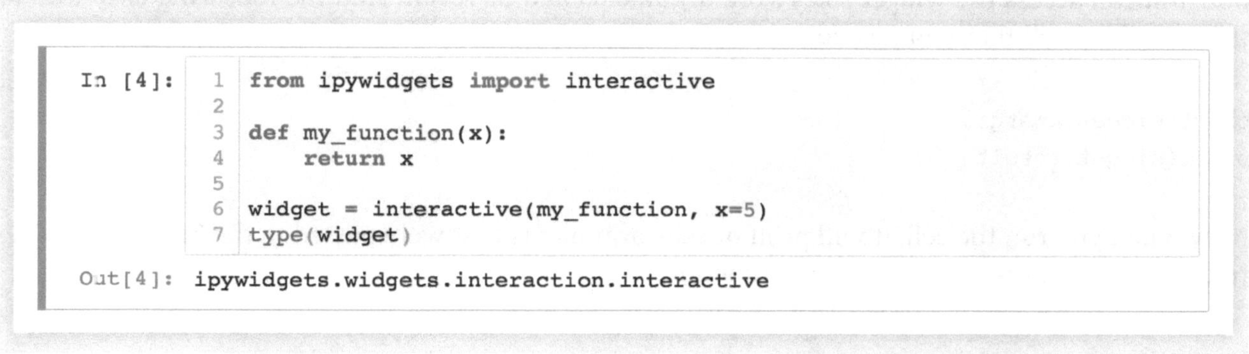

Fig. 7-7: Using interactive

If you'd like the widget to be shown, you need to import the display function. Let's update the code in the cell to be the following:

```
from ipywidgets import interactive
from IPython.display import display

def my_function(x):
    return x

widget = interactive(my_function, x=5)
display(widget)
```

Here we import the display function from IPython.display and then we call it at the end of the code. When I ran this cell, I got the slider widget:

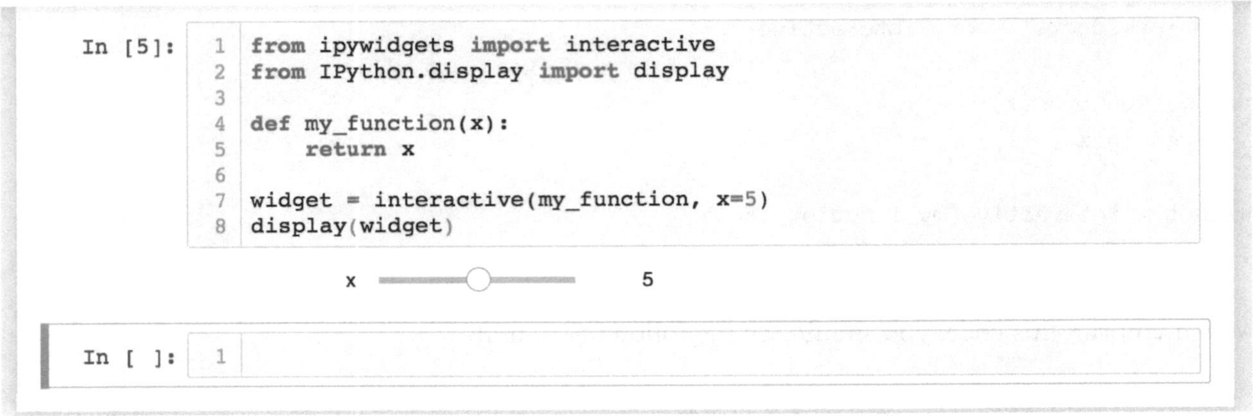

Fig. 7-8: Displaying an interactive widget

Why is this helpful? Why wouldn't you just use interact instead of jumping through extra hoops? Well the answer is that the interactive function gives you additional information that interact does not. You can access the widget's keyword arguments and its result. Add the following two lines to the end of the cell that you just edited:

```
print(widget.kwargs)
print(widget.result)
```

Now when you run the cell, it will print out the arguments that were passed to the function and the return value (i.e. result) of calling the function.

Wrapping Up

We learned a lot about Jupyter Notebook widgets in this chapter. We covered the basics of using the interact function as well as the interactive function. However there is more that you can about these functions by checking out the documentation:

- https://ipywidgets.readthedocs.io/en/stable/examples/Using%20Interact.html

Even this is just scratching the surface of what you can do with widgets in Jupyter. In the next chapter we will dig into creating widgets by hand outside of using the interact / interactive functions we learned about this in this chapter. We will learn much more about how widgets work and how you can use them to make your Notebooks much more interesting and potentially much more powerful.

Chapter 8 - Working with Widgets

What are Jupyter widgets? A widget is an "eventful python object" that in the case of Jupyter Notebook, resides in the browser and is a user interface element, such as a slider or textbox. Jupyter supports a fairly wide array of widgets including the following:

- Numeric
- Boolean
- Selection
- String
- Image
- Button
- Output
- Animation
- Date picker
- Color picker
- Controller (i.e. game controller)
- Layout

We won't cover every type of widget in this chapter, but we will get to see a fairly wide range of them in action. For a full list you can check out the following URL:

- https://ipywidgets.readthedocs.io/en/stable/examples/Widget%20List.html

Or you can run the following code in your Notebook:

```
import ipywidgets as widgets

print(dir(widgets))
```

If you have ever created a user interface in the past, then you probably already understand what a widget is. If you haven't, then let's just take a second to define what they are for.

> A widget is used to create an interactive graphical user interface for your user. The widgets synchronize stateful and stateless information between Python and Javascript.

We locked briefly at how to create widgets using the **interact** and **interactive** functions in the previous chapter. In this chapter we will create the widgets directly and learn more about how they work.

Creating a Widget

A widget can be created really easily. Let's create a simple slider for demonstration purposes. Create a new Jupyter Notebook and put the following code into a cell:

```
import ipywidgets as widgets

widgets.IntSlider()
```

When you run the cell, you should see something like this:

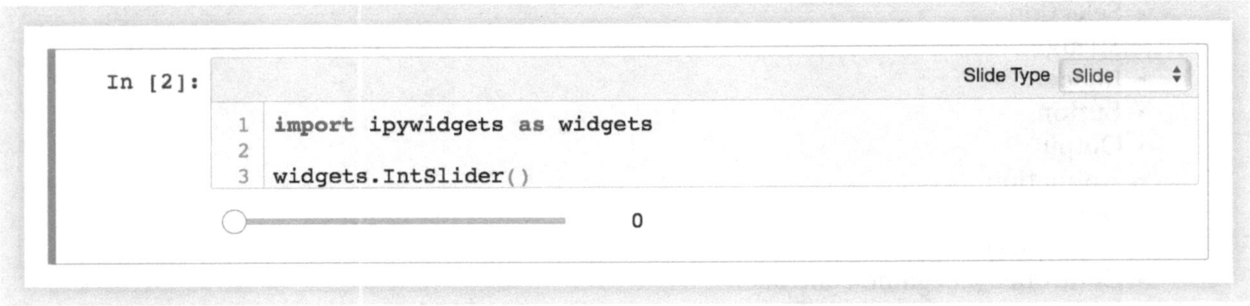

Fig. 8-1: Creating an IntSlider Widget

As you can see, the default value is zero for the slider. If you want to save the widget to a variable, then you will need to tell Jupyter to show the widget using the **display** function:

```
import ipywidgets as widgets
from IPython.display import display

btn = widgets.Button(description='Press Me')
display(btn)
```

Here we add the extra import that we need to display a widget and we create a simple Button. Note that we had to specify its **description** so that the button would have a label. Finally we called the display function and passed it the widget object. The result looks like this:

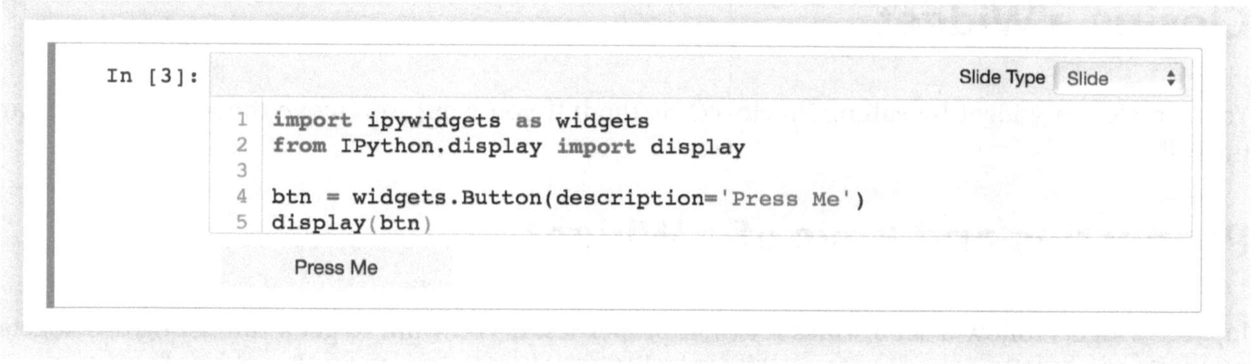

Fig. 8-2: Displaying a Widget

Now let's back up a second and create that slider again, but this time around we will use **display** to show it twice:

```
import ipywidgets as widgets
from IPython.display import display

btn = widgets.IntSlider()
display(btn)
display(btn)
```

If you put the code above into a cell in your Notebook and run it, you should see two sliders:

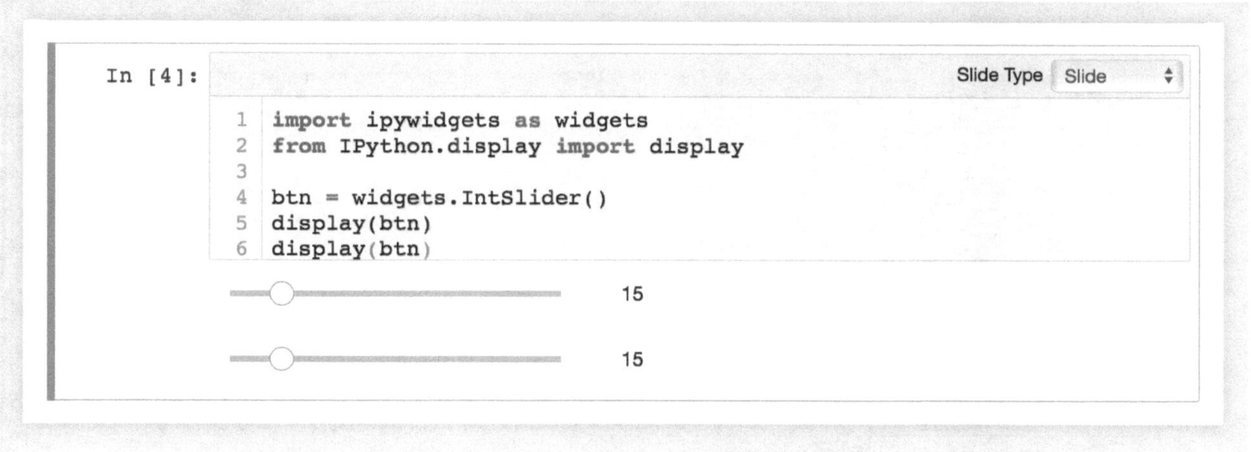

Fig. 8-3: Displaying two Widgets

Try moving around one of the sliders. You will quickly discover that when you move one slider, the other slider also moves. The reason that this happens is that we only create ONE slider object. The actual visible widgets are both pointing to the same object underneath, so when you move one you are effectively moving the other. You can think of these two sliders are two views to the same object. Of course, if you had created two **IntSliders** and assigned them to unique variable names, then you could move them independently of each other.

Closing a Widget

You can close a widget by calling its **close()** method. If you want to remove the widget, just clear the cell.

Properties and Keys of a Widget

Jupyter widgets follow a set of rules for their properties. If you want to get a full listing of widgets properties and methods, you can use Python's dir() function to introspect the widget for you:

```
dir(btn)
```

Let's say you put the code above in a new cell just below the cell that contains the code for your IntSlider widget. If you ran this new cell, you would get output like this:

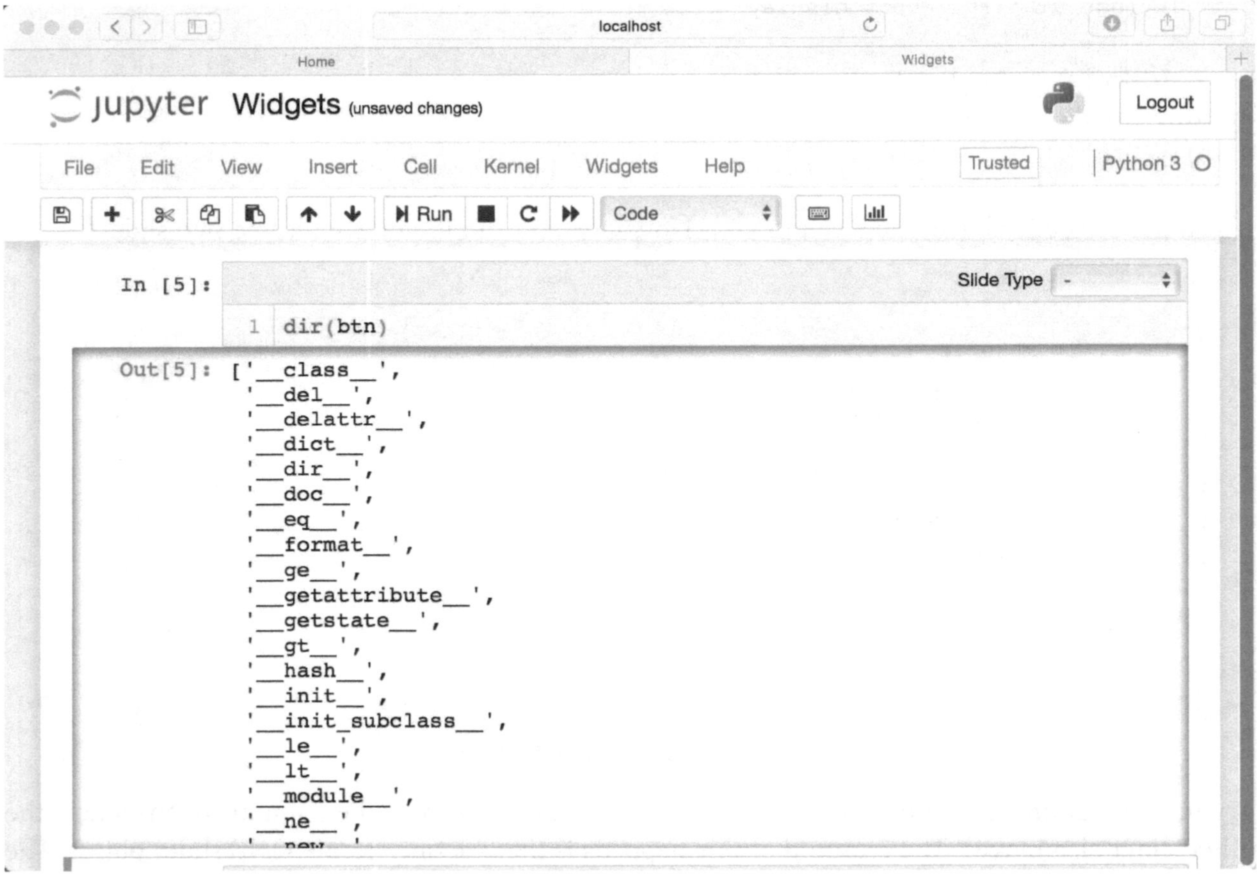

Fig. 8-4: Introspecting a widget

Try adjusting the slider to something above zero. Then create a new cell and enter the following code:

```
btn.value
```

When you run this, it will print out the current value of the slider. Widgets also have **keys**, which are such things as description, min, and max and disabled. For the full list of a widget's keys, you can consult the documentation for the widget, read the source or just run this:

```
btn.keys
```

Also worth mentioning is that you can also set a property to a new value. So if you wanted to set the slider to a new value and add a description, you could do the following:

```
btn.value = 50
btn.description = 'Hello slider'
```

If you run this code, you will see the slider update its value and description.

Widgets also support setting properties when you instantiate the widget. For example, if we wanted to, we could set a few of our Slider's properties when we create it:

```
import ipywidgets as widgets
from IPython.display import display

btn = widgets.IntSlider(value=10, description='My Slider',
                        orientation='vertical')
display(btn)
```

When you run this code, you will see that the widget looks a bit different:

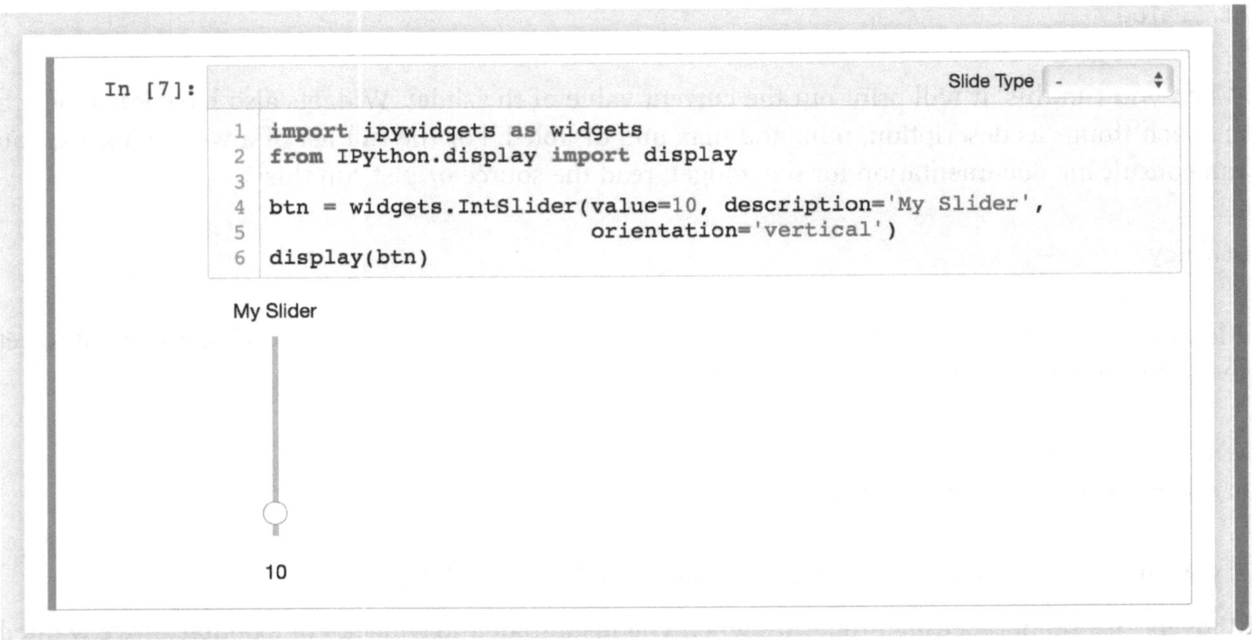

Fig. 8-5: Changing widget properties

Linking Two Widgets

Some Jupyter widgets can be linked together. For example, you can link a **FloatText** widget to a **FloatSlider** widget. What this means is that when one widget is updated, the other will be too. This is known as "synchronization of attributes". Let's take a look at a simple example:

```
text = widgets.FloatText()
slider = widgets.FloatSlider()
display(text,slider)

mylink = widgets.jslink((text, 'value'), (slider, 'value'))
```

Here we create two widgets and display them both. Then we call **widgets.jslink** and tell it to link the value of the text and slider together. When you use the **jslink** method, you are linking the widgets from the **client side**. This makes the widgets sync up more robustly because they will be using the local machine's hardware. You can also use **jsdlink**, which will create a unidirectional link between two widgets on the client side. What that means is that you can make one of the two widgets affect the second widget whereas the second widget will NOT affect the first.

Try changing the example above to use **jsdlink** like we do below:

```
text = widgets.FloatText()
slider = widgets.FloatSlider()
display(text,slider)

mylink = widgets.jsdlink((text, 'value'), (slider, 'value'))
```

Now try editing each widget's value and see how they interact. It's hard to demonstrate in the book but basically when you change the text widget it will change the slider to match. However if you change the slider's value, the text control won't change.

There are also two other methods you can use to link two widgets together:

- link
- dlink

These methods work in the same way as **jslink** and **jsdlink** respectively, except that they will talk to the server so you might experience some latency when using them. Frankly on your local machine, you probably won't see much difference between the two.

Finally I want to point out that you can also unlink the widgets by calling the link's **unlink** method:

```
mylink.unlink()
```

You can try this out by adding this code to the end of the cell where you created the linked widgets. If you do add it and re-run the cell, then you will find that the two widgets are no longer linked together.

Events

Linking widgets is closely related to widget events. An event occurs when you interact with a widget. For example, when you push a button, that is known as a **click** event. Let's look at an example of how this might work using a button widget.

```
import ipywidgets as widgets
from IPython.display import display

btn = widgets.Button(description='Test')
display(btn)


def my_event_handler(btn_object):
    print('You pressed the {} button!'.format(btn_object.description))

btn.on_click(my_event_handler)
```

Here we import the various bits and pieces we need to use widgets and display them. Then we create a simple button and a function that is named **my_event_handler**. This is the event handler which is what you would bind your widget's event to. To actually bind your button's click event to this handler, you must call **on_click** and pass it the function that you want it bound to. You will note that the event handler accepts an argument implicitly, which is the button object itself.

This allows you to access the button's properties, so in this case I went ahead and told it to print out the label of the button. The following is a screenshot of what my code and button looked like when I ran it after pressing the button:

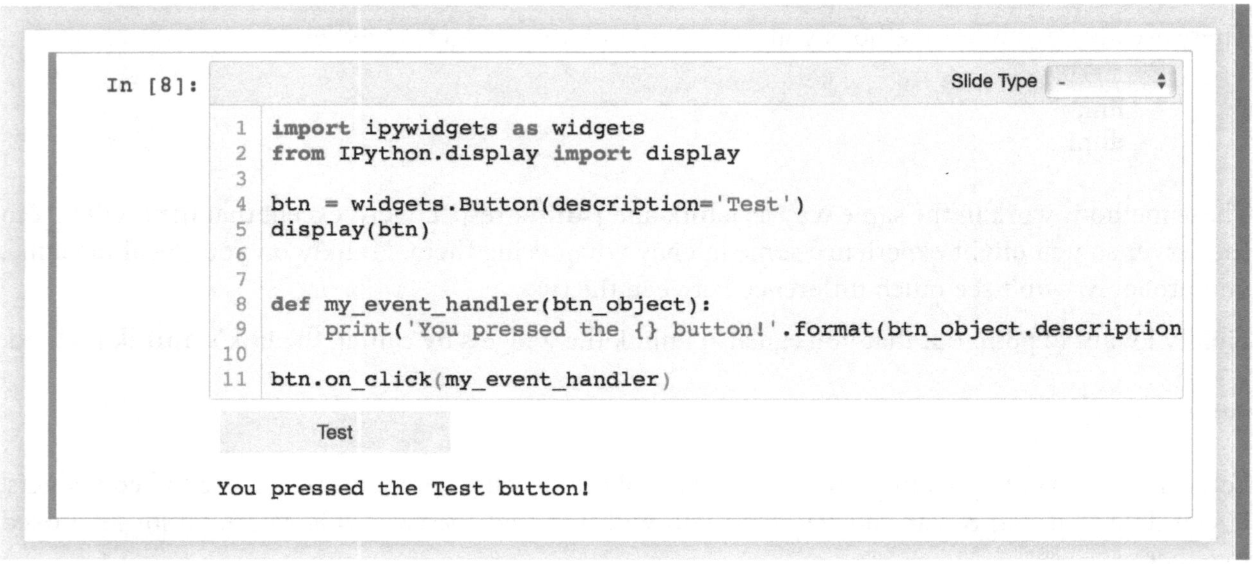

Fig. 8-6: Firing an event

What this also allows you to do is to bind multiple buttons to the same event handler. Here's how you might do that:

```
import ipywidgets as widgets
from IPython.display import display

btn = widgets.Button(description='Test')
other_btn = widgets.Button(description='Other')
display(btn)
display(other_btn)

def my_event_handler(btn_object):
    print('You pressed {}'.format(btn_object.description))

btn.on_click(my_event_handler)
other_btn.on_click(my_event_handler)
```

In this code, we create a second button called **other_btn** with a different label and bind it to the same event handler as the other button. Now you can try pressing the each button a few times and see how they behave. Here's an example session:

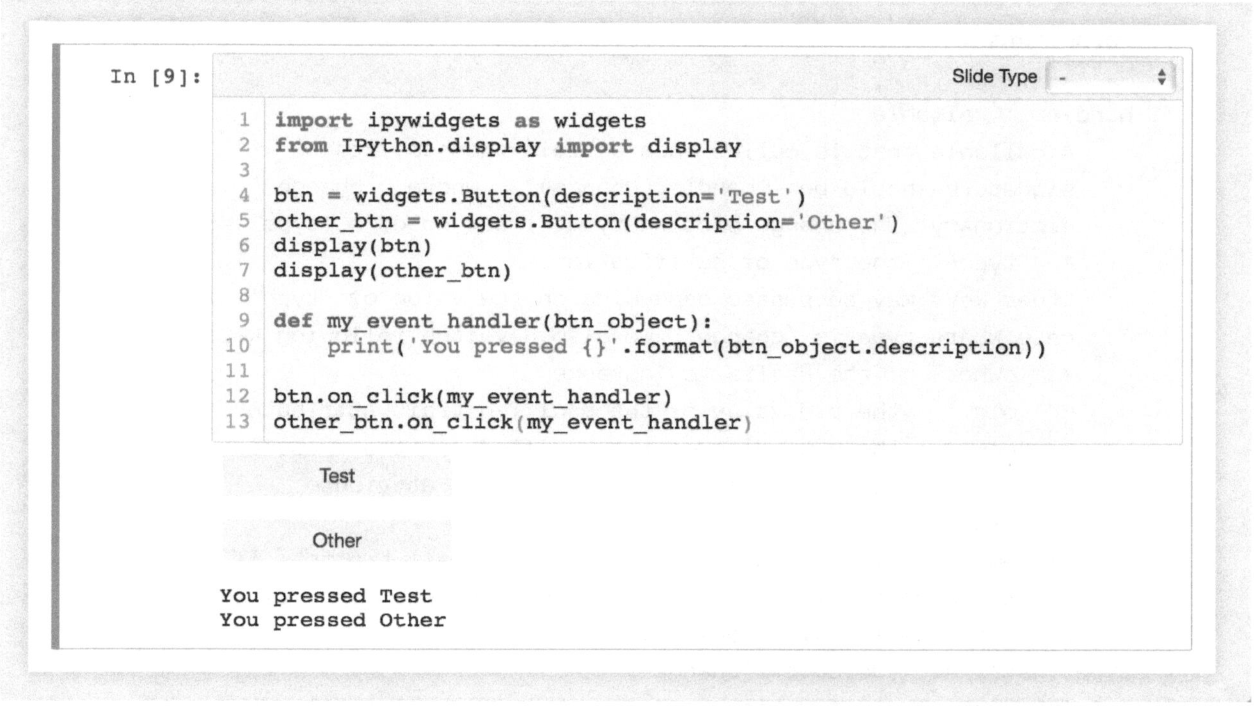

Fig. 8-7: Binding two widgets to the same handler

You can do this type of event binding with other types of widget events. You will need to look at the documentation for the widget or the source of the widget to figure out what events it supports.

Speaking of the documentation, it also mentions something that Jupyter calls **Traitlet events**. These are IPython traitlets which basically give you a different method of binding an event to a function using the **observe** method. To get an idea of how you might use a traitlet, let's run the following code in our Jupyter Notebook:

```
print(btn.observe.__doc__)
```

When I ran this code, I got the following output:

```
Setup a handler to be called when a trait changes.

        This is used to setup dynamic notifications of trait changes.

        Parameters
        ----------
        handler : callable
            A callable that is called when a trait changes. Its
            signature should be ``handler(change)``, where ``change`` is a
            dictionary. The change dictionary at least holds a 'type' key.
            * ``type``: the type of notification.
            Other keys may be passed depending on the value of 'type'. In the
            case where type is 'change', we also have the following keys:
            * ``owner`` : the HasTraits instance
            * ``old`` : the old value of the modified trait attribute
            * ``new`` : the new value of the modified trait attribute
            * ``name`` : the name of the modified trait attribute.
        names : list, str, All
            If names is All, the handler will apply to all traits.  If a list
            of str, handler will apply to all names in the list.  If a
            str, the handler will apply just to that name.
        type : str, All (default: 'change')
            The type of notification to filter by. If equal to All, then all
            notifications are passed to the observe handler.
```

So how does this work? Basically you call observe with the name of the function that you want to bind to as well as which traits you want to "observe". You can pass in a list of strings, set it to "All" or pass in a singular string. The documentation has a good example, but I am going to take it and expand it slightly to become the following:

```
int_range = widgets.IntSlider()
display(int_range)

def on_value_change(change):
    print(change)
    print(change['new'])

int_range.observe(on_value_change, names='value')
```

The difference between this and the one you will find in the documentation is that I am printing out the change object too. This will tell us what we are dealing with. In this case, the output when you change the slider looks like this:

```
{'owner': IntSlider(value=2), 'new': 2, 'old': 0, 'name': 'value', 'type': 'change'}
2
```

That tells us that the **change** argument is a dictionary of values and that the key **new** will give us the new value of the slider. So when we tell Jupyter to **observe** the **value** string, it will send in a dictionary of values. Interestingly this dictionary also contains the old value of the slider in addition to the new value. This can be useful to know in other widgets if you need to implement something like undo / redo, for example.

Layout

Jupyter widgets also have a **layout** attribute that they expose which allows you to set a number of CSS properties that you may use to control how widgets are laid out. These properties include size, display, box model, positioning and more. You can use the layout feature to make your widgets change sizes based on the available space.

Let's look at a simple example:

```
from ipywidgets import Button, Layout
from IPython.display import display

layout = Layout(width='50%', height='100px')

btn = Button(description='(50% width, 100px height) button',
             layout=layout)
display(btn)
```

Here we import our Button and a Layout. We set up the Layout such that it will make the widget take up 50% of the available width and 100 pixels high. Then we set the button's layout argument to the layout that we just created. This is what the result looks like:

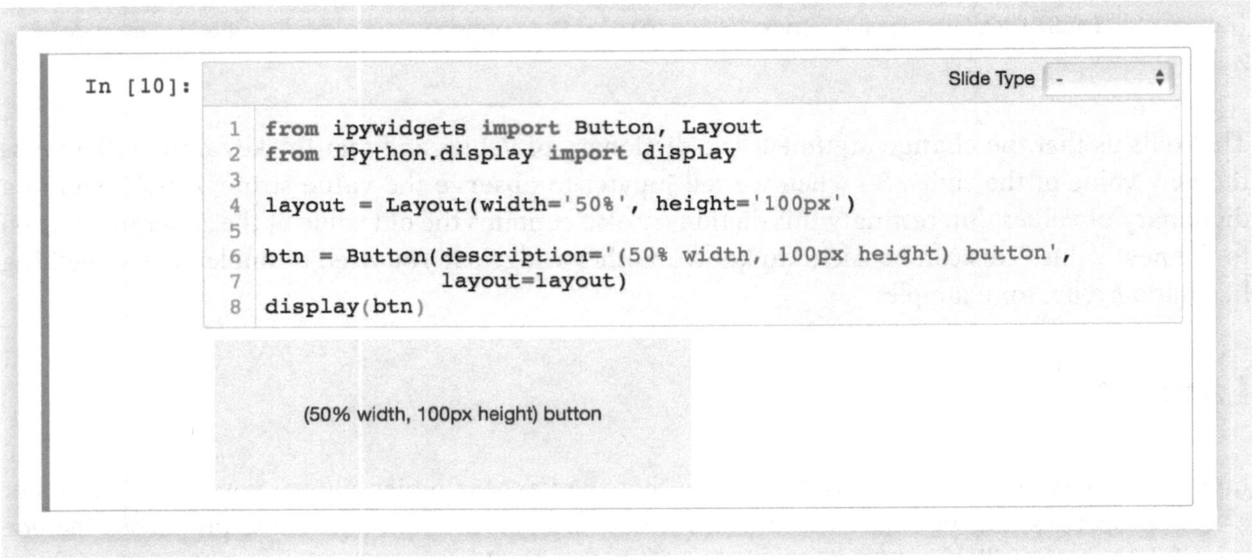

Fig. 8-8: Using a layout to resize a widget

You can apply layouts by creating a layout instance like we did in the previous example or you can have a widget use another widget's layout directly. To demonstrate, let's add the following code to the bottom of the cell that we just created in the previous example:

```
btn2 = Button(description='Another button', layout=btn.layout)
display(btn2)
```

Here we set this new button's layout to **btn.layout**, which basically makes our new button use the same layout object that the original button is using. You should end up seeing the button's like this:

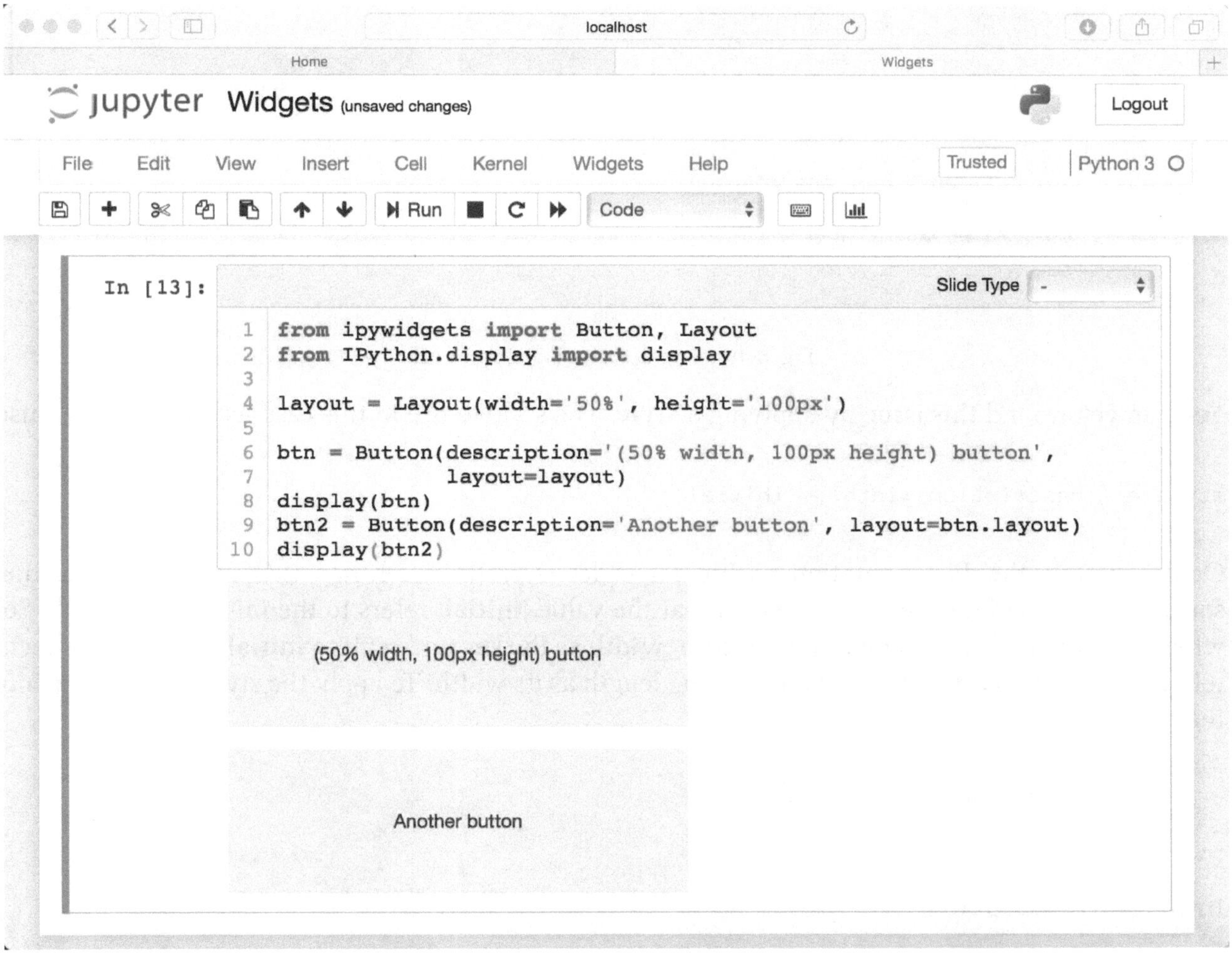

Fig. 8-9: Applying layout to second button

Styling

Interestingly, some widgets allow you to put in a description that is too long to be shown.

```
from ipywidgets import IntSlider

IntSlider(description='A really long description')
```

When you run this code, you will find that Jupyter cuts off some of the text:

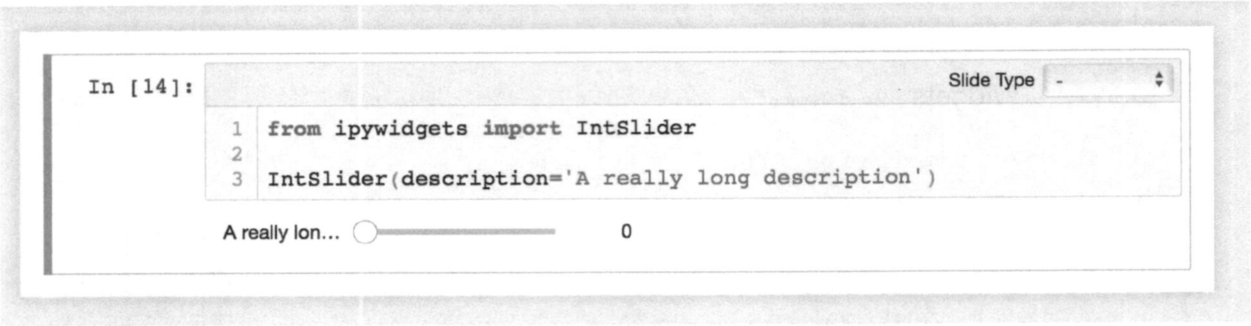

Fig. 8-10: Long descriptions get cut off

You can get around this issue by applying a **style**. The style to use in this case would look like this:

```
style = {'description_width': 'initial'}
```

Oddly enough, the documentation on Jupyter styles is pretty much non-existent. Looking at the source code in **widget_int.py**, it appears that the value, **initial**, refers to the initial label width. So when you create a style that has **description_width** as the key and set it to **initial**, you are, in effect, telling Jupyter to use the widget label's string length as its width. To apply the style, you can just do the following:

```
from ipywidgets import IntSlider

style = {'description_width': 'initial'}
IntSlider(description='A really long description', style=style)
```

And now your widget will look like this:

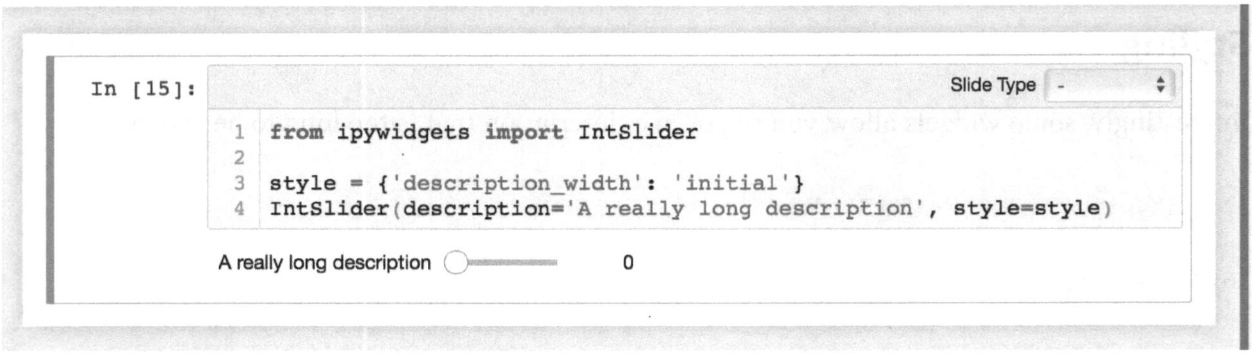

Fig. 8-11: Long description, short slider

Of course, the problem with this solution is that now your slider looks too small. We can solve that issue by using a helper function!

Arranging Widgets

There are some helper functions like **HBox** and **VBox** that you can use for combining widget and laying them out visually. The HBox will add widgets to it one at a time horizontally. You can think of it as lining up individual pieces in a horizontal line from left-to-right. Let's use an HBox and a Label widget to solve our problem:

```
from ipywidgets import HBox, Label, IntSlider

label = Label('A really long description')
my_slider = IntSlider()

HBox([label, my_slider])
```

Here we import the pieces we need, create a couple of widgets and then add them to our HBox. The result is as follows:

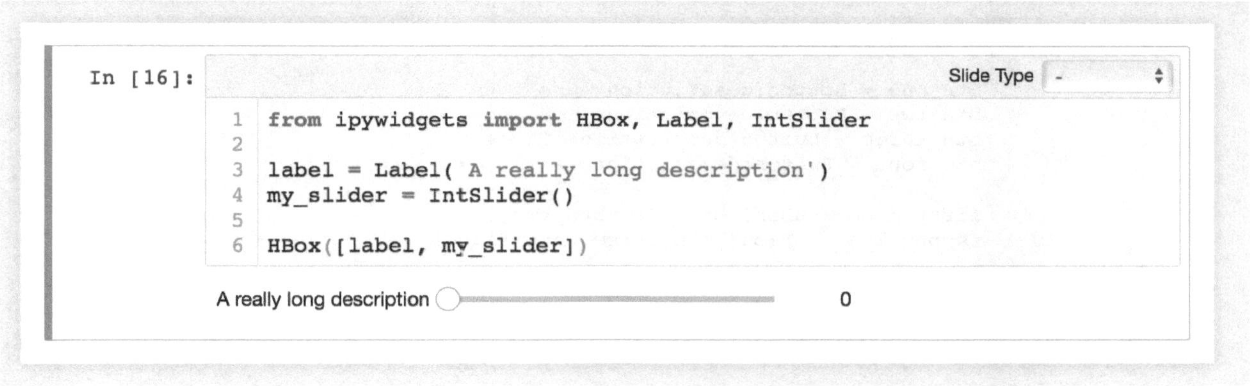

Fig. 8-12: Using an HBox

As you might expect, you can use a combination of HBox and VBox layouts to make complex layouts of your widgets. For example, you could add a couple of widgets to one HBox and a couple more to a second HBox and then add both HBoxes to a VBox to create a grid. Let's go ahead and do that so you can see how that might work.

```
from ipywidgets import Button, HBox, VBox

btn_one = Button(description='One')
btn_two = Button(description='Two')
btn_three = Button(description='Three')
btn_four = Button(description='Four')

first_line = HBox([btn_one, btn_two])
second_line = HBox([btn_three, btn_four])

VBox([first_line, second_line])
```

Here we create four buttons and two HBoxes. The HBoxes each hold two buttons apiece. Finally we add the HBoxes to the VBox and this is what we end up with:

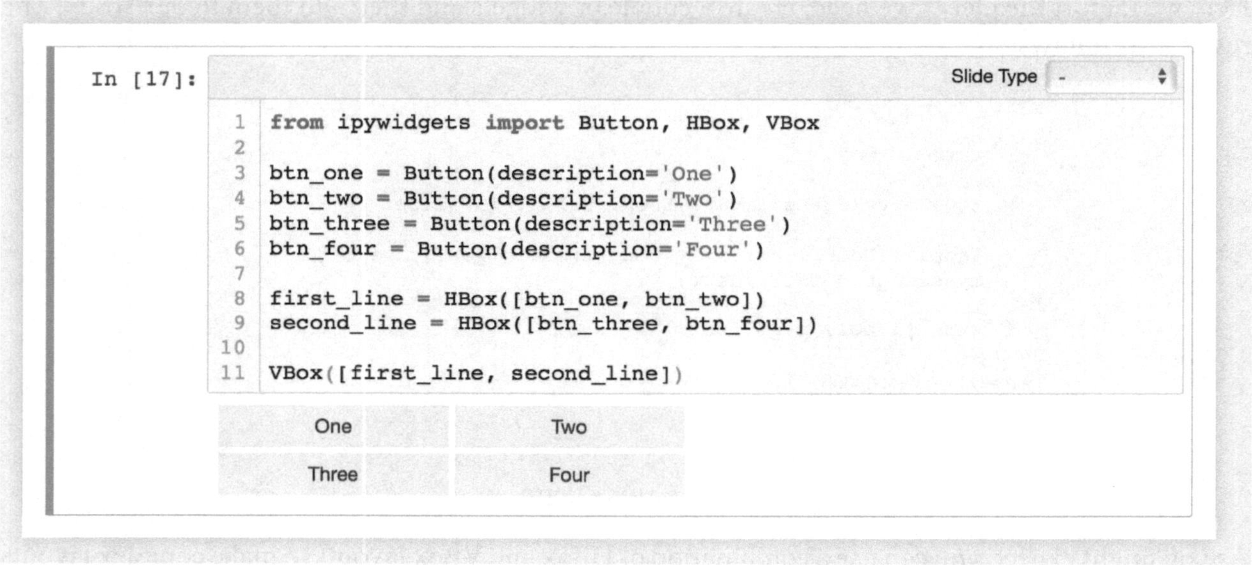

Fig. 8-13: Laying out multiple widgets

You can also build complex layouts with another widget called the **FlexBox**. There is actually a really good tutorial on this topic in the documentation, so I will leave that one for you to read as an exercise. I also want to mention that there is one other widget for creating layouts called the **GridBox**.

In my experience using wxPython, a cross-platform desktop user interface toolkit, I have found that using VBox and HBox type containers is more than enough for creating complex layouts of my widgets and the more advanced layout tools tend to make things more difficult unless you are already planning to do a grid-like interface. You are more than welcome to give these other types of layouts a try as they definitely have their place.

Wrapping Up

In this chapter we learned a lot about how to create and use Jupyter Widgets. We also learned how we can display, style and arrange them. There are lots of other things you can learn about widgets on by checking out the documentation on the topic or reading a few tutorials on the web. For example, Jupyter supports the ability for you to create your own custom widgets. It also supports the use of asynchronous widgets. I highly recommend using widgets in your Notebooks to give them some pizazz and to make them more useful too!

Chapter 9 - Slideshows

Jupyter Notebook can be turned into a slide presentation that is kind of like using Microsoft Powerpoint, except that you can run the slide's code live! It's really neat how well it works. The only con in my book is that there isn't a lot of theming that can be applied to your slides, so they do end up looking a bit plain.

In this chapter, we will look at two methods of creating a slideshow out of your Jupyter Notebook. The first method is by using Jupyter Notebook's built-in slideshow capabilities. The second is by using a plug-in called RISE.

Let's get started!

Creating a Slideshow

The first thing we need to do is to create a new Notebook. Once you have that done and running, let's create three cells so that we can have three slides. Your Notebook should now look like the following:

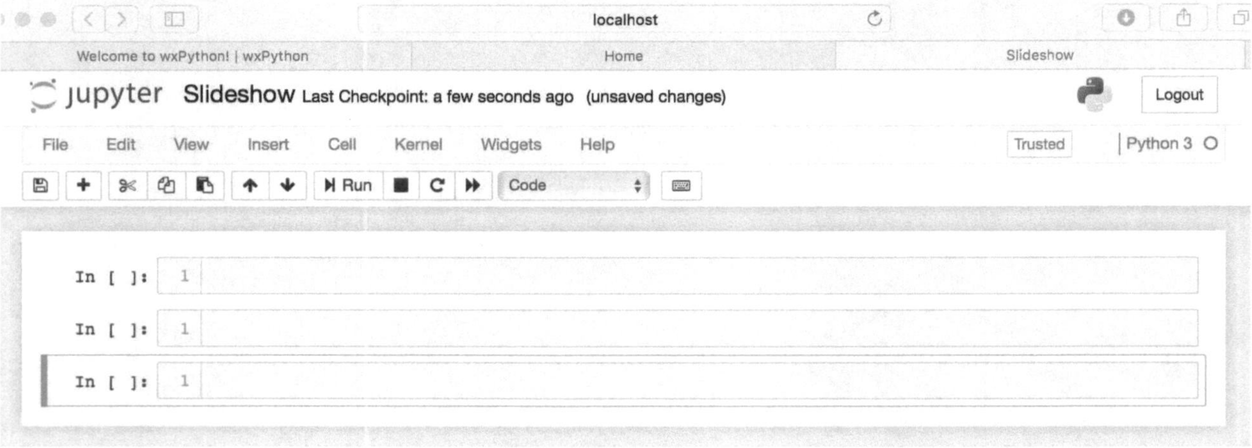

Fig. 9-1: An empty Notebook with 3 cells

Now let's turn on the "slideshow" tools. Go to the **View** menu and then click on the **Cell Toolbar** menu option. You will find a sub-menu in there that is called **Slideshow**. Choose that. Now your Notebook's cell should look like this:

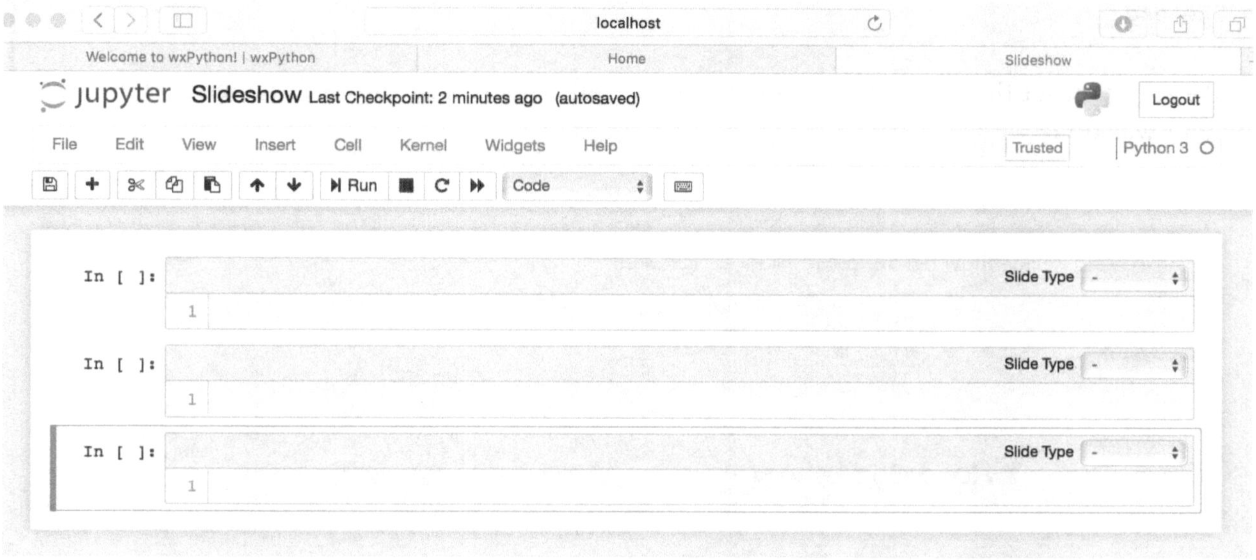

Fig. 9-2: An empty slideshow

There are now little comboboxes on the top right of each cell. These widgets give you the following options:

- Slide
- Sub-Slide
- Fragment
- Skip
- Notes

You can just create a series of Slides if you like, but you can make the slideshow a bit more interesting by adding Sub-Slides and Fragments. Sub-slides are just slides that are below the previous one while Fragments are basically fragments within the previous slide. As an aside, I have actually never used Fragments myself. Anyway you can also set a slide to Skip, which just allows you to skip a slide or Notes, which are just speaker notes.

Let's add some text to our first cell. We will add the text "# Hello Slideshow" to it and set the cell type to Markdown. Note the pound sign at the beginning of the text. This will cause the text to be a heading.

In cell two, we can add a simple function. Let's use the following code:

```
def double(x):
    print(x * 2)

double(4)
```

For the last cell, we will add the following text:

```
# The end
```

Make sure you set that to be a Markdown cell as well. This is what my cells ended up looking like when I was done:

Fig. 9-3: Getting the slideshow ready

To make things simple, just set each of the cell's individual comboboxes to **Slide**.

Now we just need to turn it into an actual slideshow. To do that, you will need save your Notebook and shut down the Jupyter Notebook server. Next you will need to run the following command:

```
jupyter nbconvert slideshow.ipynb --to slides --post serve
```

When you do that, you should see something like the following in your web browser:

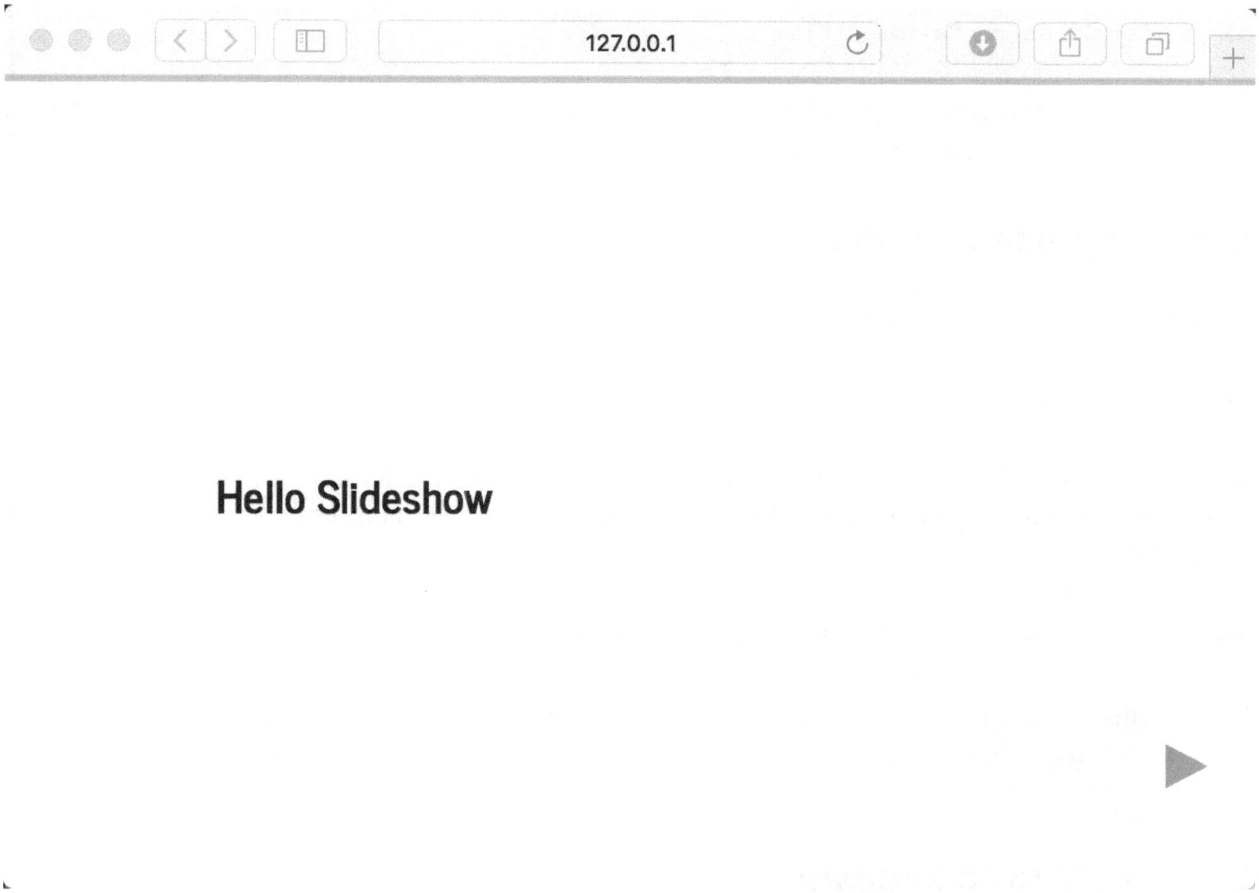

Fig. 9-4: Running the slideshow

To navigate your slideshow, you can use your left and right arrow keys or you can use spacebar to go forward and shift_spacebar to go back. This creates a pretty nice and simple slideshow, but it doesn't allow you to run the cells. For that, we will need to use the RISE plugin!

Getting Started with RISE

Reveal.js - Jupyter/IPython Slideshow Extension (RISE) is a plugin that uses *reveal.js* to make the slideshow run live. What that means is that you will now be able to run your code in the slideshow without exiting the slideshow. The first item that we need to learn about is how to get RISE installed.

Installing rise with conda

If you happen to be an Anaconda user, then this is the method you would use to install RISE:

```
conda install -c conda-forge rise
```

This is the easiest method of installing RISE. However most people still use regular CPython, so next we will learn how to use pip!

Installing rise with pip

You can use Python's pip installer tool to install RISE like this:

```
pip install RISE
```

You can also do python -m pip install RISE is you want to. Once the package is installed, you have a second step of installing the JS and CSS in the proper places, which requires you to run the following command:

```
jupyter-nbextension install rise --py --sys-prefix
```

If you somehow get a version of RISE that is older than 5.3.0, then you would also need to enable the RISE extension in Jupyter. However, I recommend just using the latest version so you don't have to worry about that.

Using RISE for a SlideShow

Now that we have RISE installed and enabled, let's re-open the Jupyter Notebook we created earlier. Your Notebook should now look like this:

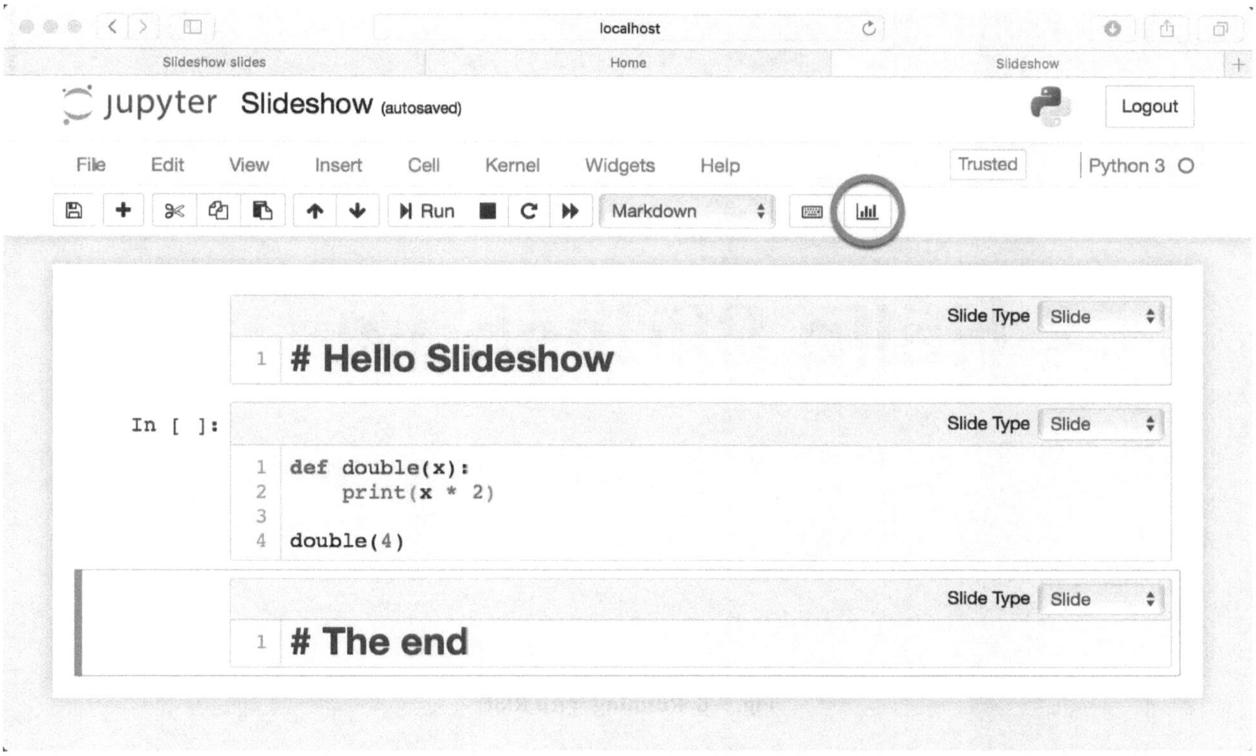

Fig. 9-5: Adding RISE

You will notice that I circled a new button that was added by RISE to your Notebook. If you mouse over that button you will see that it has a tooltip that appears that says "Enter/Exit RISE Slideshow". Click it and you should see a slideshow that looks a lot like the previous one. The difference here is that you can actually edit and run all the cells while in the slideshow. Just double-click on the first slide and you should see it transform to the following:

Fig. 9-6: Running with RISE

After you are done editing, press SHIFT+ENTER to run the cell. Here are the primary shortcuts you will need to run the slideshow effectively:

- SPACEBAR - Goes forward a slide in the slideshow
- SHIFT+SPACEBAR - Goes back a slide in the slideshow
- SHIFT+ENTER - Runs the cell on the current slide
- DOUBLE-CLICK - To edit a Markdown cell

You can view all the Keyboard shortcuts by going to the **Help** menu when not in Slideshow mode and clicking the **Keyboard Shortcuts** option. Most if not all of these shortcuts should work inside of a RISE slideshow.

If you want to start the slideshow on a specific cell, just select that cell and then press the Enter Slideshow button.

RISE also works with Notebook widgets. Try creating a new cell with the following code from the widget's chapter:

```
from ipywidgets import interact

def my_function(x):
    return x

# create a slider
interact(my_function, x=20)
```

Now start the slideshow on that cell and try running the cell (SHIFT+ENTER). You should see something like this:

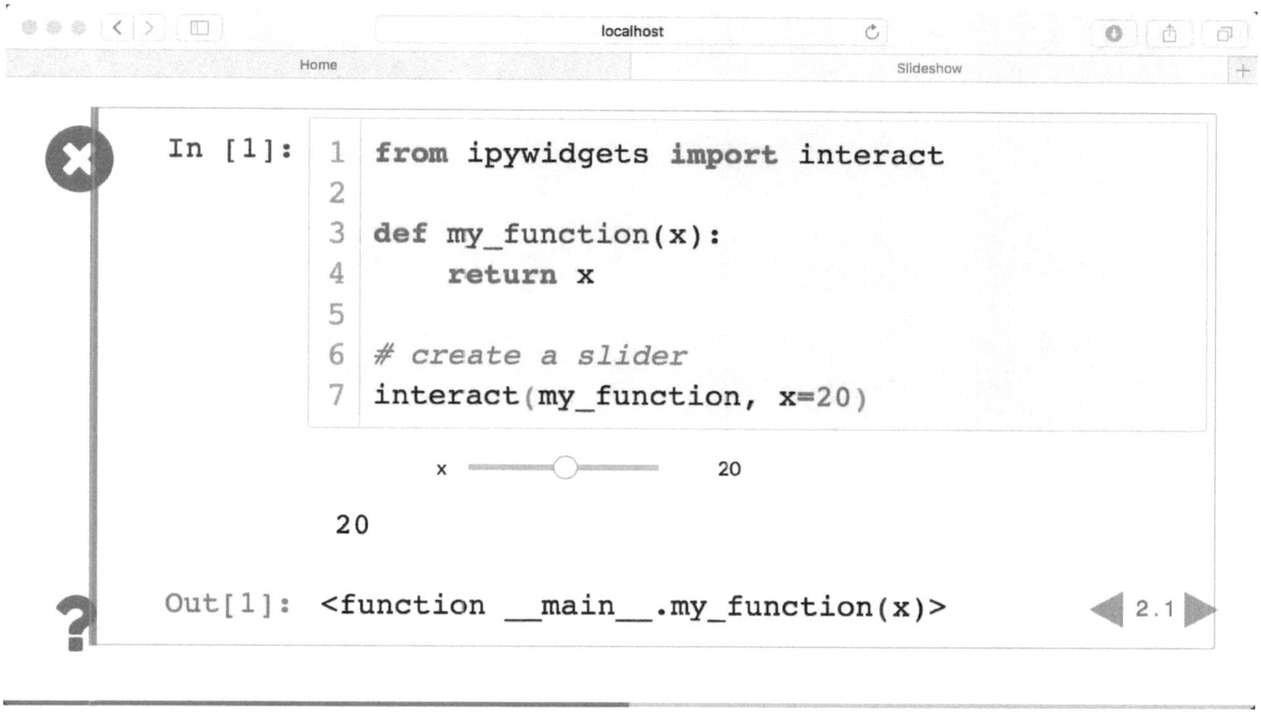

Fig. 9-7: Using a widget in RISE

You can use RISE to add neat widgets, graphs and other interactive elements to your slideshow that you can edit live to demonstrate concepts to your attendees. It's really quite fun and I have used RISE personally for presenting intermediate level material in Python to engineers.

RISE also has several different themes that you can apply as will as minimal support for slide transitions. See the documentation for full information:

- https://rise.readthedocs.io/en/docs_hot_fixes/customize.html

Wrapping Up

In this chapter we learned about two good methods for creating presentations out of our Jupyter Notebooks. You can use Jupyter directly via their **nbconvert** tooling to generate a slideshow from the cells in your Notebook. This is nice to have, but I personally like RISE better. It makes the presentations so much more interactive and fun. I highly recommend it. You will find that using Jupyter Notebook for your presentations will make the slides that much more engaging and it is so nice to be able to fix slides during the presentation too!

Chapter 10 - Debugging

Debugging is an important concept. The concept of debugging is trying to figure out what is wrong with your code or just trying to understand the code. There are many times where I will come to unfamiliar code and I will need to step through it in a debugger to grasp how it works. Most Python IDEs have good debuggers built into them. I personally like Wing IDE for instance. Others like PyCharm or PyDev. But what if you want to debug the code in your Jupyter Notebook? How does that work?

In this chapter we will look at a couple of different methods of debugging a Notebook. The first one is by using Python's own **pdb** module.

Using pdb

The pdb module is Python's debugger module. Just as C++ has gdb, Python has pdb.

Let's start by opening up a new Notebook and adding a cell with the following code in it:

```
def bad_function(var):
    return var + 0

bad_function("Mike")
```

If you run this code, you should end up with some output that looks like this:

```
---------------------------------------------------------------------------
TypeError                                 Traceback (most recent call last)
<ipython-input-1-2f23ed1cac1e> in <module>()
      2         return var + 0
      3
----> 4 bad_function("Mike")

<ipython-input-1-2f23ed1cac1e> in bad_function(var)
      1 def bad_function(var):
----> 2         return var + 0
      3
      4 bad_function("Mike")

TypeError: cannot concatenate 'str' and 'int' objects
```

What this means is that you cannot concatenate a string and an integer. This is a pretty common problem if you don't know what types a function accepts. You will find that this is especially true when working with complex functions and classes, unless they happen to be using type hinting. One way to figure out what is going on is by adding a breakpoint using pdb's **set_trace()** function:

```
def bad_function(var):
    import pdb
    pdb.set_trace()
    return var + 0

bad_function("Mike")
```

Now when you run the cell, you will get a prompt in the output which you can use to inspect the variables and basically run code live. If you happen to have Python 3.7, then you can simplify the example above by using the new **breakpoint** built-in, like this:

```
def bad_function(var):
    breakpoint()
    return var + 0

bad_function("Mike")
```

This code is functionally equivalent to the previous example but uses the new **breakpoint** function instead. When you run this code, it should act the same way as the code in the previous section did.

You can read more about how to use pdb here:

- https://docs.python.org/3/library/pdb.html

You can use any of pdb's command right inside of your Jupyter Notebook. Here are some examples:

- w(here) - Print the stack trace
- d(own) - Move the current frame X number of levels down. Defaults to one.
- u(p) - Move the current frame X number of levels up. Defaults to one.
- b(reak) - With a *lineno* argument, set a break point at that line number in the current file / context
- s(tep) - Execute the current line and stop at the next possible line
- c(ontinue) - Continue execution

Note that these are single-letter commands: w, d, u and b are the commands. You can use these commands to interactively debug your code in your Notebook along with the other commands listed in the documentation listed above.

ipdb

IPython also has a debugger called **ipdb**. However it does not work with Jupyter Notebook directly. You would need to connect to the kernel using something like **Jupyter console** and run it from there to use it. If you would like to go that route, you can read more about using Jupyter console here:

- https://jupyter-console.readthedocs.io/en/latest/

However there is an IPython debugger that we can use called **IPython.core.debugger.set_trace**. Let's create a cell with the following code:

```
from IPython.core.debugger import set_trace


def bad_function(var):
    set_trace()
    return var + 0


bad_function("Mike")
```

Now you can run this cell and get the ipdb debugger. Here is what the output looked like on my machine:

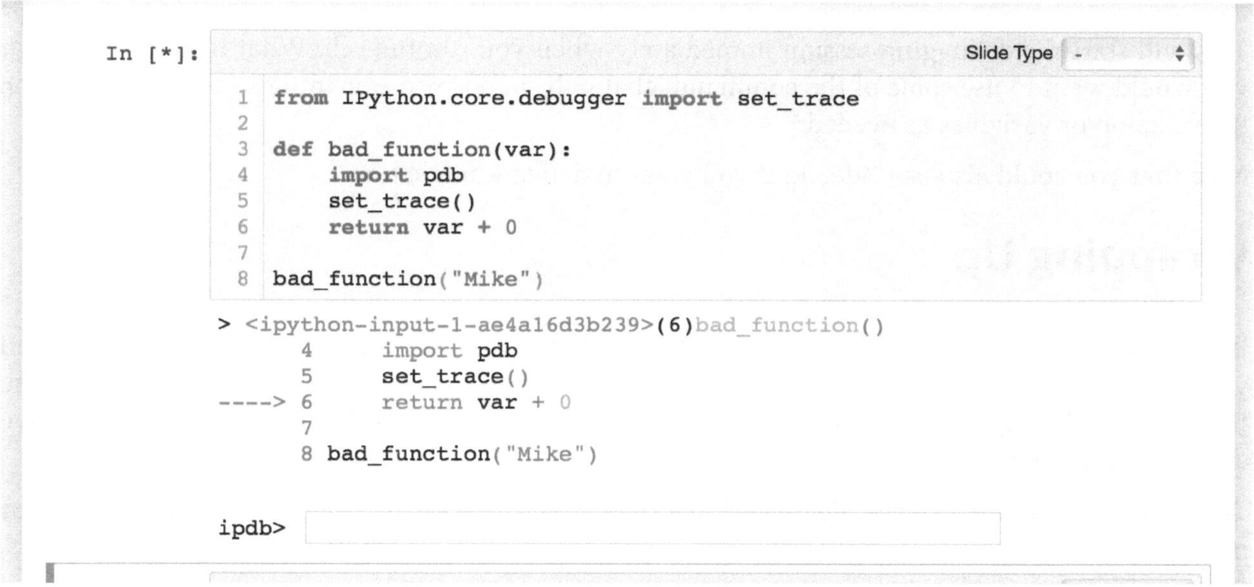

Fig. 10-1: Using the IPython Debugger

The IPython debugger uses the same commands as the Python debugger does. The main difference is that it provides syntax highlighting and was originally designed to work in the IPython console.

There is one other way to open up the **ipdb** debugger and that is by using the **%pdb** magic. Here is some sample code you can try in a Notebook cell:

```
%pdb

def bad_function(var):
    return var + 0

bad_function("Mike")
```

When you run this code, you should end up seeing the TypeError traceback and then the ipdb prompt will appear in the output, which you can then use as before.

What about %%debug?

There is yet another way that you can open up a debugger in your Notebook. You can use %%debug to debug the entire cell like this:

```
%%debug

def bad_function(var):
    return var + 0

bad_function("Mike")
```

This will start the debugging session immediately when you run the cell. What that means is that you would want to use some of the commands that pdb supports to step into the code and examine the function or variables as needed.

Note that you could also use %debug if you want to debug a single line.

Wrapping Up

In this chapter we learned of several different methods that you can use to debug the code in your Jupyter Notebook. I personally prefer to use Python's pdb module, but you can use the IPython.core.debugger to get the same functionality and it could be better if you prefer to have syntax highlighting.

There is also a newer "visual debugger" package called the PixieDebugger from the **pixiedust** package:

- https://github.com/pixiedust/pixiedust

I haven't used it myself. Some reviewers say it is amazing and others have said it is pretty buggy. I will leave that one up to you to determine if it is something you want to add to your toolset.

As far as I am concerned, I think using pdb or IPython's debugger work quite well and should work for you too.

Chapter 11 - Testing

The more you do programming, the more you will here about how you should test your code. You will hear about things like Extreme Programming and Test Driven Development (TDD). These are great ways to create quality code. But how does testing fit in with Jupyter? Frankly, it really doesn't. If you want to test your code properly, you should write your code outside of Jupyter and import it into cells if you need to. This allows you to use Python's **unittest** module or **py.test** to write tests for your code separately from Jupyter. This will also let you add on test runners like **nose** or put your code into a Continuous Integration setup using something like Travis CI or Jenkins.

However all is now lost. You can do some testing of your Jupyter Notebooks even though you won't have the full flexibility that you would get from keeping your code separate. We will look at some ideas that you can use to do some basic testing with Jupyter.

Execute and Check

One popular method of "testing" a Notebook is to run it from the command line and send its output to a file. Here is the example syntax that you could use if you wanted to do the execution on the command line:

```
jupyter-nbconvert --to notebook --execute --output output_file_path input_file_path
```

Of course, we want to do this programmatically and we want to be able to capture errors. To do that, we will take our Notebook runner code from chapter 5 and re-use it. Here it is again for your convenience:

```
# notebook_runner.py

import nbformat
import os

from nbconvert.preprocessors import ExecutePreprocessor


def run_notebook(notebook_path):
    nb_name, _ = os.path.splitext(os.path.basename(notebook_path))
    dirname = os.path.dirname(notebook_path)
```

```
    with open(notebook_path) as f:
        nb = nbformat.read(f, as_version=4)

    proc = ExecutePreprocessor(timeout=600, kernel_name='python3')
    proc.allow_errors = True

    proc.preprocess(nb, {'metadata': {'path': '/'}})
    output_path = os.path.join(dirname, '{}_all_output.ipynb'.format(nb_name))

    with open(output_path, mode='wt') as f:
        nbformat.write(nb, f)

    errors = []
    for cell in nb.cells:
        if 'outputs' in cell:
            for output in cell['outputs']:
                if output.output_type == 'error':
                    errors.append(output)

    return nb, errors

if __name__ == '__main__':
    nb, errors = run_notebook('Testing.ipynb')
    print(errors)
```

You will note that I have updated the code to run a new Notebook. Let's go ahead and create a Notebook that has two cells of code in it. After creating the Notebook, change the title to **Testing** and save it. That will cause Jupyter to save the file as **Testing.ipynb**. Now enter the following code in the first cell:

```
def add(a, b):
    return a + b

add(5, 6)
```

And enter the following code into cell #2:

```
1 / 0
```

Now you can run the Notebook runner code. When you do, you should get the following output:

```
[{'ename': 'ZeroDivisionError',
  'evalue': 'integer division or modulo by zero',
  'output_type': 'error',
  'traceback': ['\x1b[0;31m\x1b[0m',
                '\x1b[0;31mZeroDivisionError\x1b[0mTraceback (most recent call '
                'last)',
                '\x1b[0;32m<ipython-input-2-bc757c3fda29>\x1b[0m in '
                '\x1b[0;36m<module>\x1b[0;34m()\x1b[0m\n'
                '\x1b[0;32m----> 1\x1b[0;31m \x1b[0;36m1\x1b[0m '
                '\x1b[0;34m/\x1b[0m '
                '\x1b[0;36m0\x1b[0m\x1b[0;34m\x1b[0m\x1b[0m\n'
                '\x1b[0m',
                '\x1b[0;31mZeroDivisionError\x1b[0m: integer division or '
                'modulo by zero']}]
```

This indicates that we have some code that outputs an error. In this case, we did expect that as this is a very contrived example. In your own code, you probably wouldn't want any of your code to output an error. Regardless, this Notebook runner script isn't enough to actually do a real test. You need to wrap this code with testing code. So let's create a new file that we will save to the same location as our Notebook runner code. We will save this script with the name "test_runner.py". Put the following code in your new script:

```
import unittest

import runner


class TestNotebook(unittest.TestCase):

    def test_runner(self):
        nb, errors = runner.run_notebook('Testing.ipynb')
        self.assertEqual(errors, [])


if __name__ == '__main__':
    unittest.main()
```

This code uses Python's **unittest** module. Here we create a testing class with a single test function inside of it called **test_runner**. This function calls our Notebook runner and asserts that the errors list should be empty. To run this code, open up a terminal and navigate to the folder that contains your code. Then run the following command:

```
python test_runner.py
```

When I ran this, I got the following output:

```
F
======================================================================
FAIL: test_runner (__main__.TestNotebook)
----------------------------------------------------------------------
Traceback (most recent call last):
  File "test_runner.py", line 10, in test_runner
    self.assertEqual(errors, [])
AssertionError: Lists differ: [{'output_type': u'error', 'ev... != []

First list contains 1 additional elements.
First extra element 0:
{'ename': 'ZeroDivisionError',
 'evalue': 'integer division or modulo by zero',
 'output_type': 'error',
 'traceback': ['\x1b[0;31m---------------------------------------------------------\
-----------------\x1b[0m',
               '\x1b[0;31mZeroDivisionError\x1b[0m                                 '
               'Traceback (most recent call last)',
               '\x1b[0;32m<ipython-input-2-bc757c3fda29>\x1b[0m in '
               '\x1b[0;36m<module>\x1b[0;34m()\x1b[0m\n'
               '\x1b[0;32m----> 1\x1b[0;31m \x1b[0;36m1\x1b[0m '
               '\x1b[0;34m/\x1b[0m \x1b[0;36m0\x1b[0m\x1b[0;34m\x1b[0m\x1b[0m\n'
               '\x1b[0m',
               '\x1b[0;31mZeroDivisionError\x1b[0m: integer division or modulo '
               'by zero']}

Diff is 677 characters long. Set self.maxDiff to None to see it.

----------------------------------------------------------------------
Ran 1 test in 1.463s

FAILED (failures=1)
```

This clearly shows that our code failed. If you remove the cell that has the divide by zero issue and re-run your test, you should get this:

```
.
----------------------------------------------------------------------
Ran 1 test in 1.324s

OK
```

By removing the cell (or just correcting the error in that cell), you can make your tests pass.

The py.test Plugin

I discovered a neat plugin you can use that appears to help you out by making the workflow a bit easier. I am referring to the py.test plugin for Jupyter, which you can learn more about here:

- https://github.com/computationalmodelling/nbval

Basically it gives py.test the ability to recognize Jupyter Notebooks and check if the stored inputs match the stored outputs and also that Notebooks run without error. After installing the **nbval** package, you can run it with py.test like this (assuming you have py.test installed):

```
py.test --nbval
```

Frankly you can actually run just py.test with no commands on the test file we already created and it will use our test code as is. The main benefit of adding nbval is that you won't need to necessarily add wrapper code around Jupyter if you do so.

Testing within the Notebook

Another way to run tests is to just include some tests in the Notebook itself. Let's add a new cell to our Testing Notebook that contains the following code:

```
import unittest

class TestNotebook(unittest.TestCase):

    def test_add(self):
        self.assertEqual(add(2, 3), 5)
```

This will test the **add** function in the first cell eventually. We could add a bunch of different tests here. For example, we might want to test what happens if we add a string type with a None type. But you may have noticed that if you try to run this cell, you get to output. The reason is that we aren't instantiating the class yet. We need to call **unittest.main** to do that. So while it's good to run that cell to get it into Jupyter's memory, we actually need to add one more cell with the following code:

```
unittest.main(argv=[''], verbosity=2, exit=False)
```

This code should be put in the last cell of your Notebook so it can run all the tests that you have added. It is basically telling Python to run with verbosity level of 2 and not to exit. When you run this code you should see the following output in your Notebook:

```
test_add (__main__.TestNotebook) ... ok

----------------------------------------------------------------------
Ran 1 test in 0.003s

OK

<unittest.main.TestProgram at 0x7fbc8fffc0d0>
```

You can do something similar with Python's **doctest** module inside of Jupyter Notebooks as well.

Wrapping Up

As I mentioned at the beginning, while you can test your code in your Jupyter Notebooks, it is actually much better if you just test your code outside of it. However there are workarounds and since some people like to use Jupyter for documentation purposes, it is good to have a way to verify that they are working correctly. In this chapter you learned how to run Notebooks programmatically and verify that the output was as you expected. You could enhance that code to verify certain errors are present if you wanted to as well.

You also learned how to use Python's unittest module in your Notebook cells directly. This does offer some nice flexibility as you can now run your code all in one place. Use these tools wisely and they will serve you well.

Chapter 12 - JupyterLab

JupyterLab is the latest package from Project Jupyter. In some ways, it is kind of a replacement for Jupyter Notebook. However the Jupyter Notebook is a separate project from JupyterLab. I like to think of JupyterLab as a kind of web-based Integrated Development Environment that you an use to to work with Jupyter Notebooks as well as using terminals, text editors and code consoles. You might say JupyterLab is a more powerful version of Jupyter Notebook.

Anyway, here are a few of the things that JupyterLab is capable of:

- Code Consoles - These are coding scratchpads that you can use for running code interactively, kind of like Python's IDLE
- Kernel-backed documents - These allow you to enable code in any text file (Markdown, Python, R, etc) that can then be run in the Jupyter kernel
- Mirrored Notebook cell outputs - This let's you create simple dashboards
- Multiple views of the same document - Gives you the ability to live edit documents and see the results in real-time

JupyterLab will allow you to view and handle multiple types of data. You can also display rich output from these formats using various visualizations or Markdown.

For navigation, you can use customizable keyboard shortcuts or key maps from vim, emacs and even SublimeText.

You can add new behavior to your JupyterLab instance via extensions. This includes theming support, file editors and more.

Installation

You can use **conda**, **pip** or **pipenv** to install JupyterLab.

conda

If you want to use conda, then you will want to use the following command:

```
conda install -c conda-forge jupyterlab
```

pip

If you prefer using Python's native installer, pip, then this is the command you want:

```
pip install jupyterlab
```

Note: If you are using pip install –user, then you will need to add the user-level bin directory to your PATH environment variable to be able to launch jupyterlab.

pipenv

The **pipenv** tool is a new package that can be used to create a Python virtual environment and download a package into it. If you happen to have it installed, then you can use the following two commands to get JupyterLab:

```
pipenv install jupyterlab
pipenv shell
```

Note that calling the **shell** command is required if you want to launch JupyterLab from within the virtualenv that you installed it into.

Running JupyterLab

Now that we have JupyterLab installed, we should try running it. You can use either

```
jupyter-lab
```

or

```
jupyter lab
```

to run it. When I ran either of these commands, I got the following initial web application:

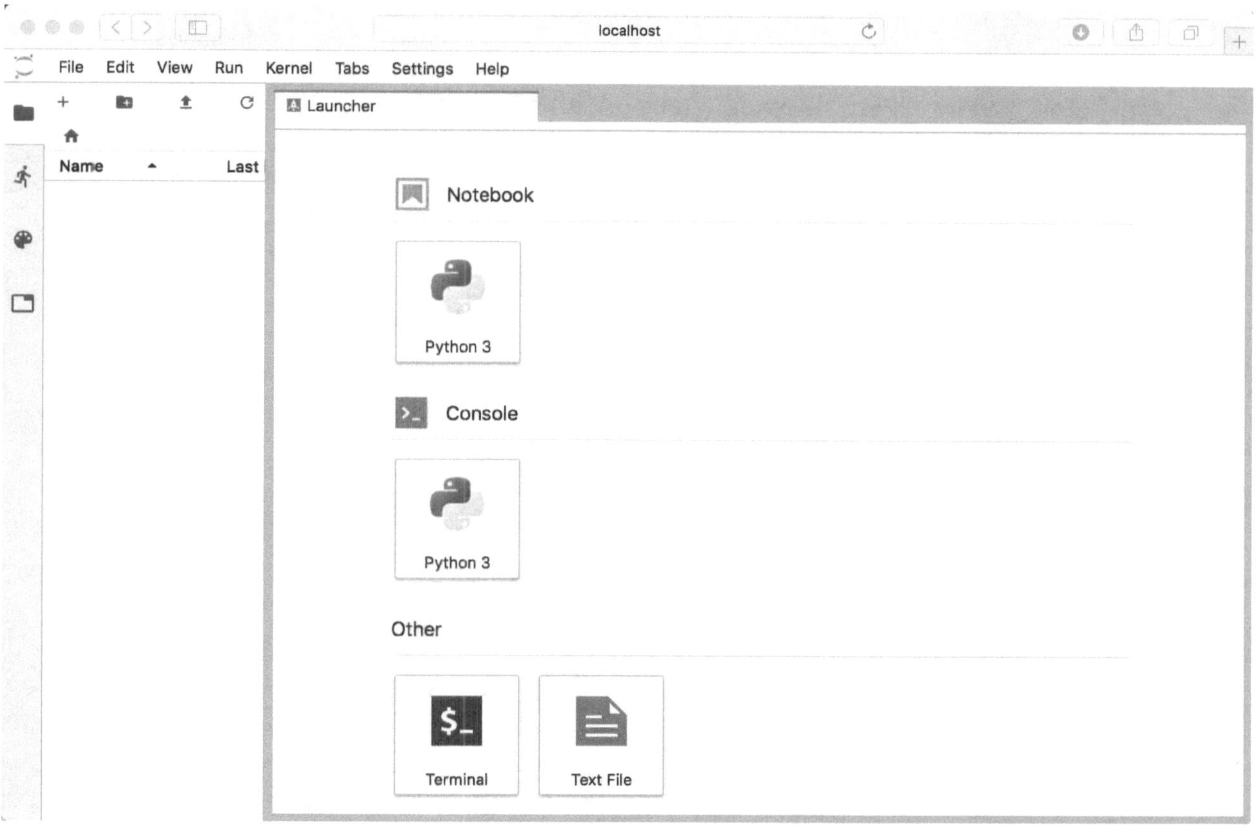

Fig. 12-1: Initial Landing Page for a New JupyterLab

The tab on the right is called the **Launcher**. This is one place you can go to start a new Notebook, Code Console, Terminal or Text File. New documents are opened as new tabs. You will note that when you create a new Notebook or other item that the Launcher disappears. If you would like to open a second document, just click the "+" button on the left, which I have circled below:

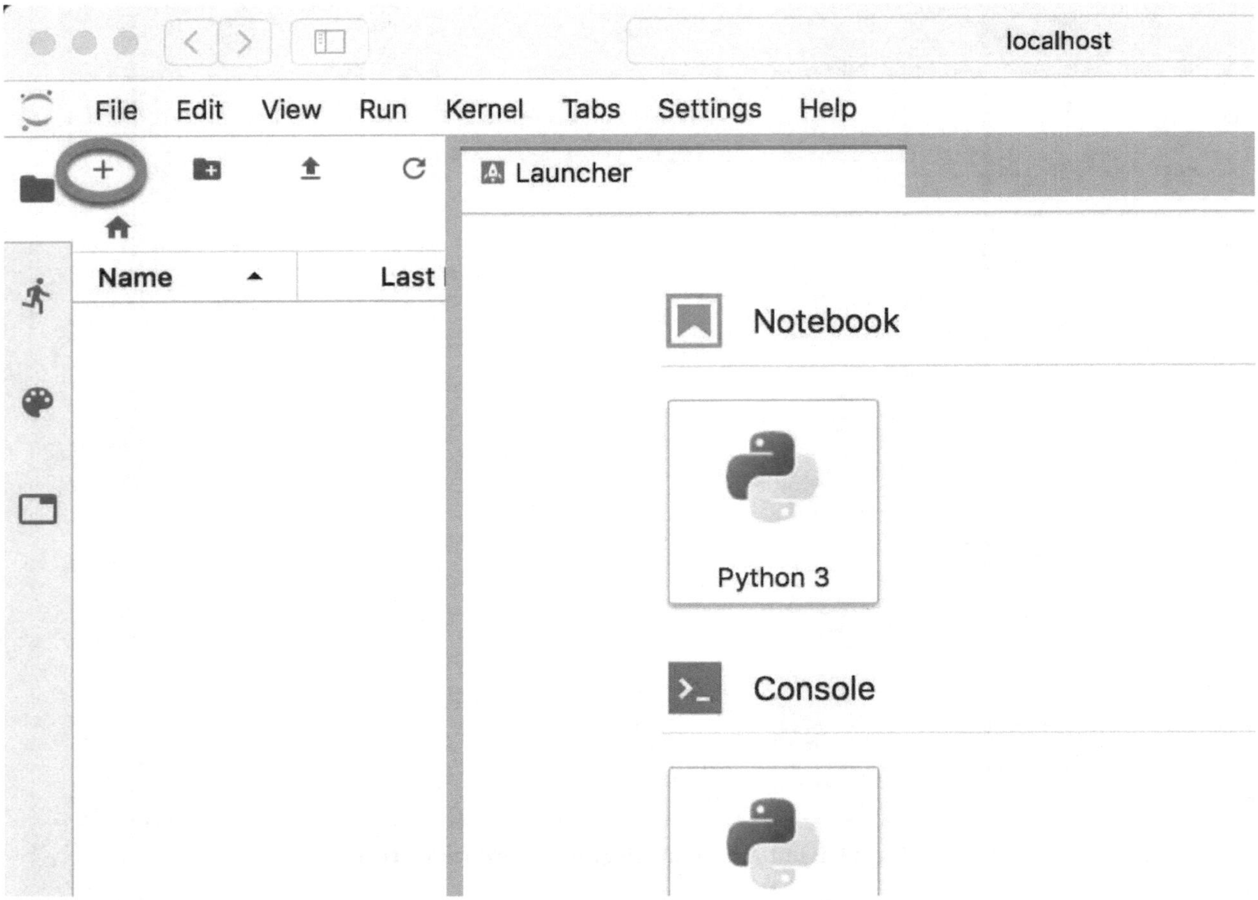

Fig. 12-2: Adding a new item in JupyterLab

Let's open a Notebook and then click the plus button. If you do that, your screen should look something like this:

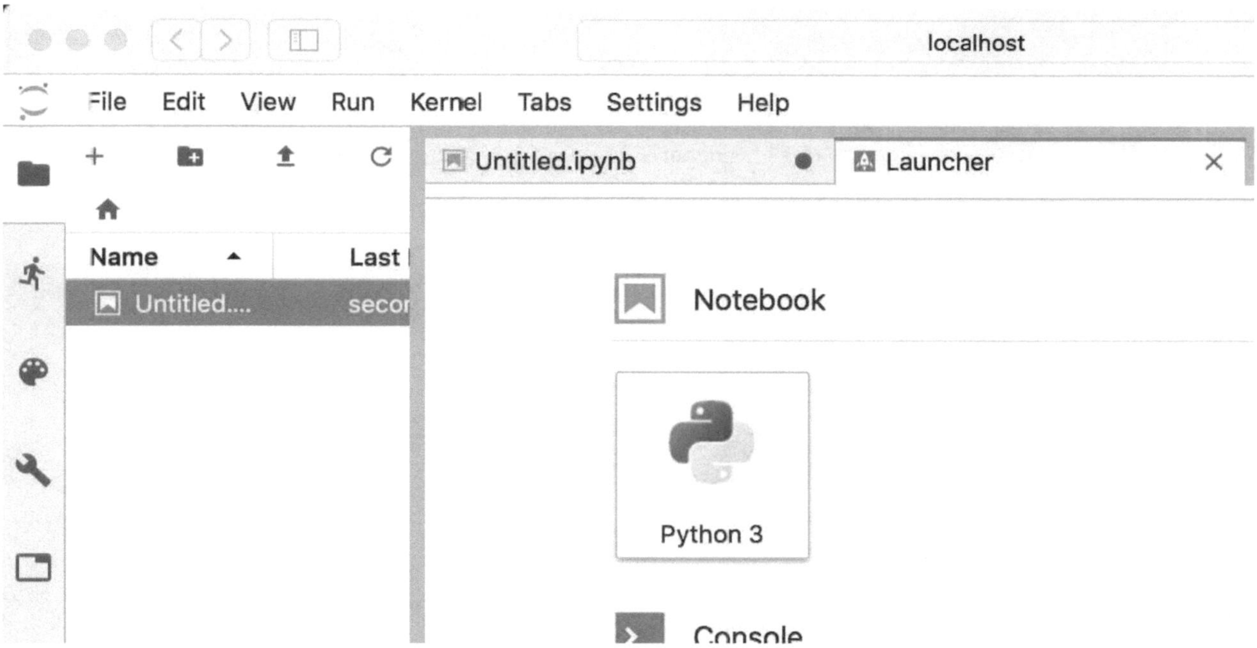

Fig. 12-3: Multiple Tabs in JupyterLab

You can also create new items by using the **Menu** that runs along the top of the screen. Just go to **File** –> **New** and then choose the type of item you would like to create. Most of the menu items should be familiar to you if you have used Jupyter Notebook. There are some new entries here that are specific to JupyterLab however. For example:

- New Launcher - Launches a new launcher
- Open From Path - Open a document from a path other than the one you started in
- Save Notebook As… - Let's you save the currently selected Notebook with a new filename
- Export Notebook As… - Let's you export your Notebook to a different format, such as PDF, Markdown, etc

Explore the menu and see what else you can find. It's pretty self-explanatory.

The File Browser

The tree on the left is known as the **File Browser**. It shows you the files that are available to you from the location that you launched JupyterLab from. Just click the folder icon to make the tree collapse so that the tab can fill the browser:

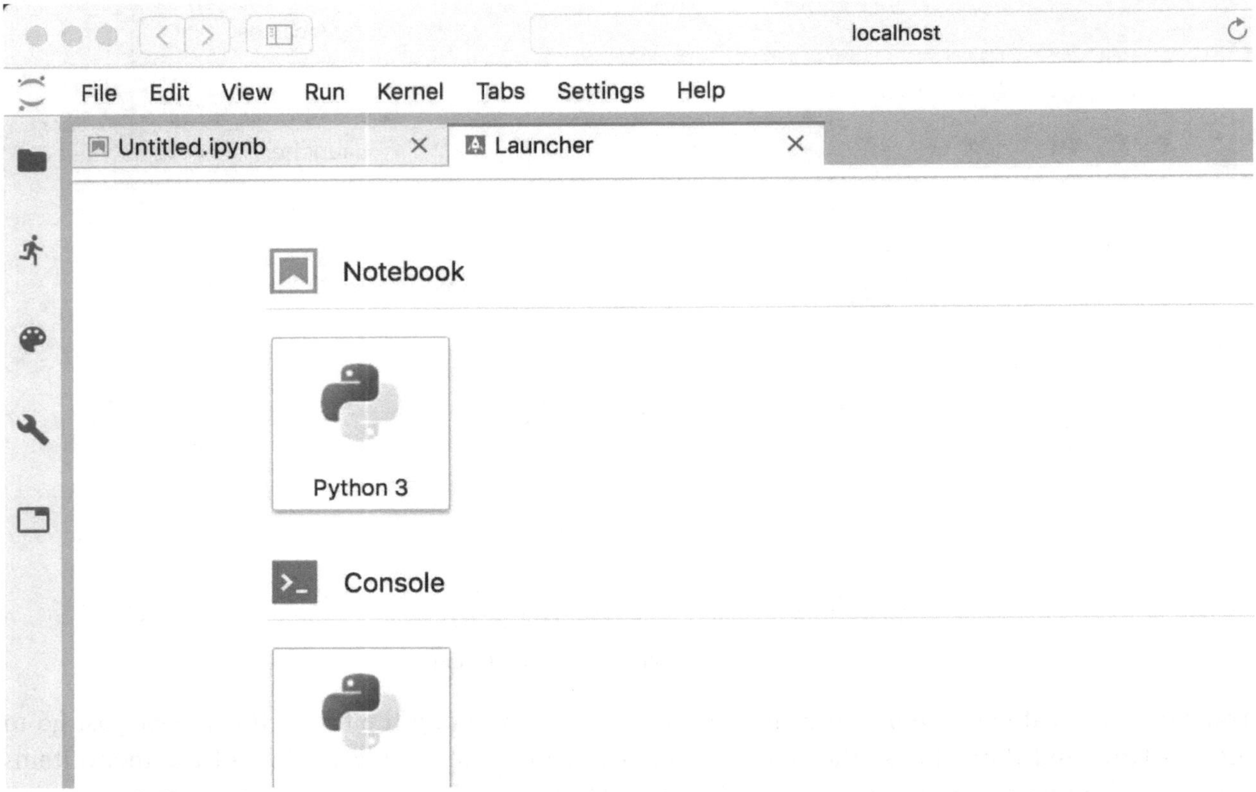

Fig. 12-4: File Browser Minimized

You will note that you can create new folders in the File Browser as well by clicking the folder+ icon (circled below):

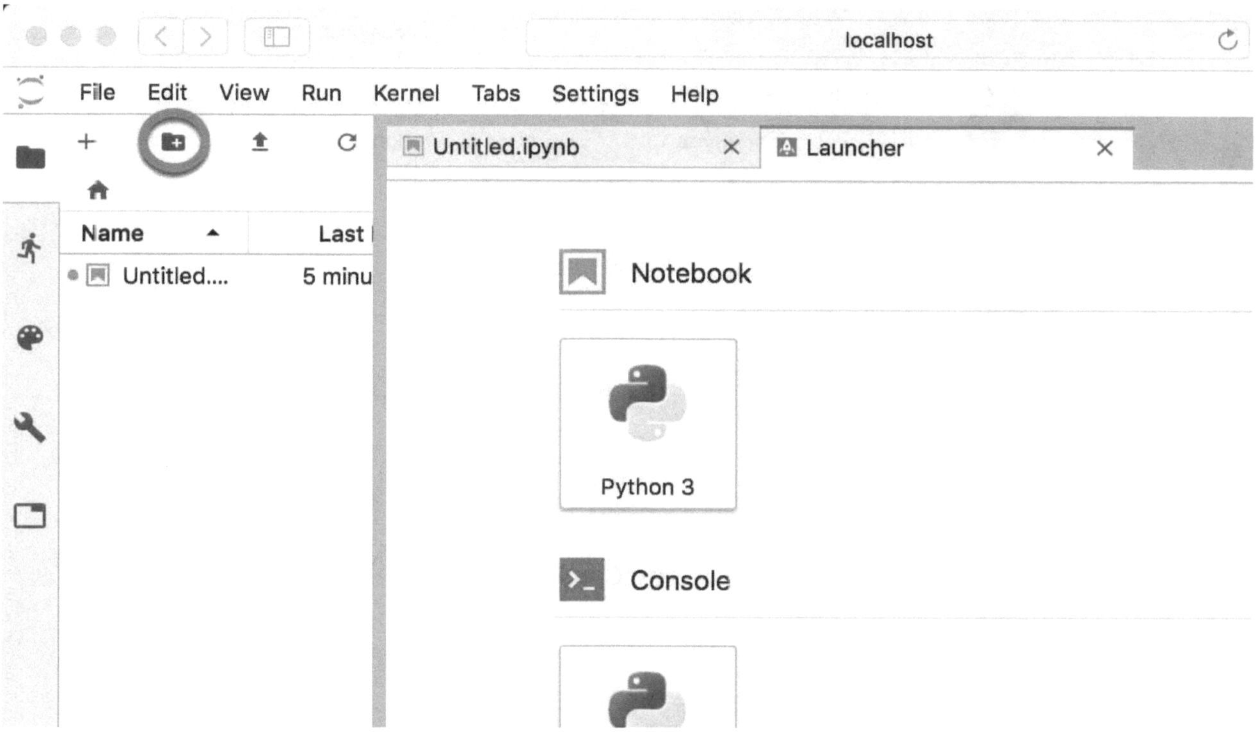

Fig. 12-5: Creating a New Folder

If you need to add a file to JupyterLab from another location on your computer, then you will want to click on the **Upload** button:

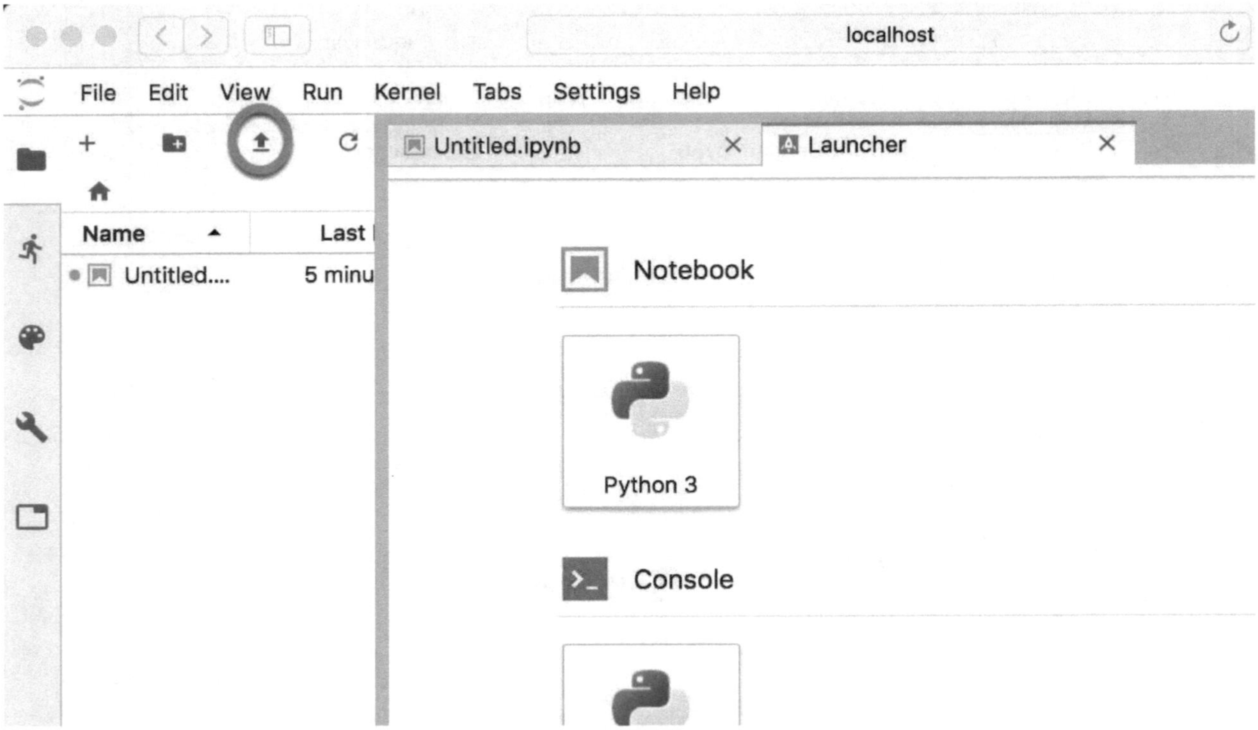

Fig. 12-6: Uploading / Saving a File to the Workspace

When you do, it will pop open a File Open dialog:

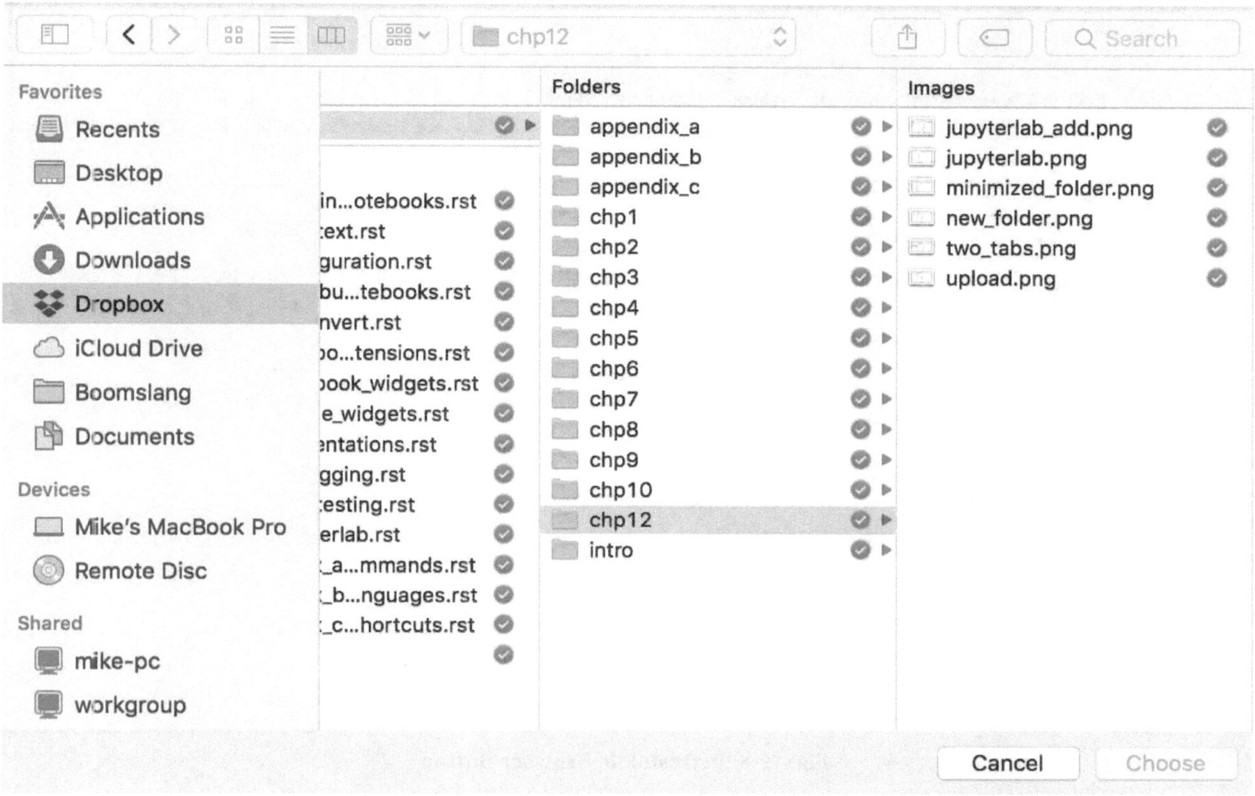

Fig. 12-7: Upload Dialog

Just use this as you would if you were opening a file in another program. Just remember that instead of opening a file, you are "uploading" or "copying" it to your JupyterLab workspace.

Finally there is a refresh button that you can use to refresh the workspace if you happened to copy a file into the workspace by using a method other than the Upload button:

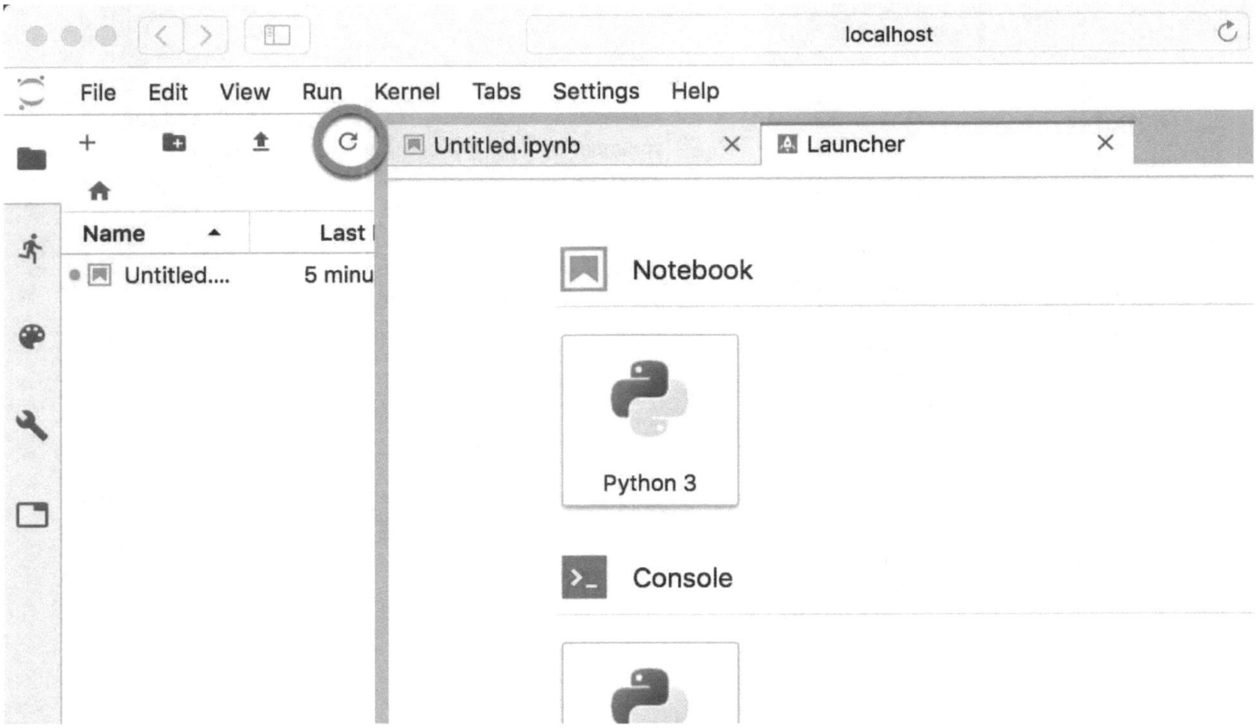

Fig. 12-8: Refresh File Browser Button

Special URLS

As with Jupyter Notebook, JupyterLab allows users to copy URLS into the browser to open a specific Notebook or file. However JupyterLab has also added the ability to manage workspaces and file navigation via URLs.

For example, if you want to use file navigation, you can use the special keyword **tree** to do so. Here is an example URL using an untitled Notebook:

```
http://localhost:8888/lab/tree/Untitled.ipynb
```

If you were to try this out, you would see the normal Jupyter Notebook interface instead of seeing the Notebook inside of JupyterLab.

Workspaces

The default workspace doesn't have a name, but it can be found at **/lab**. If you would like to clone your workspace, you can use the following format:

```
http://localhost:8888/lab/workspaces/test?clone
```

This will copy your current workspace into a workspace named **test**. If you want to copy the test workspace into your default workspace, the URL would look like this:

```
http://localhost:8888/lab?clone=test
```

You can also reset a workspace using the **reset** URL parameter. When you reset a workspace, you are clearing it of its contents. Here is an example of resetting the default workspace:

```
http://localhost:8888/lab/workspaces/lab?reset
```

Creating and Using Notebooks

JupyterLab obviously supports Notebooks as well. In fact, earlier in this chapter, you saw the Launcher and how you can use it to open a new Notebook or other file type. The Notebooks in JupyterLab behave the same way as they do when run separately from JupyterLab.

The Cell Inspector

Let's create a Notebook inside of our JupyterLab instance. Go to the Launcher and choose a kernel. You will have Python 2 or Python 3 by default. Once you have created it, you should see a new tab named "Untitled.ipynb" like this:

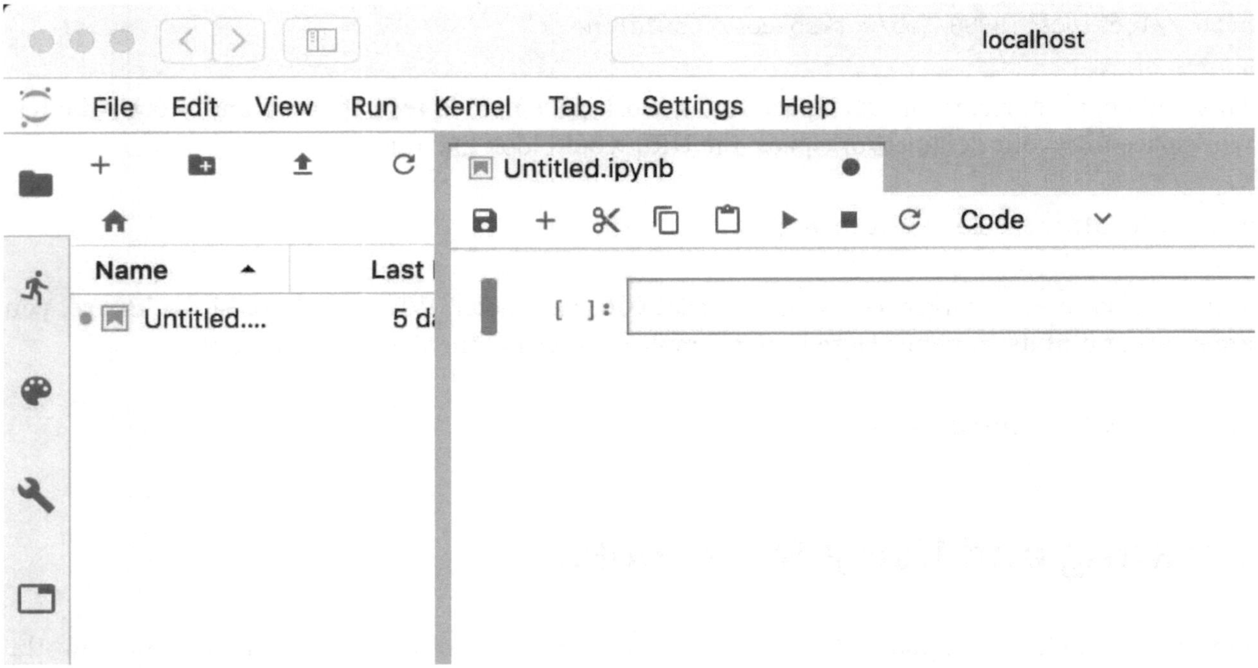

Fig. 12-9: An Empty Notebook

As you can see, we have a Notebook with a single cell. Let's add the following code to the slide:

```
def adder(a, b):
   return a + b

adder(2, 3)
```

Now let's click the little wrench that is in the toolbar on the left. Here's a screenshot with the button circled:

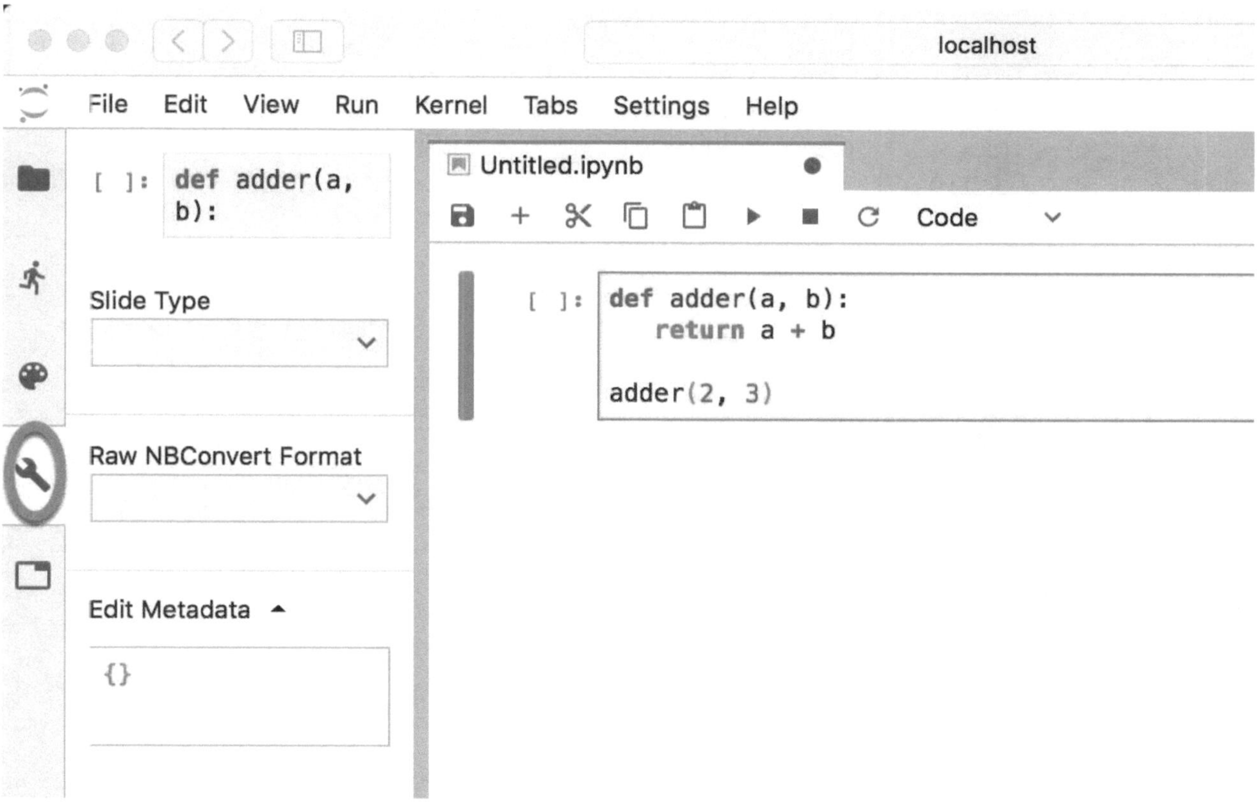

Fig. 12-10: The Cell Inspector

When you click that wrench, your screen should look like the above. This is called the **Cell Inspector**. This is where you can set up your Notebook for presentation purposes. You can set which cells are slides or sub-slides. Pretty much anything that we talked about in Chapter 9 relating to the Notebook itself can also be done here. You will also note that the Cell Inspector will display any metadata that JupyterLab / Notebook is adding to the cells.

If you would like to see that in action, then try setting your first cell to a **Slide**. Now you should see the Metadata field populated like this:

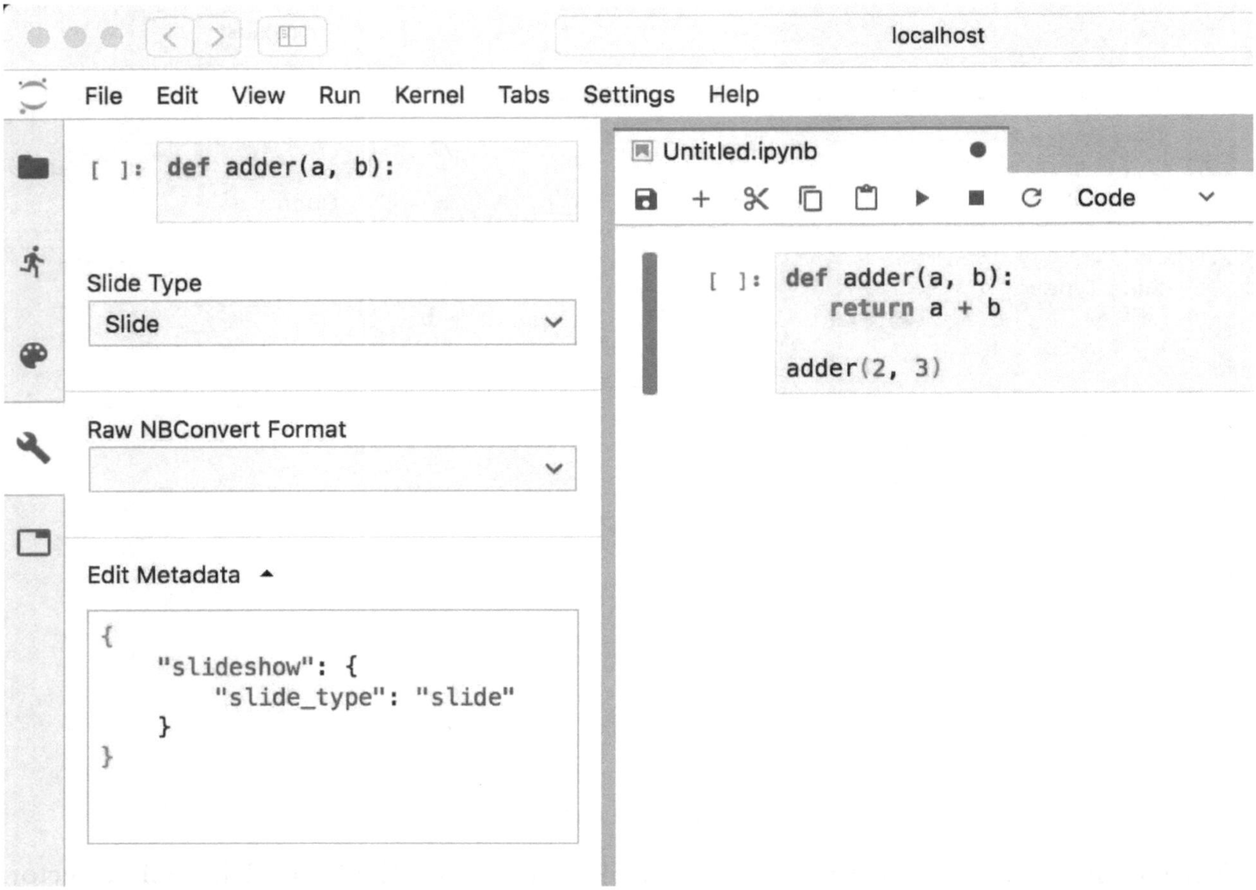

Fig. 12-11: The Cell's Metadata

Using Files

You can use JupyterLab's File Browser and File menu to work with files and directories on your system. This allows you to open, create, delete, rename, download / upload, copy and share files and directories. You can find the File Browser in the left sidebar:

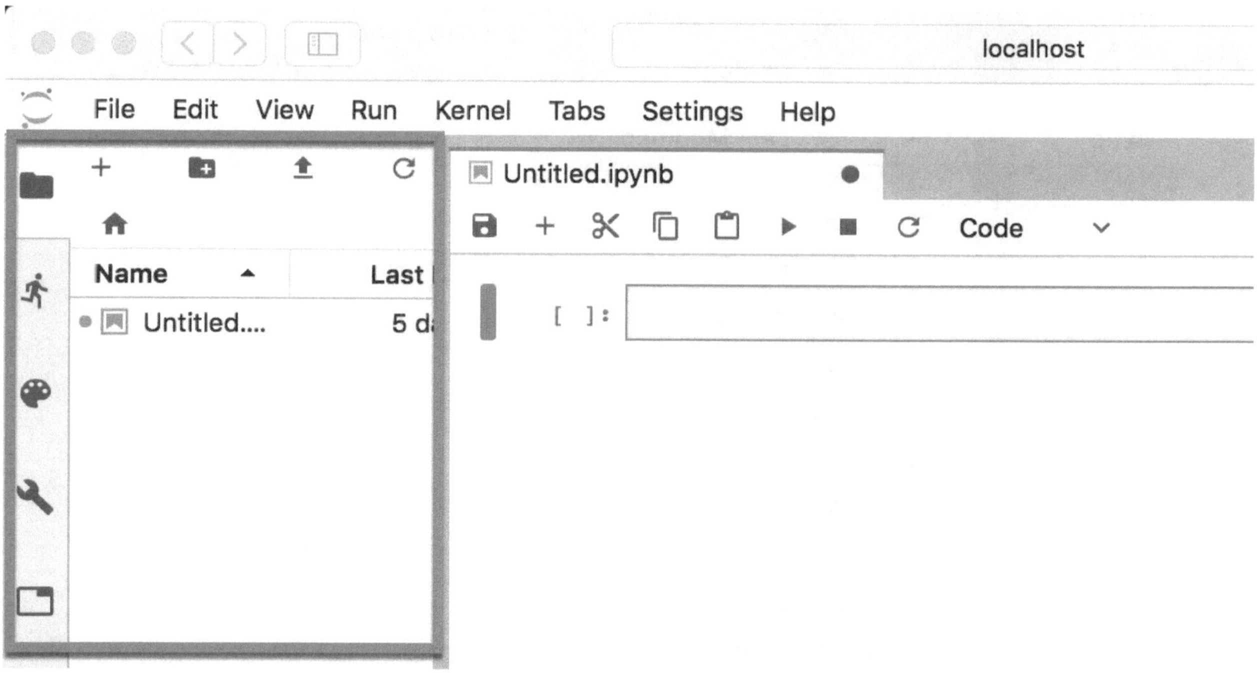

Fig. 12-12: The File Browser

If you have files in your browser, you can open it by just double-clicking the file as you would normally do in your system's file browser. You may also drag a file from the File Browser into the work area (on the right) which will cause it to open.

Many of the file types that JupyterLab supports also have multiple viewers and editors. You can open a Markdown file in an editor or view it as HTML, for example. If you want to open the file in a non-default viewer/editor, just right-click the file and choose "Open With..." from the context menu:

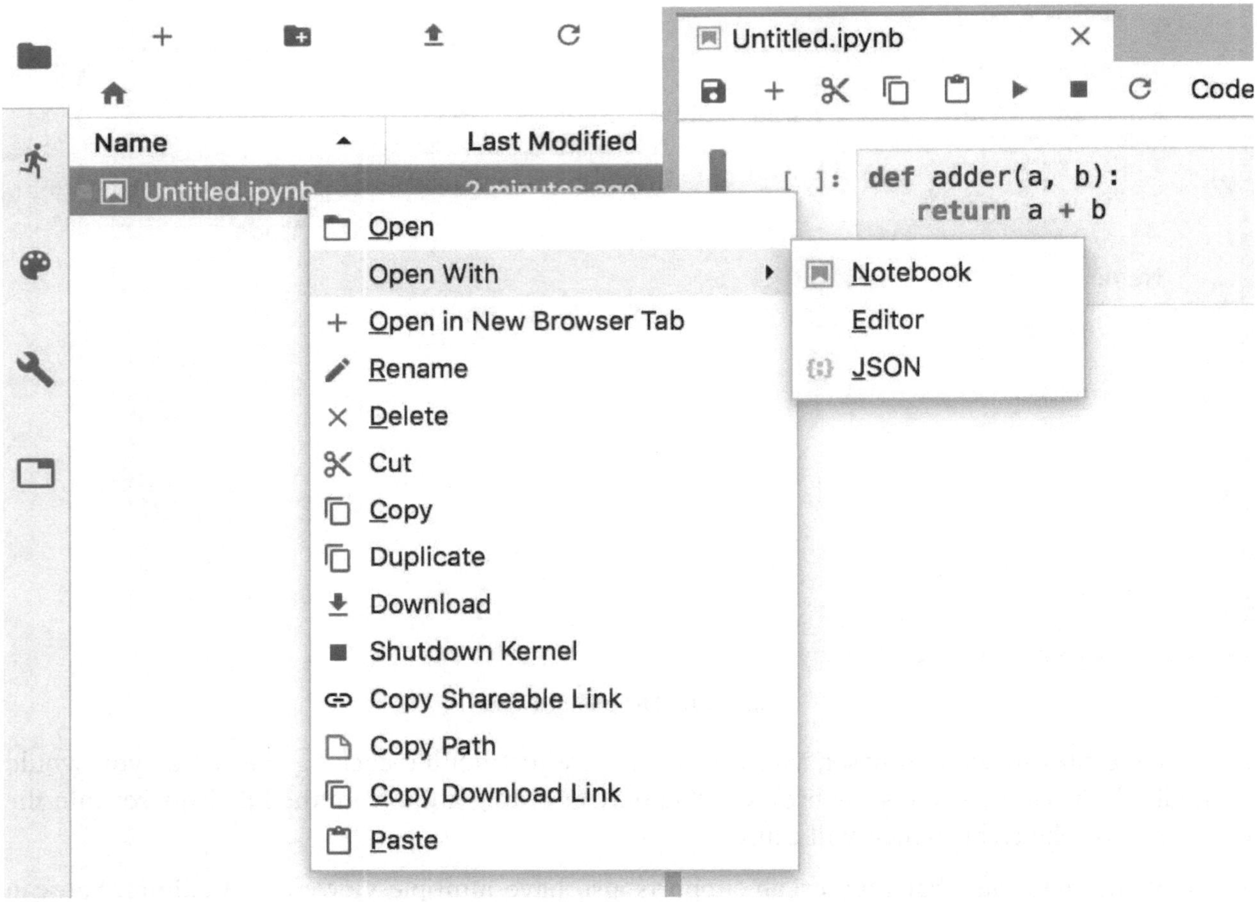

Fig. 12-13: Context Menu for Files

Note that you can open a single file into multiple viewers/editors and they will remain in sync.

The Text Editor

JupyterLab comes with a built-in text editor that you can use to create or open text files. Open up the Launcher and instead of creating a Notebook, go to the bottom of the Launcher and create a text file.

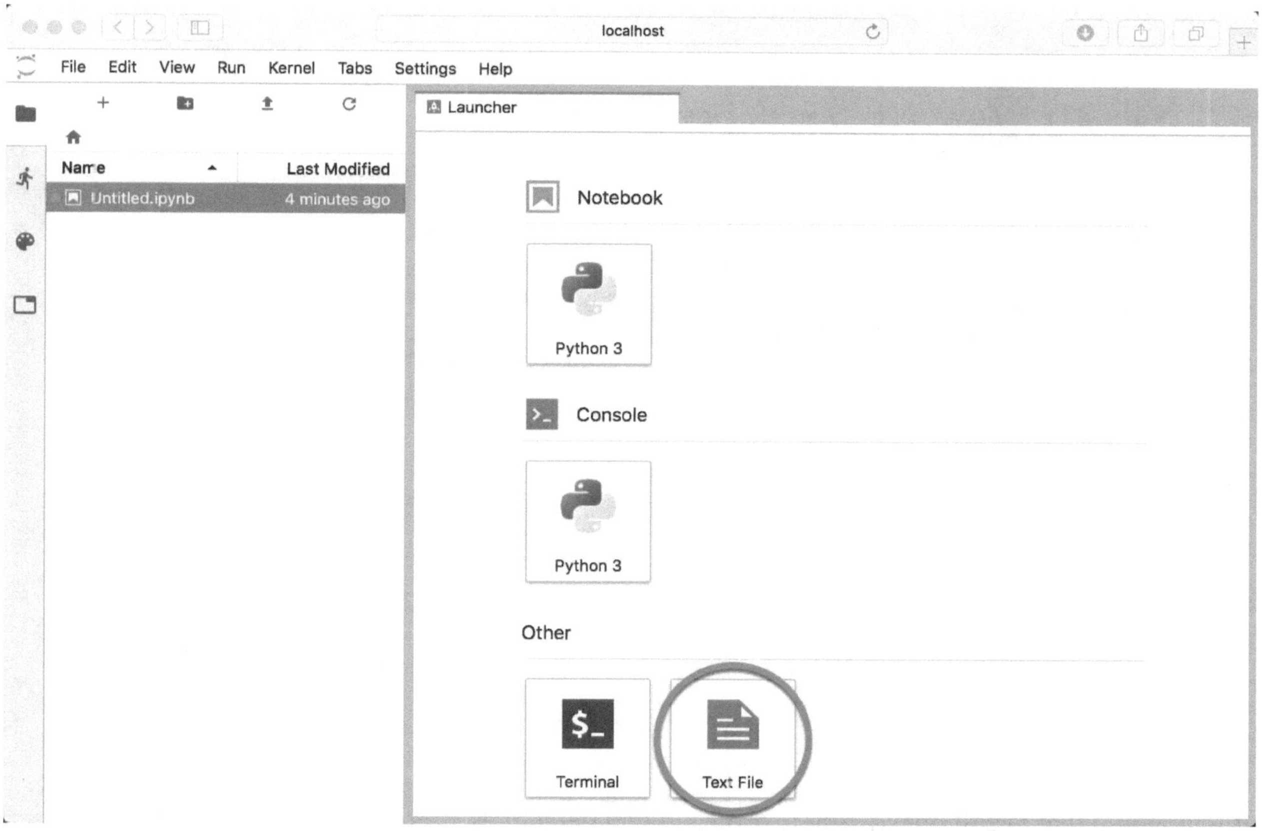

Fig. 12-14: Launch the Text Editor

It will create an **untitled.txt** file by default. But you can go to the **File** menu and use **Save As...** to save it as something else. This allows you to create Python files, Markdown and pretty much anything else you would like to. It even provides syntax highlighting for some file types, although code completion is not supported. You may also create files via the **File** menu.

The text editor also supports configurable indentation (tabs vs. spaces), key maps and basic theming. Just go to the **Settings** menu to view or edit them:

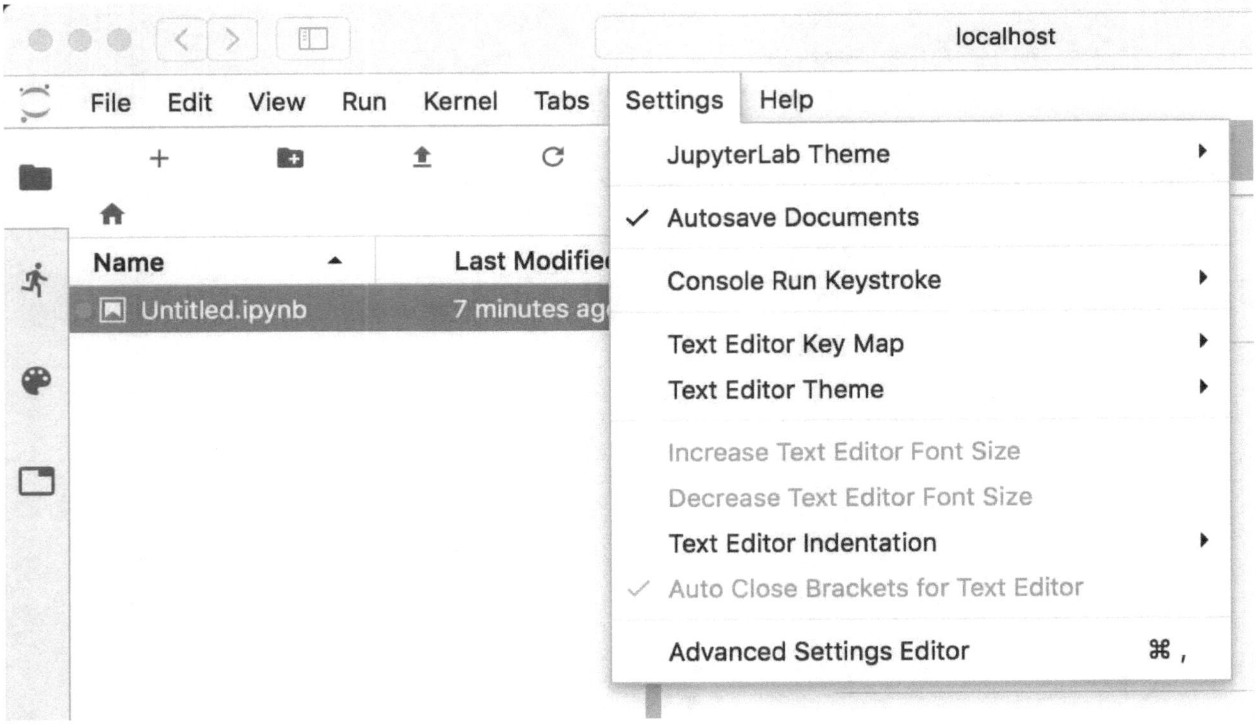

Fig. 12-15: File Settings

If you would like to edit an existing text file, all you need to do is double-click it in the File Browser.

Interactive Code Consoles

One of the newer features to JupyterLab is the **Code Console**, which is basically a REPL in your browser. It will let you run code interactively in the currently selected kernel. The "cells" of a code console show the order in which the code was run. To create a new Code Console, click the **+** button in the File Browser and select the kernel of your choice:

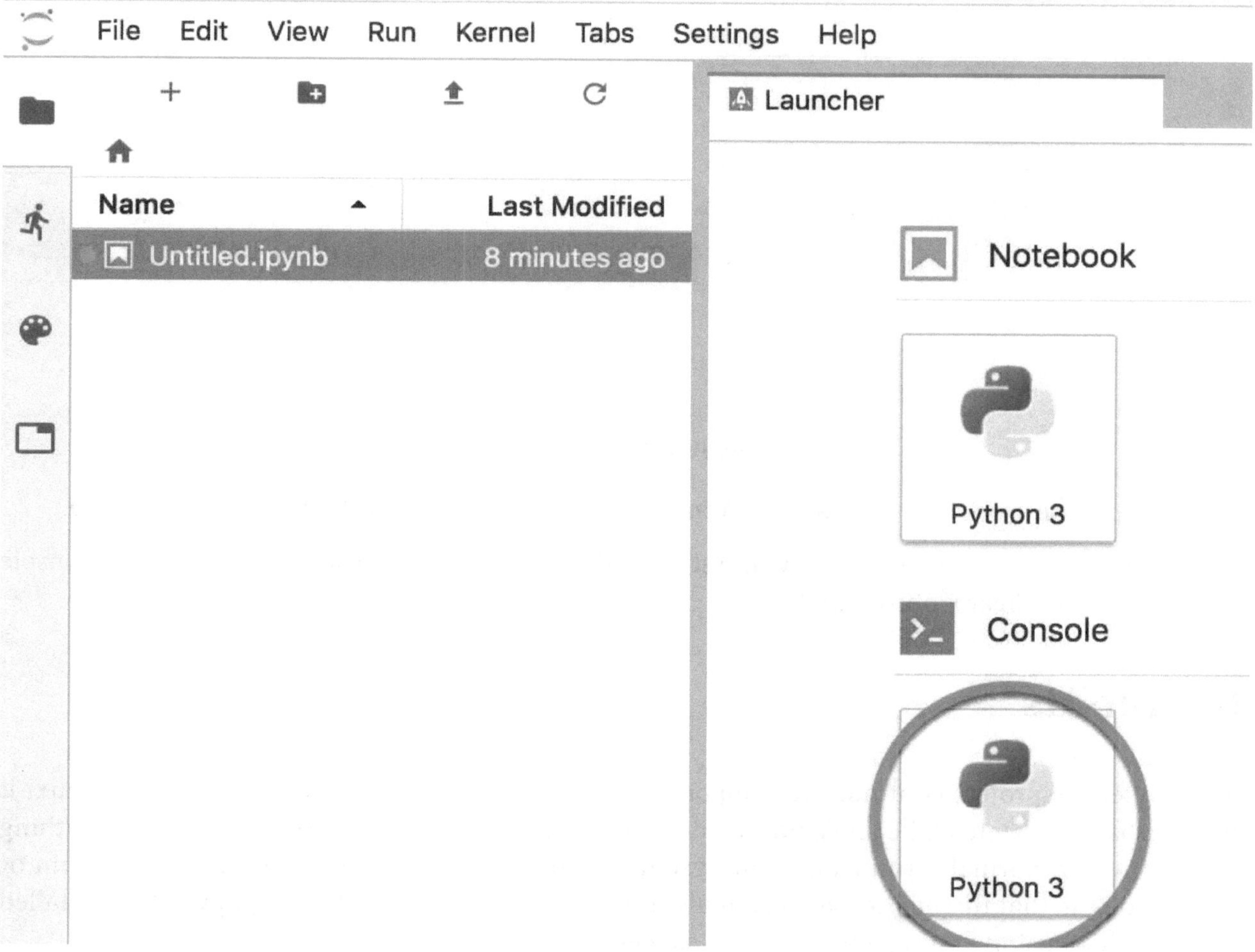

Fig. 12-16: Code Console Launcher

Enter some code. Here's an example if you are having some trouble thinking of any on your own:

```
print( Hello Console!')
```

Now press **Shift+Enter** to run the code. You should see the following output if everything worked correctly:

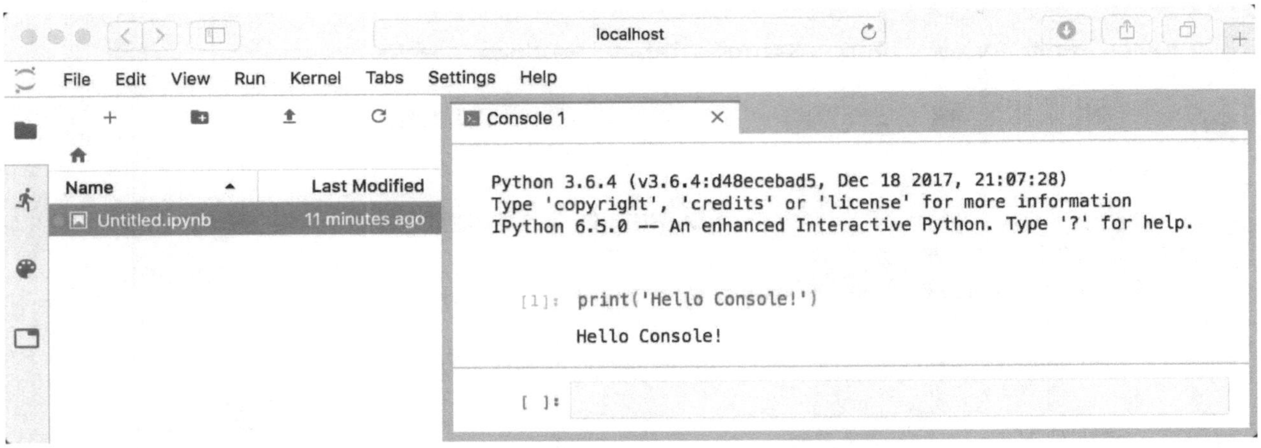

Fig. 12-17: Code Console

Code completion works via the **Tab** key. You can also bring up tooltips by pressing **Shift+Tab**.

If you need to clear the code console without restarting the kernel, you can right click on the console itself and select "Clear Console Cells".

Terminals

The JupyterLab project continues its support of system shells in the browser. For Mac / Linux, it supports bash, tsch, etc while on Windows, it supports Powershell. These terminals can run anything that you would normally run from your system's terminal, including other programs like vim or emacs. Do note that the JupyterLab terminals run on the system that you have JupyterLab installed to, so it will be using your user's privileges as well.

Anyway, if you would like to see a terminal in action, just start up the Launcher by pressing the "+" button in the File Browser. Then select the Terminal:

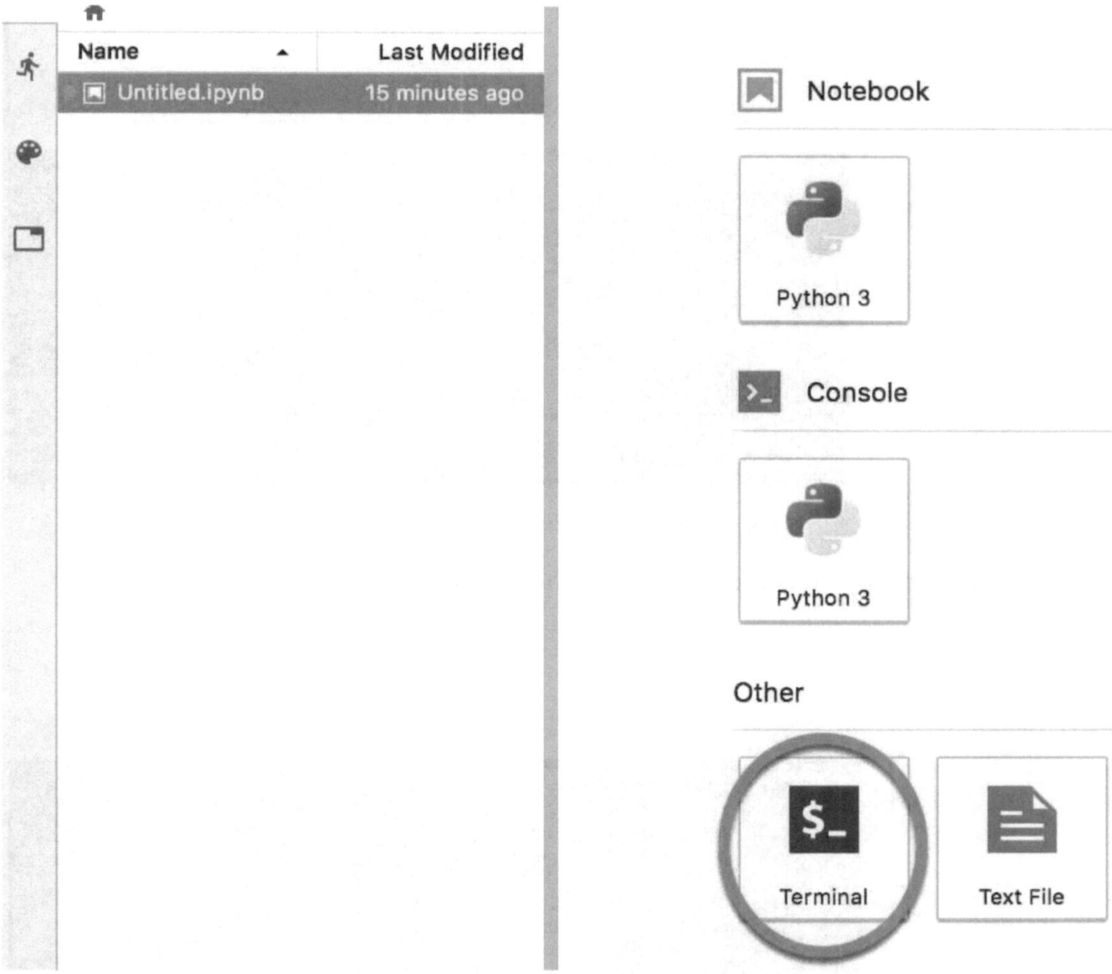

Fig. 12-18: Terminal Launcher

If you close the terminal tab, JupyterLab will leave it running in the background. Here is a terminal running:

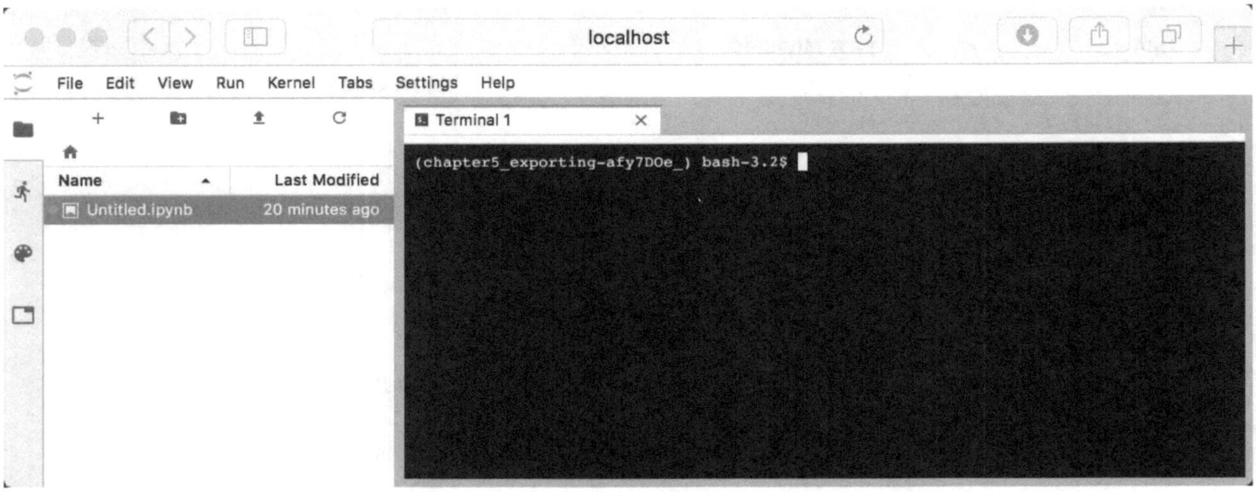

Fig. 12-19: Running Terminal

If you would like to re-open your terminal, just go to the **Running** tab:

Fig. 12-20: Running Apps

Then select the terminal from the list of running applications.

The Command Palette

The user actions in JupyterLab all go through a central command system. This includes the commands used by the menu bar, context menus, keyboard shortcuts and more. You can access the available commands via the **Command Palette**, which you will find under the **Commands** tab:

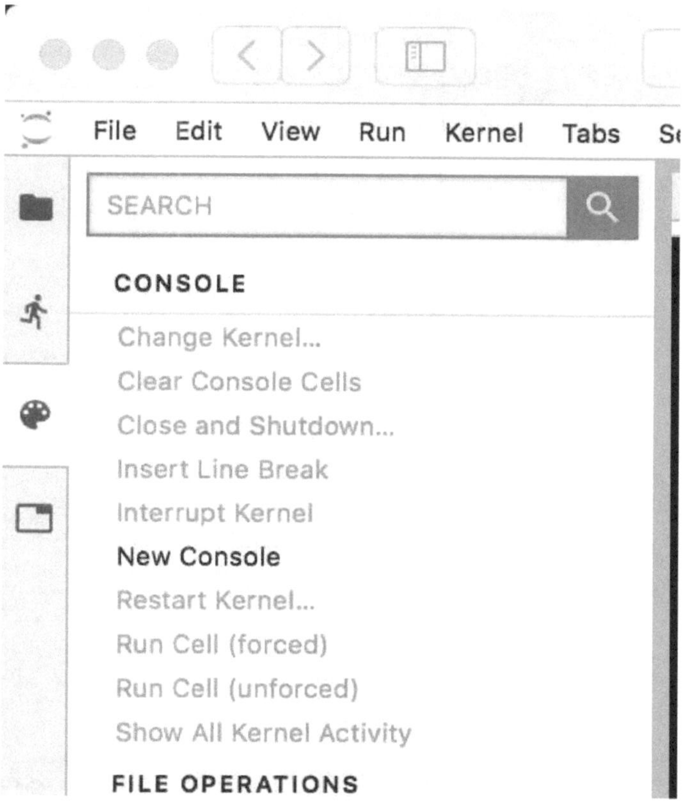

Fig. 12-21: The Command Palette

Here you can search for commands and execute them directly instead of hunting for them in the menu system. You can also bring up the Command Palette with the following keyboard shortcut: **Command/Ctrl Shift C**

Supported File Types

JupyterLab supports quite a few filetypes that it can display or allow you to edit. This allows you to layout rich cell output in a Notebook or Code Console. For files, JupyterLab will detect the data format by looking at the extension of the file or the entire filename if the extensions does not exist. Note that multiple editors / viewers can be associated with a single file type. For example, you can edit a Markdown file and view it as HTML. Just right-click a file and go to the **Open With** context menu item to view the editors and viewers that are available to you for that file type:

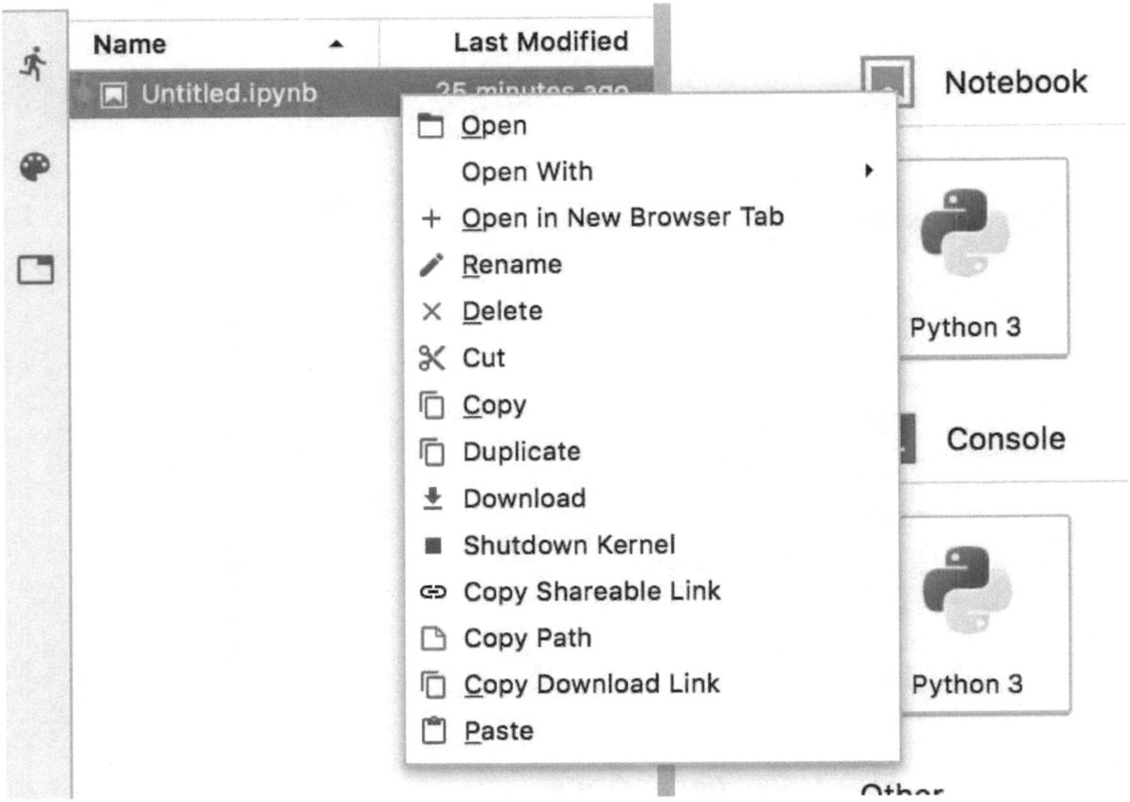

Fig. 12-22: Using Open With

You can use Python code to display different data formats in your Notebook or Code Console. Here is an example:

```
from IPython.display import display, HTML
display(HTML('<h1>Hello from JupyterLab</h1>'))
```

When you run this code in a Notebook, it should look like this:

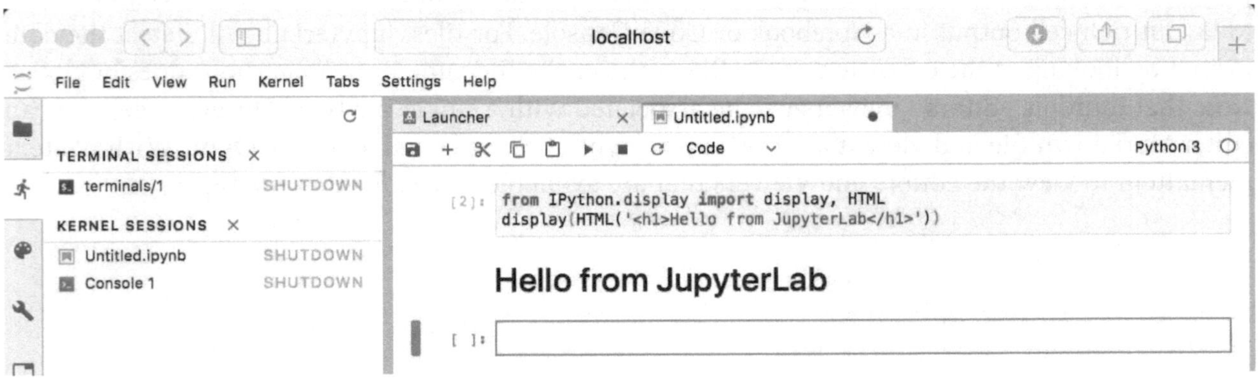

Fig. 12-23: Running HTML in a Notebook

For a full list of file types that are supported by JupyterLab, I recommend checking out the following page:

- https://jupyterlab.readthedocs.io/en/stable/user/file_formats.html

This should always be up-to-date and more useful then if I were to list out the items myself.

A Word on Extensions

As you might expect, JupyterLab supports extensions and was designed with extensibility in mind. Extensions can customize the user's experience or enhance one or more parts of JupyterLab. For example, you could add new items to the menu or command palette or add some new keyboard shortcuts. JupyterLab itself is actually a collection of extensions.

If you want to create an extension for JupyterLab, then you will need to be familiar with Javascript or be willing to learn. The extensions need to be in the npm packaging format. To install pre-made extensions, you are required to have **Node.js** installed on your machine. Be sure to check out their website for proper installation instructions for your operating system:

- https://nodejs.org/en/

Installing / Uninstalling Extensions

Once you have Node.js installed, then you can install an extension to JupyterLab by running the following command:

```
jupyter labextension install the-extension-name
```

If you require a specific version of the extension, then the command would look like this:

```
jupyter labextension install the-extension-name@1.2
```

Where "1.2" is the version you require. You can also extensions that are gzipped tarballs or a URL to a gzipped tarball.

To get a list of currently installed JupyterLab extensions, just run

```
jupyter labextension list
```

In the event that you want to uninstall an extension, you can easily do so like this:

```
jupyter labextension uninstall the-extension-name
```

You may also install or uninstall multiple extensions by listing the names of the packages after the install or uninstall command. Since JupyterLab rebuilds after each installation, this can take quite a while. To speed things up a bit when installing or uninstalling multiple extensions, you can include the **–no-build** flag. Then once the installation or uninstall is complete, you will need to run the build command yourself, like this:

```
jupyter lab build
```

Disabling Extensions

If you don't want to uninstall an extension but you would like to disable it, that is easy to do too. Just run the **disable** command:

```
jupyter labextension disable the-extension-name
```

Then when you want to re-enable it, you can run the **enable** command:

```
jupyter labextension enable the-extension-name
```

Wrapping Up

The JupyterLab package is really amazing. You can do a lot more with it than you could with just a Jupyter Notebook. However the user interface is also more complex so the learning curve will be a bit steeper. However I think it is worth learning how to use it as the ability to edit documents and view them live is really helpful when creating a presentation or doing other types of work. At the very least, I would give it a try in a virtual environment to see whether or not it will fit your workflow.

Appendix A - Magic Commands

Jupyter Notebook is built on top of the IPython kernel by default. You can install and run other kernels if you would like to create a Notebook that uses a language other than Python. This chapter assumes that you are using Python, however. The IPython kernel comes with a set of built-in magic commands. There are two different types of magic commands:

- Line magics
- Cell magics

Note that we won't be covering every single magic in this book, let alone this chapter. There is a full listing of all the magics in the IPython documentation. You are encouraged to go read that documentation should you need to know more:

- https://ipython.readthedocs.io/en/stable/interactive/magics.html

In this chapter, we will just go over a selection of the magics that are available to you so you can have a better understanding of how you might use them and how they might benefit you.

Before we get started, let's talk about the definition of a **magic** command. In the IPython kernel, a magic command must use a special syntax element for the magic that is not a valid unary operator in Python. The syntax used in IPython is the percent sign: %

Other languages may use a different character for their magic syntax. Note that you can add your own magic commands to IPython if you want to.

If you would like to get a list of all available magic commands, try running the following command in IPython or in a Jupyter Notebook cell:

```
%lsmagic
```

Here is the output I received when I ran the command in a Notebook:

Appendix A-1: A listing of magic commands

Please note that this chapter isn't going to go into depth for each and every one of the magic commands. I will highlight the ones that I think will be useful to use in the Notebook, but also realize that these magics were mostly originally designed for IPython itself, so some may not even apply to the Notebooks.

Now that that is out of the way, let's learn about some of these magic commands!

Line Magics

Line magics are denoted by having a single percent (%) sign as their prefix. They only operate on a single line of input.

%alias

This magic will allow you to create an alias for a system command, such as Linux's **echo** command. Note that aliases have a lower precedence than magic functions and Python's own normal variables. So if you create a magic that has the same name as a Python variable, you won't be able to execute your alias until you delete the variable. See the IPython documentation for additional information.

%alias_magic

Allows the developer to create an alias for an existing line or cell magic. One of the examples I like from the documentation shows how to alias the **timeit** magic. Put the following code into a cell in Jupyter Notebook:

```
%alias_magic t timeit
```

When you run this cell, you have aliased the %timeit magic. This allows you to do fun things like time how long it takes to do a one-liner in subsequent cells. So in the next cell, try entering the following code and running it:

```
%t [x for x in range(10)]
```

When I ran it, I got the following:

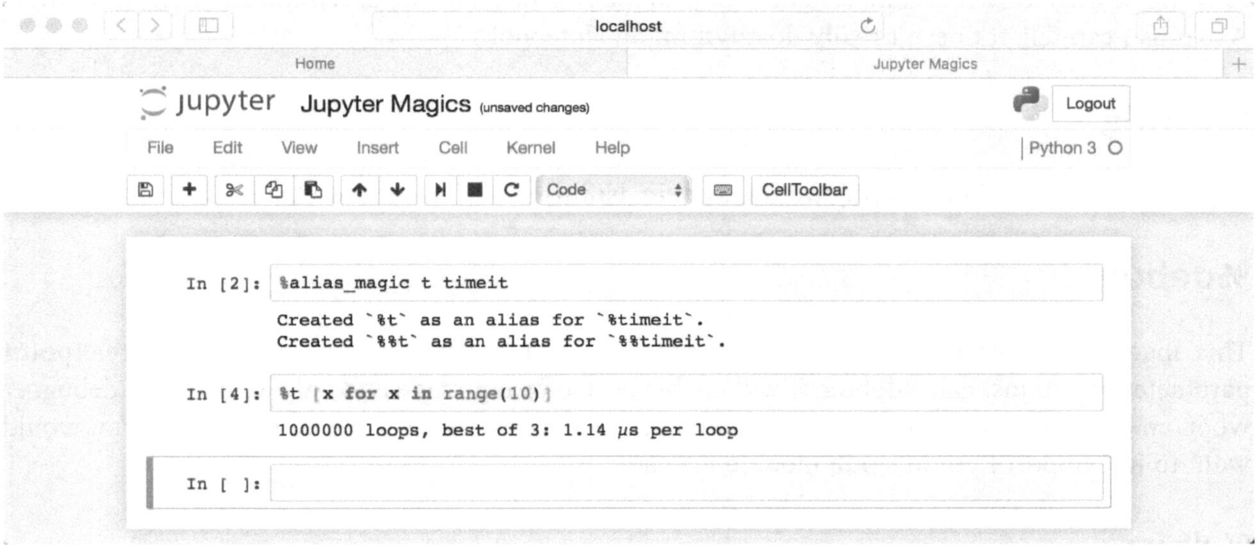

Appendix A-2: The %alias_magic

%autocall

Makes functions callable without the need of having to type the parentheses. This magic has 3 modes:

- 0 - fully disabled
- 1 - active, but does not apply if there are no arguments on the line
- 2 - Active always. Even when there are arguments present, the callable object is still called

%automagic

This magic will make magic functions callable without the need of the % prefix. When called without arguments, it will just toggle on and off.

%bookmark

Manages IPython's bookmark system. Probably not that useful in a Notebook context.

%cd

Changes the current working directory.

%colors

This can be used to switch color schemes for prompts, info system and exception handlers in IPython. As far as I can tell, it doesn't really do anything in Notebooks.

%config

Exposes most of IPython's configuration system. Not used by Jupyter Notebooks.

%debug

This magic activates the interactive debugger. You can set break points via the **–breakpoint** parameter. If you just call **%debug**, it will enable post-mortem mode and only activate the debugger when an exception is raised. As far as I can tell, this magic doesn't work in Notebooks. You would want to just import Python's **pdb** module instead.

%dhist

Prints the history of visited directories.

%dirs

This magic returns the current directory stack.

%doctest_mode

Toggles doctest mode on and off. Probably doesn't really affect Notebooks all that much since there really aren't prompts in Notebooks like there are in the IPython shell.

%edit

In IPython, it will bring up an editor and then execute the resulting code. In Jupyter Notebook, it appears to just create a temporary file, outputs its location and then runs it:

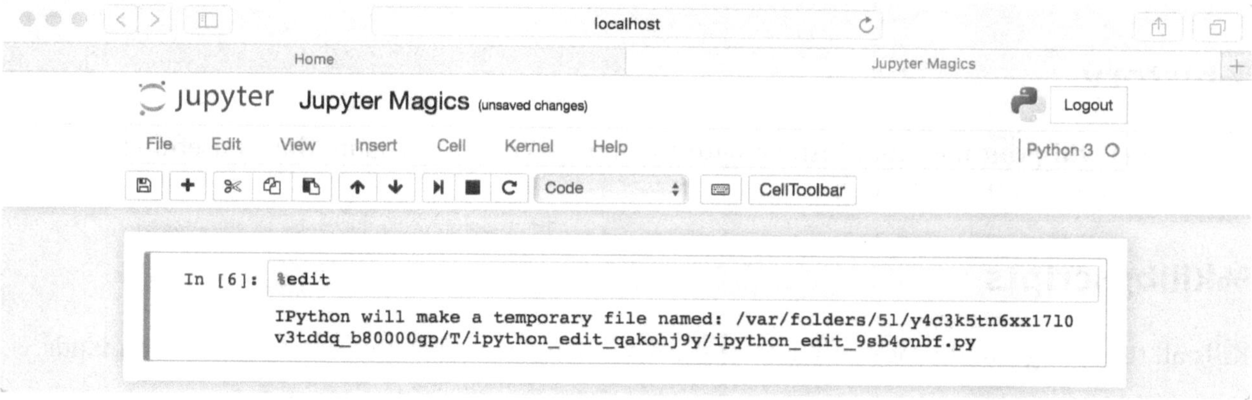

Appendix A-3: The %edit magic

This is useful in IPython because it lets you edit multi-line code. Since it does not open an editor in the Notebook because the Notebook is already an editor, it's really not that helpful in this context.

%env

Used to get, set or list environment variables. Here is the output of just running the command in Jupyter Notebook:

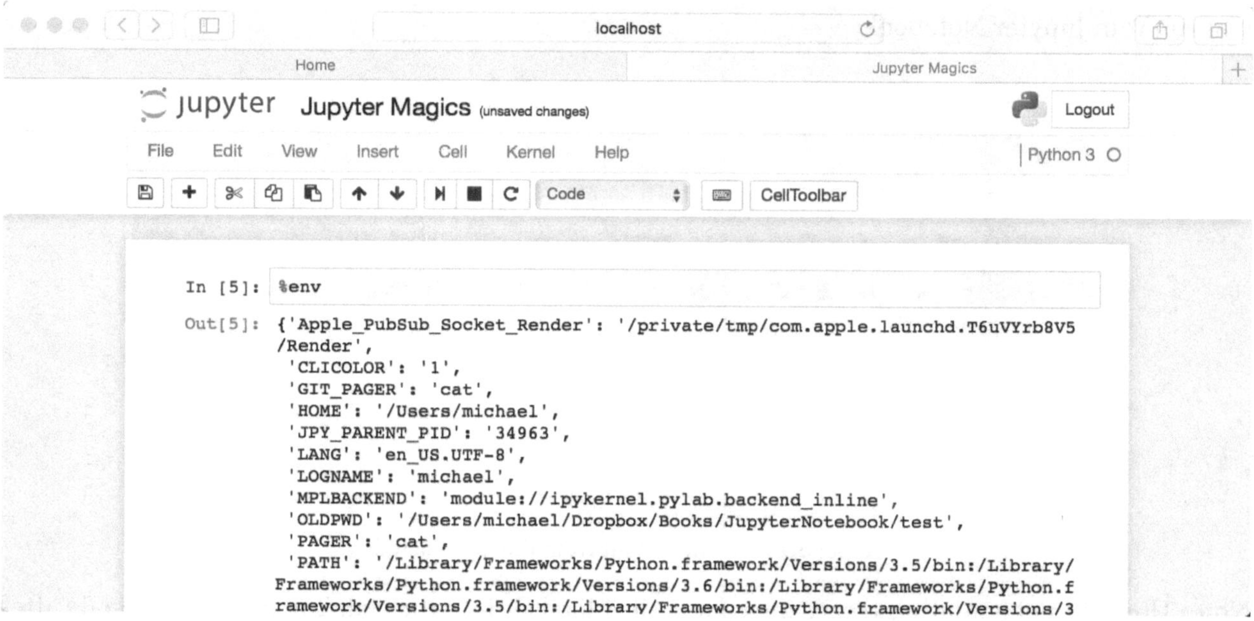

Appendix A-4: The output from the %env magic

%gui

Will enable or disable IPython's GUI event loop integration. This allows you to run wxPython, PyQt4, PyGTK, Tk and Cocoa (OSX) in IPython. After doing a bit of research, this magic isn't actually compatible with Jupyter Notebook.

%history

This magic will print the input history with the most recent last. Again, this is useful in IPython, but not so much in the Notebook.

%killbgscripts

Kills all the background process that were started when you called any **%%script%%** commands.

%load

Used to load code in a Python file into the current frontend. This allows you to load a Python file into a Notebook cell. Here is how you run the magic:

```
%load my_script.py
```

This assumes that the script, **my_script.py**, is in the same folder that your Notebook is saved in. You could also pass a full path to the magic instead. Here's an example of what it looks like when you run it in Jupyter Notebook:

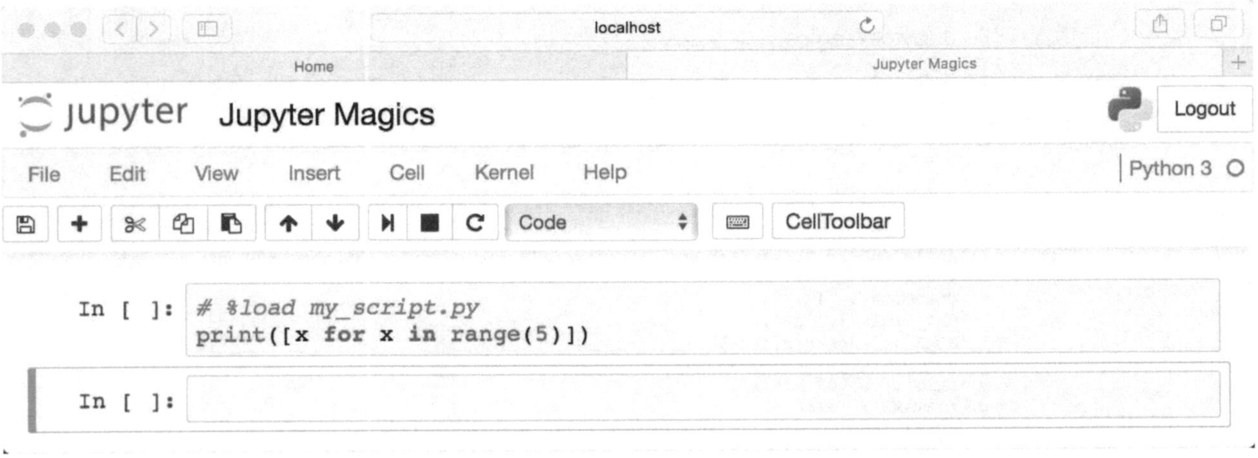

Appendix A-5: The output from the %env magic

Note: This will not actually execute the code. It just loads it into the cell. You can run the code after it is loaded, however.

%load_ext

Loads an IPython extension by its module name.

%loadpy

This is an alias of **%load**.

%logoff

Use this magic to temporarily turn logging off. Note that you must start logging before calling this magic.

%logon

Restarts logging. Used when you have called **%logoff** to restart logging.

%logstart

Starts logging anywhere within your session. You can set the log file name and log mode as well. See the official documentation for full details.

%logstate

Outputs the status of the logging system.

%logstop

Fully stops logging and closes the log file. You will need to use **%logstart** to restart logging if that is desired.

%lsmagic

Outputs a listing of the currently available magic functions.

%macro

Allows you to define a macro for future re-execution.

%magic

Prints out information about the magic function system.

%matplotlib

Sets up **matplotlib** to work interactively. This basically enables graphs to be shown interactively within IPython and Jupyter Notebook. This magic appears to be on by default in the Notebook.

Let's look at a simple example. Enter the following into a Notebook cell:

```
import matplotlib.pyplot as pyplot

def create_plot():
    pyplot.plot(list(range(5)))
    pyplot.title = 'matplotlib sample'
    pyplot.ylabel = 'Increasing numbers'
    pyplot.show()

create_plot()
```

When you run this in Jupyter Notebook, it looks like this:

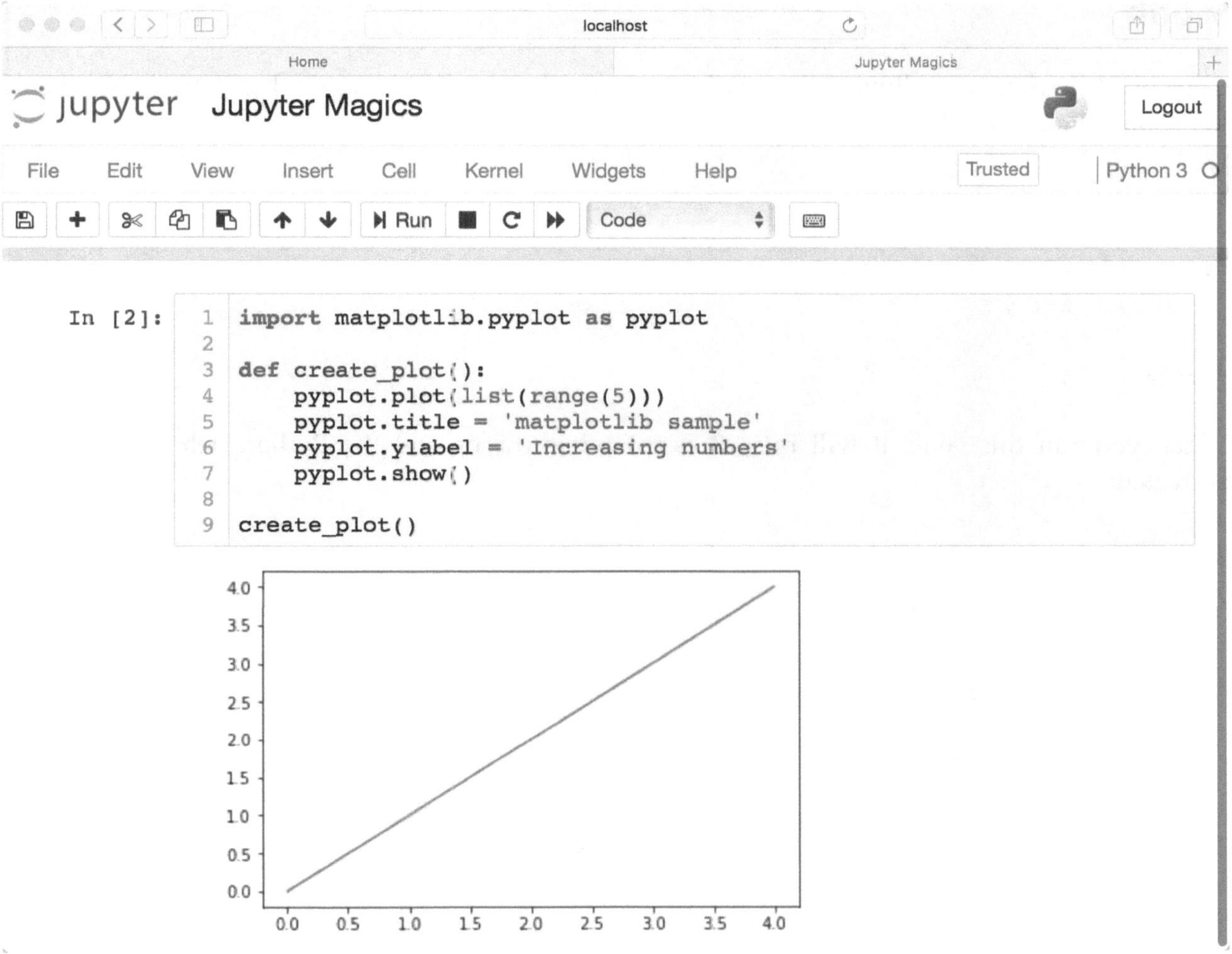

Appendix A-6: Matplotlib magic

%notebook

Exports and converts IPython notebooks. Probably doesn't apply to Jupyter Notebooks. You should just use the **nbconvert** utility if you need to transform your Notebook into something else.

%page

This magic will "pretty print" the object and display it.

%pastebin

Uploads the code to Github's Gist paste bin and returns the URL to the newly created Gist.

%pdb

Controls the automatic calling of the pdb interactive debugger. This does work in Jupyter Notebook. Let's look at an example:

```
%pdb

def divide(x, y):
    return x / y

divide(1, 0)
```

When you run this code, it will raise a **ZeroDivisionError** and the Python debugger will get activated:

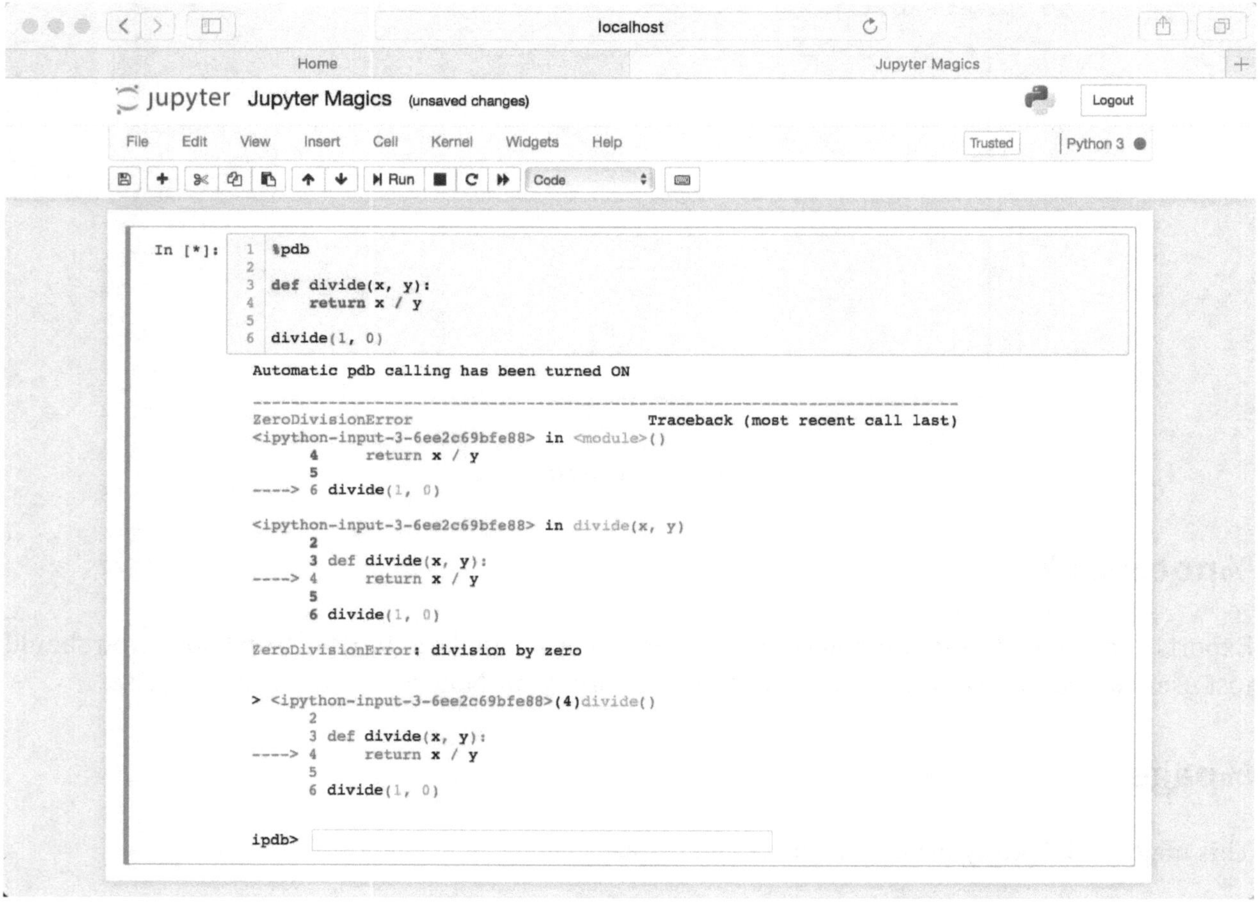

Appendix A-7: The %pdb magic

You can then interact with the debugger interactively in your Notebook using pdb's commands. Note that I had to reduce the font size for this example due to the Notebook being rather large, so be sure to try running this yourself.

%pdef

Prints out the call signature for any callable object. If the object happens to be a class, it will print out the constructor's information instead.

%pdoc

Prints out the docstring of the object. In the case of a class, it will print both the class and its constructor's docstrings.

%pfile

Print (or runs through pager) the file where an object is defined. Check the documentation for usage.

%pinfo

Provides detailed information about the object.

%pinfo2

Provides extra detailed information about the object.

%pip

Intercepts the usage of the pip command and tells the user to run it outside of IPython.

%popd

Change to the directory that was popped off the top of the stack.

%pprint

Toggles pretty printing on / off.

%precision

Sets the floating point precision used for pretty printing. You can set either integer precision or use a format string.

%profile

This magic is **deprecated** since IPython 2.0 and should not be used. Use the **%prun** magic instead.

%prun

Runs the statement through the Python code profiler. This magic has several options you can use. See the documentation for the most up-to-date information.

%psearch

Searches the object in namespaces by wildcard.

%psource

Prints (or runs through pager) the source code for an object.

%pushd

Places the current directory on the stack and then changes to that directory.

%pwd

Returns the current working directory path.

%pycat

Displays a syntax-highlighted file through a pager. This is very similar to the cat utility but assumes the file to be a Python source code file and apply Python syntax highlighting to it.

%pylab

Loads **numpy** and **matplotlib** to work interactively.

%quickref

Shows a quick reference sheet in IPython. Has no effect in Jupyter Notebooks.

%recall

Repeats a command or gets command to input line for editing. Has no effect in Jupyter Notebooks.

%rehashx

Updates the alias table with all the executable files in the $PATH environment variable.

%reload_ext

Reloads an IPython extension by its module name.

%rerun

Will re-run the previous input. Has no effect in Jupyter Notebooks.

%reset

Resets the namespace by removing all names defined by the user, including IPython's input and output history. Not sure why you would need or ever use this in Jupyter Notebook.

%reset_selective

Resets the namespace by removing the names defined by the user. Leaves IPython's input and output history alone. Not sure why you would need or ever use this in Jupyter Notebook.

%run

Runs the named file inside of IPython as a program. Does not work in Jupyter Notebooks.

%save

Saves a set of lines or a macro to the given filename. Does not appear to work correctly in Jupyter Notebooks.

%sc

Does shell capture. In other words, it will run the shell and capture its output. However this is **deprecated**.

%set_env

Set environment variables.

%sx

Shell execute. Runs shell commands and captures the output. !! is a short-hand way of calling this command.

%system

Shell execute. Does the same thing as **%sx**.

%tb

Prints the last traceback with the currently active exception mode.

%time

Times the execution of the Python statement or expression. Try entering the following into a Notebook cell:

```
%time

[x for x in range(10)]
```

Now run the cell. Your output should look like this:

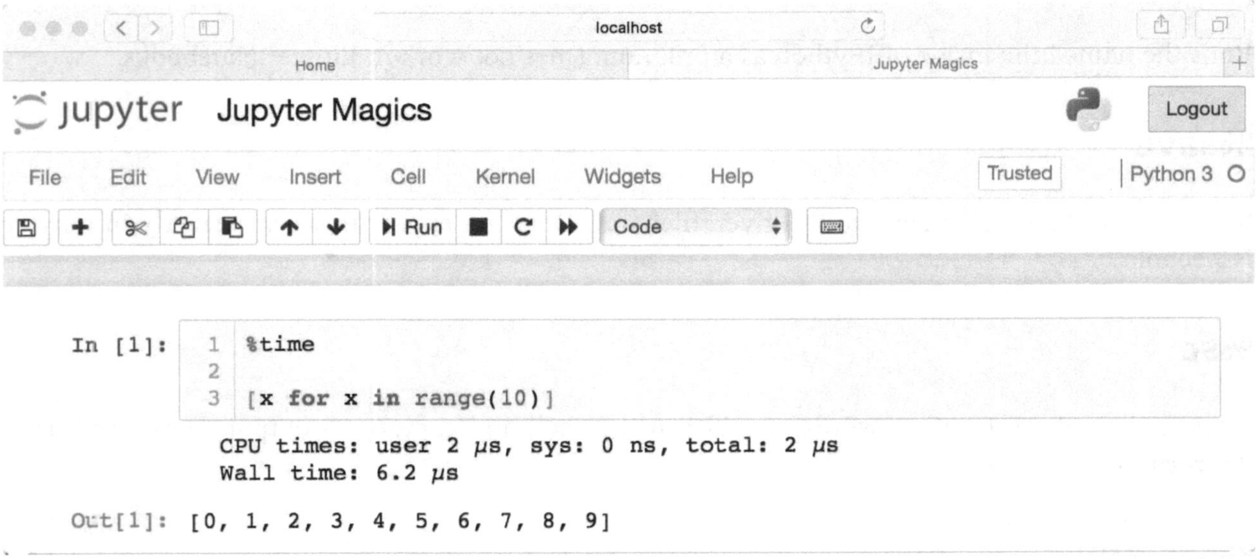

Appendix A-8: The %time magic

%timeit

You can also use the **%timeit** magic to time your code. It will use Python's **timeit** module to time your code. Here's an example of its use:

```
%timeit [x for x in range(10)]
```

And here is what it looks like when you run it in a Notebook:

Appendix A-9: The %timeit magic

%unalias

Removes an alias.

%unload_ext

Unloads an IPython extension by its module name. Note that not all extensions can be unloaded. The extension must implement **unload_ipython_extension** for it to be unloaded.

%who

Prints all interactive variables in IPython. Does not work in Jupyter Notebook.

%who_ls

Return a sorted list of all interactive variables. Also does not work in Jupyter Notebook.

%whos

Like the **%who** magic, but gives some extra information about each variable. The documentation isn't really specific and since it doesn't work with Jupyter Notebook, it won't be covered here either.

%xdel

Deletes a variable, attempting to clear it from anywhere within IPython's machinery that holds a reference to said variable.

%xmode

Switch modes for the exception handlers.

Cell Magics

A **cell magic** is denoted by a double percent sign (%%) prefix. It operates on multiple lines of input in contrast to a line magic.

%%bash

Runs the cells with bash in a subprocess. This is also a shortcut way of saying %%script bash

%%capture

Using this magic, you can run the cell and capture its stdout, stderr and IPython's rich display() calls.

%%html

This will render the cell as a block of HTML. In other words, you can use basic HTML in your Notebook cell if you use this magic.

%%javascript

Runs the cell block as Javascript code.

%%js

Runs the cell block as Javascript code.

%%latex

Will render the cell as a block of latex. When using Jupyter Notebook, this magic will only render using the subset of latex that is defined in **MathJax**.

%%perl

This magic will run the cells with perl in a subprocess. This is also a shortcut for %%script perl

%%pypy

Runs the cells with pypy in a subprocess. Note: PyPy is a faster alternative implementation of Python that uses a Just-in-Time (JIT) compiler. See https://pypy.org/ for more information.

%%python

Runs the cells with Python in a subprocess. This is a shortcut for %%script python.

%%python2

Runs the cells with python2 in a subprocess. This is a shortcut for %%script python2.

```
%%python2

for i in range(3):
    print i
```

Note that this is one way to run Python 2 in a Python 3 Notebook:

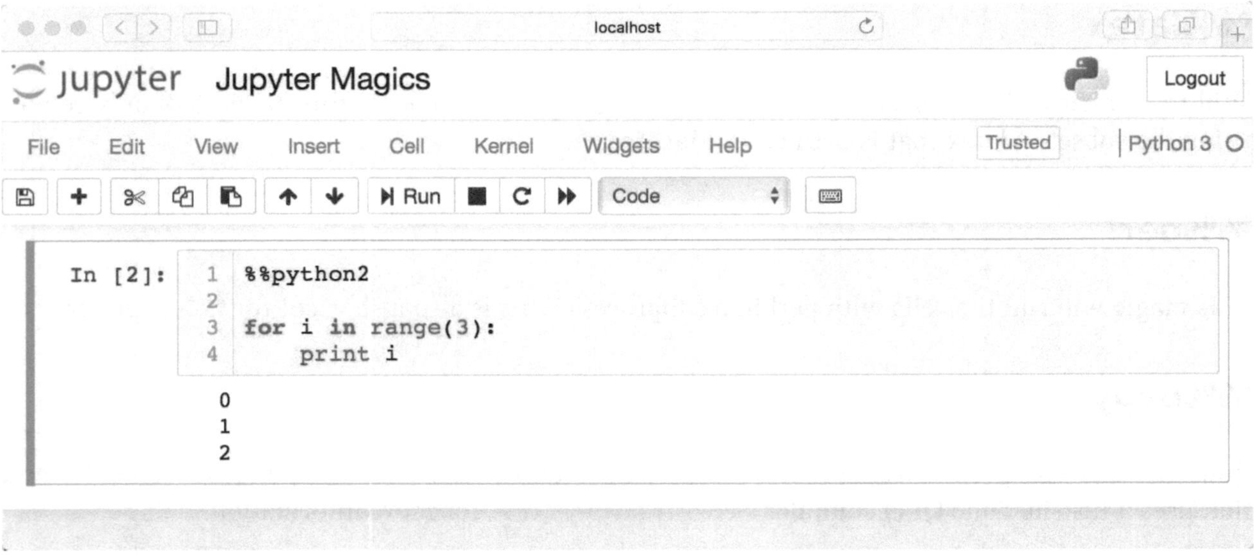

Appendix A-10: The %%python2 magic

%%python3

Runs the cells with python3 in a subprocess. This is a shortcut for %%script python3.

%%ruby

Runs the cells with ruby in a subprocess. This is a shortcut for %%script ruby.

%%script

Will run the cell using a shell command. Just pass this command something like **bash** or **python** to make this magic execute.

%%sh

Run the cells with **sh** in a subprocess. This is a shortcut for %%script sh

%%svg

This will render the cell as an SVG literal.

%%writefile

This magic will write the contents of the cell to a file. Try adding the following code to a cell in Jupyter Notebook. Make sure you update the path as needed for your system:

```
%%writefile /Users/michael/Desktop/test.py

for i in range(3):
    print(i)
```

Now run the cell. The output should look like this:

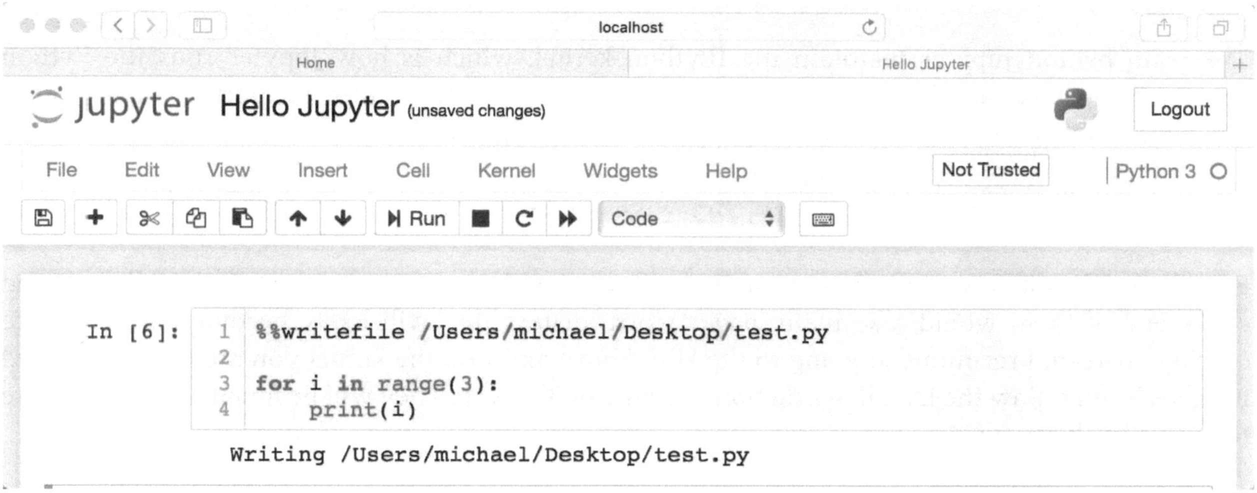

Appendix A-11: The %%writefile magic

If you go to the location that you specified, you should now have a file named **test.py** with the contents of that cell, minus the **%%writefile** line.

Wrapping Up

In this chapter we learned how to use IPython's magic commands in Jupyter Notebook. There are lots of magics that do useful things for you and can make doing certain things easier in your Notebooks. Check out the full documentation for the most up-to-date information or just try using some of these in your Notebooks to see how they work:

- https://ipython.readthedocs.io/en/stable/interactive/magics.html

Appendix B - Running Other Programming Languages

The team behind Jupyter maintain the IPython kernel, which is how Jupyter runs the Python programming language by default. The Jupyter Community has added support for many other languages. You can find a list of the languages that are supported here:

- https://github.com/jupyter/jupyter/wiki/Jupyter-kernels

Each kernel has its own installation method, which means that covering how to install each and every one of them would take many pages worth of text that will likely become obsolete quite quickly. Instead, I recommend going to the URL above and find the kernel you are most interested in there. Then follow the install instructions that are on the web. They will be much more up-to-date than this book can be.

Adding a New Language

For this book, I thought it would be fun to show how you can use the Ruby programming language in Jupyter. Just go to the following URL as it has the latest installation information for your operating system:

- https://github.com/SciRuby/iruby

Once you are done installing the dependencies for your operating system, you will need to run the following two commands:

```
gem install cztop iruby
iruby register --force
```

The first command uses Ruby's package manager to install a couple of Ruby packages. In this case, we want to instapp cztop and iruby, the latter of which is the Ruby kernel for Jupyter. Once installed, you need to register it.

Running Ruby

Now that we have everything set up, you should be able to start up Jupyter Notebook:

```
jupyter notebook
```

Jupyter is now running. Go ahead and create a new Notebook and then go to the **New** button and you should see Ruby in the list of new Notebook options:

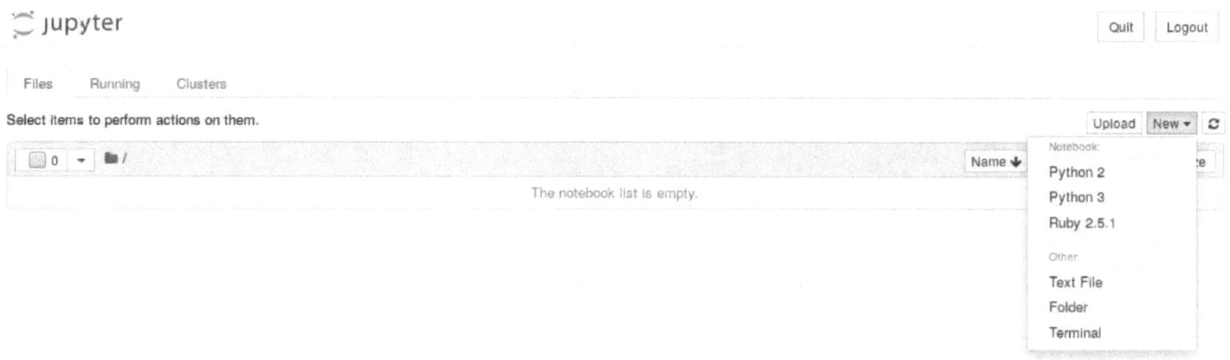

Appendix B-1: Creating a Ruby Notebook

Go ahead and create a new Ruby Notebook. Let's enter the following code into a cell that I took from Ruby's website to see if the Notebook works:

```
cities  = %w[ London
            Oslo
            Paris
            Amsterdam
            Berlin ]
visited = %w[Berlin Oslo]

puts "I still need " +
     "to visit the " +
     "following cities:",
     cities - visited
```

When I ran this cell, I ended up with the following output:

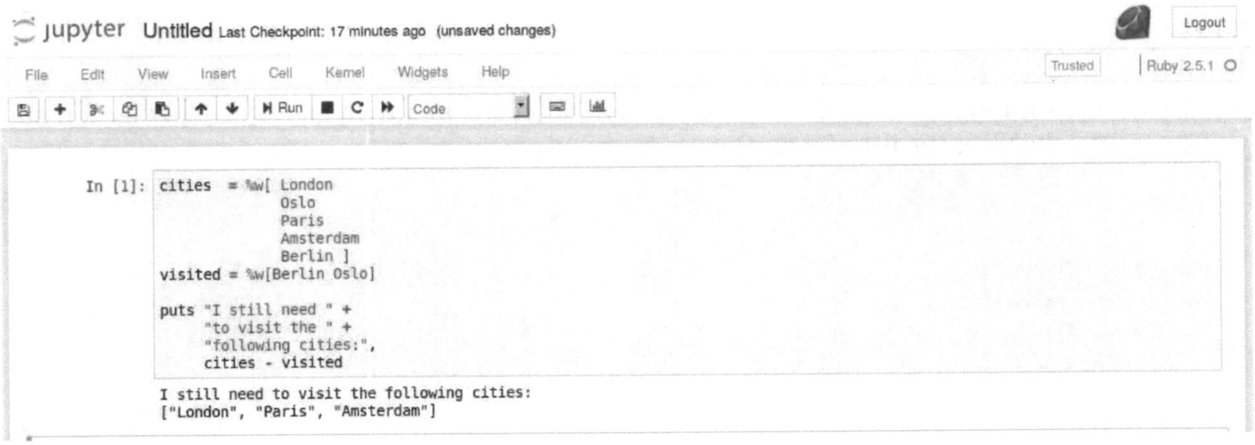

Appendix B-2: Running Ruby code

Running Multiple Languages

You can also run multiple languages in one Notebook by using IPython magics, such as **%%ruby** and **%%python3**. Let's create a new Notebook based on Python 3. Once you have that running, add the following code to the first cell:

```
%%ruby

cities  = %w[ London
          Oslo
          Paris
          Amsterdam
          Berlin ]
visited = %w[Berlin Oslo]

puts "I still need " +
     "to visit the " +
     "following cities:",
     cities - visited
```

Now create a second cell and add the following code:

```
%%python3

print('Hi from Jupyter!')
```

Technically since we are running a Python 3 based Notebook, we don't need the **%%python3**, but I prefer to be explicit. Now run both cells and you should get the following output:

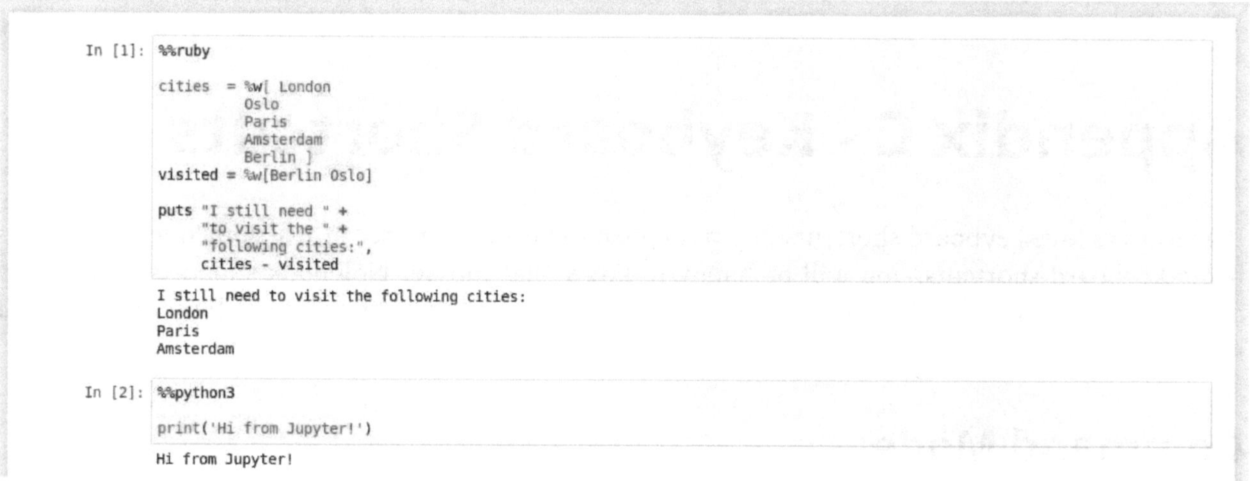

Appendix B-3: Running Ruby and Python 3

Wrapping Up

At this point you should have a good idea for how to add a new language to your Jupyter installation. You have also learned how to use the new language within Jupyter as well as how to run multiple languages in a single Notebook.

Appendix C - Keyboard Shortcuts

Power users love keyboard shortcuts. If you happen to be a power user or just someone who enjoys using keyboard shortcuts, you will be happy to know that Jupyter Notebook supports quite a few of them. But before we get started learning about them, we need to know about Jupyter's different modes.

Command Mode

Command mode will bind the keyboard to Notebook level actions. You can tell if you are in Command mode by looking at the color of the box that encircles your selected cell. If it is blue, you are in Command mode. Here is a screenshot:

Appendix C-1: Command mode

Note that you can't really tell the difference in this screenshot or the one in the next section if you are reading the paperback version of this book. Use the PDF or open Jupyter Notebook so you can see the difference for yourself.

Edit Mode

Edit mode is when you are actually editing the cell. When you are in this mode, you will notice that the cell selection color is now green:

Appendix C-2: Edit mode

Commonly Used Shortcuts

Here are some of the common shortcuts you might use in **Command Mode**:

- CTRL + ENTER - run the selected cell
- A - insert a new cell above the selected cell

- B - insert a new cell below the selected cell
- C - Copy the currently selected cell
- V - Paste the cell
- D, D - Press D twice to delete a cell
- 0, 0 - Press zero twice to restart kernel
- Y - Change the cell's mode to code
- M - Change the cell's mode to markdown

Here are some of the common shortcuts you might use in **Edit Mode**:

- CTRL + / - Toggles commenting of the line
- TAB - Used for code completion
- SHIFT + TAB - Show tooltip

Opening the Command Palette

If you want to learn more about the keyboard shortcuts, you can open the **Command Palette**:

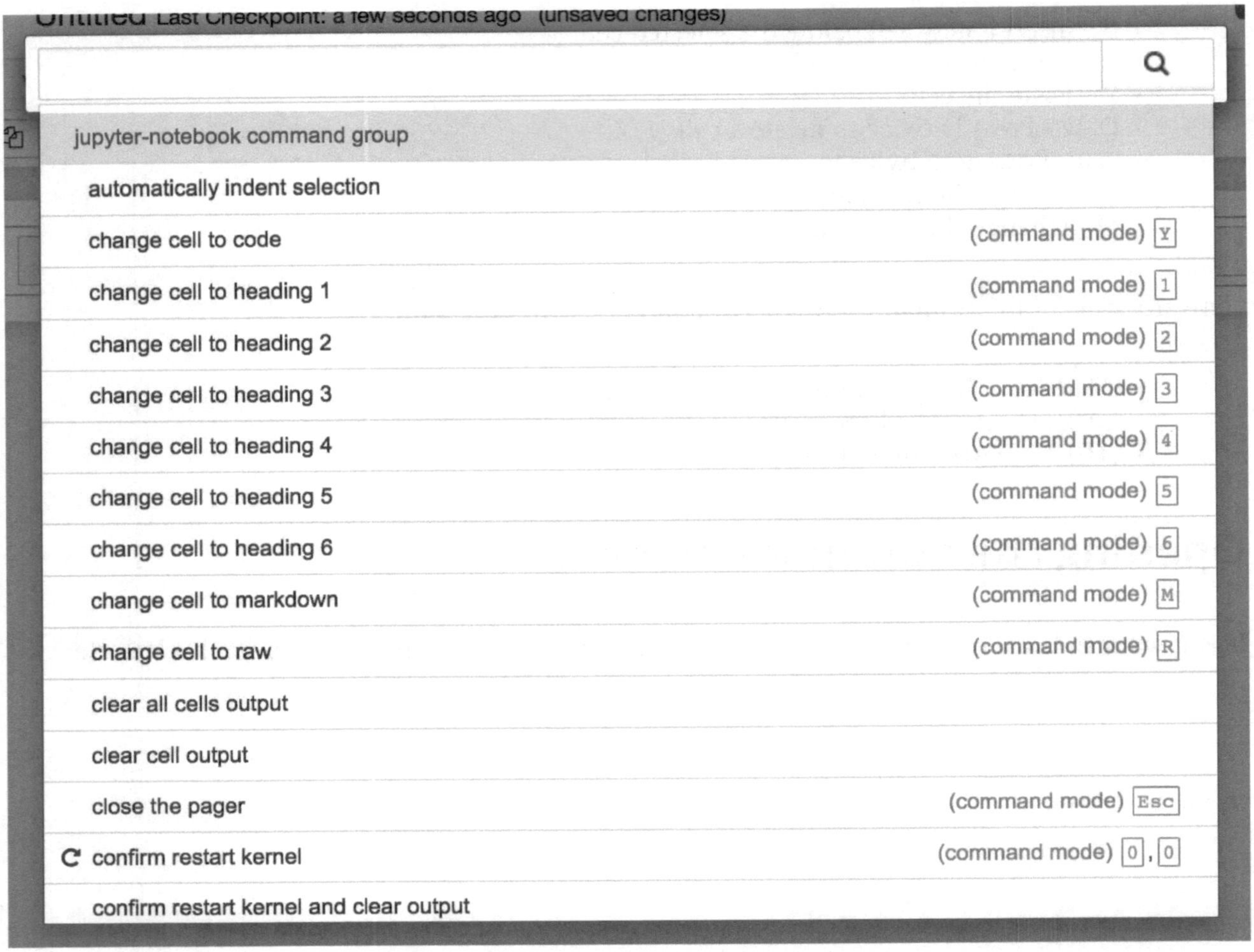

Appendix C-3: The Command Palette

You can use either of the following shortcuts to open the palette:

- Ctrl-Shift-F
- Ctrl-Shift-P

View all Shortcuts

While in **Command mode**, just press the letter **H** and you should see the following:

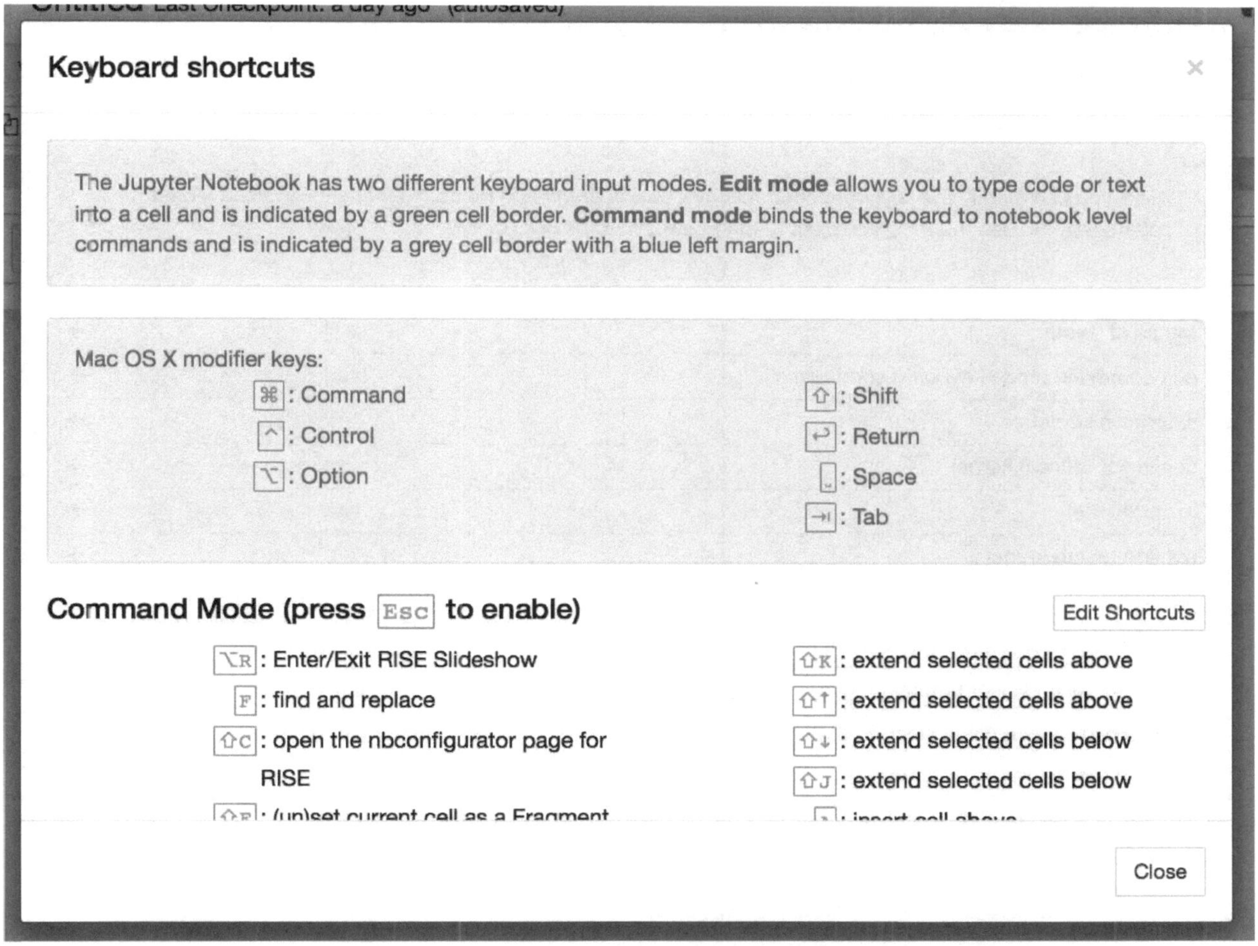

Appendix C-4: Viewing all the Keyboard Shortcuts

Editing Shortcuts

To edit the keyboard shortcuts, you can either open the shortcuts dialog by pressing **H** in Command mode or go to the **Help** menu and choose **Edit Keyboard Shortcuts**. You should see the following dialog when you do so:

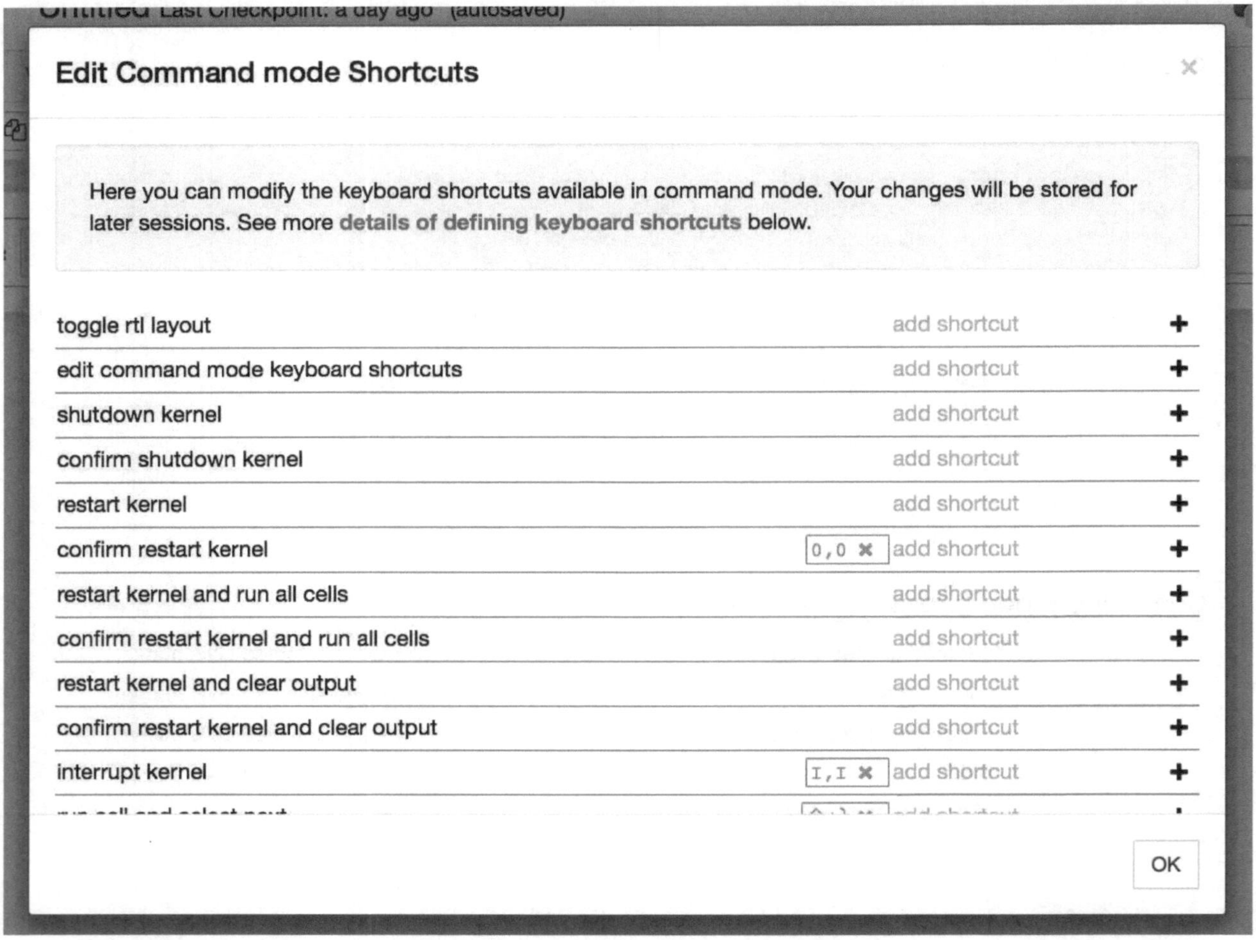

Appendix C-5: Editing Keyboard Shortcuts

Wrapping Up

This appendix's focus was on learning about some of the keyboard shortcuts you can use with Jupyter Notebook. You also learned about the Command Palette and how to edit your shortcuts.

Afterword and Thanks

This book was really interesting for me to write as I hadn't really used Jupyter Notebook a great deal before I started writing this book. Fortunately the documentation for the project is quite good overall and the package is quite intuitive. I hope you have found this book helpful in learning how to use Jupyter Notebook effectively.

To review, we learned about the following:

- Creating Notebooks
- Configuration
- Distributing Notebooks
- Exporting / Converting Notebooks
- Installing / Managing Extensions
- Creating / Working with Widgets
- Presentations (RISE)
- Debugging
- Testing

Special thanks for to the Jupyter Project team who made this all possible. I also want to thank all my readers and the people who backed this book on Kickstarter. Thanks so much for your support and encouragement while writing this book. Writing is a lonely hobby and having a great readership is an amazing asset.

Thanks, Mike

Made in United States
Troutdale, OR
05/05/2025

31127846R00091